LAKELAND
FELLRANGER

MID-WESTERN FELLS

MARK RICHARDS

HarperCollinsPublishers Ltd.
77-85 Fulham Palace Road
London
W6 8JB

The Collins website address is:
www.collins.co.uk

Collins is a registered trademark of
HarperCollinsPublishers Ltd.

First published in 2004

10 09 08 07 06 05 04

10 9 8 7 6 5 4 3 2 1

ISBN 0 00 711368 4

Colour reproduction by Colourscan, Singapore
Printed and bound in Singapore by Imago

(cover) Scafell Crag from the west ridge of Lingmell
(title page) Bowfell from Black Wars on Pike o'Blisco

CONTENTS

Key to maps and diagrams   GRID NORTH IS TOP OF EVERY MAP

contours 15m/30ft intervals, shown only to indicate relief

crags and scree

enclosure boundaries

trees and woodland

becks or gills

lake or tarn

roads and buildings

▲ summit cairn

27 car parking, cross-reference number with table on page 10

B bus stop

3 route number as described in the text

- - - - - - - strongly marked path

- - - - - - - intermittent path

••••••••••••• no path author's recommended route

- - - - path negotiates difficult ground/mild scrambling

**The hand-drawn maps and diagrams in this guide are based upon
HARVEY SUPERWALKER: LAKELAND WEST**

LAKELAND FELLRANGER

CALDBECK

Northern Fells

COCKERMOUTH

PENRITH

KESWICK

North-Western Fells

Near Eastern Fells

Central Fells

Western Fells

EGREMONT

Far Eastern Fells

Mid-Western Fells

AMBLESIDE

Southern Fells

KENDAL

Eight title divisions of the English Lake District

BROUGHTON-IN-FURNESS

A personal passion

My earliest memories of Lakeland came through studying artistic essays and books of the picturesque that my mother had acquired. They portrayed the romance of a majestic landscape that had formed the backdrop to her youth. Born in north Lancashire, she naturally knew of Lakeland as a special place, though she had little opportunity to visit.

At a similar time, through the tales of Black Bob, the *Dandy* wonder dog, comic strip stories of a shepherd's adventures on the hills above Selkirk, I gained a love of both pen and ink drawing and the hills of the Scottish Borders, all distantly set in a romantic land of my own very youthful dreams. For I was born in rural west Oxfordshire and the magic that my mother clung to was becoming increasingly real to me.

Holidays were always allied to my parents' roots. My father's Cornish ancestry gave me early seaside trips to that wonderful coastline and, as my teenage years unfolded, a regular busman's holiday to a fell farm on Lord Shuttleworth's Leck Hall estate gave me the hands-on feel and flavour of rough fell country. My first fragmentary taste of what Lakeland itself was all about came, when I was twelve years old, on a day-trip to Ambleside and Great Langdale, when I remember purchasing *The Southern Fells*, Book Four of Alfred Wainwright's *A Pictorial Guide to the Lakeland Fells*. That book was periodically perused as my formative life as a young farmer kept my attention firmly on the needs of a 150-acre farm of cattle and corn. Socially I revelled in the activities of the Young Farmers' movement. I remember an exchange with the Alnwick club gave me a chance to climb The Cheviot in smooth-soled leather shoes, my first real fell climb. After masterminding two ploughing marathons – 100, then 200 acres turned from stubble to tilth in 24 hours – in my early twenties I sought new adventures. I joined the Gloucestershire Mountaineering Club and got to grips with Snowdonia, Scotland and yes, at long last, the Lakeland Fells. Rock climbing and long days in all weathers ridge walking put me in touch with the thrill of high places.

That first Wainwright guide focused my mind on a love of wild places, Lakeland in particular. Quickly I now acquired the remainder of the series and, feeling far removed from the beauty of it all, I took to drawing from my own black and white photographs, mimicking AW. Within a year of joining the Mountaineering Club I had become a firm friend of the legend himself, spending regular weekends at Kendal Green, joining him on his original exploration of the *Coast to Coast Walk*, *The Outlying Fells (see page 228 for my one moment of recognition)*, *Westmorland Heritage* and supplying numerous photographs of Scottish mountains he was unable to reach for his *Scottish Mountain Drawings* series. As my walking progressed and his faltered, so my trips to Kendal became fewer. Marriage, a family and farming brought responsibilities so time constraints deflected my attention from AW and the Lakeland I loved.

I remained in farming until almost forty, during which time I had several walking guides published. AW nurtured my first title, a very pictorial map-guide to the Cotswold Way back in 1973. This was followed by guides to the North Cornwall Coast, Offa's Dyke Path, a three-part exploration of the Peak District National Park and Hadrian's Wall, as well as many small guides and articles, including a happy sequence of *Out of the Way* pieces for *The Countryman*, a journal I had known from childhood, published on my doorstep. All along gnawing at the back of my mind was the sense that some day I should prepare my own complete survey of the Lakeland Fells. Having edited a little magazine, *Walking Wales,* for one year, I found I could ignore it no longer and, with the support and encouragement of HarperCollins, to whom I will be forever grateful, I moved to Cumbria to begin *Lakeland Fellranger*.

From fireside to fellside

The Mid-Western Fells are in many respects the rugged mountain heart of Lakeland, defined by four high passes: the on-foot and saddleback Stake and Styhead, the motorable Wrynose and Hardknott. The group features the highest ground, many of the most revered crags and certainly some of the best loved fells. The valley bases too are Meccas for lovers of the finest of all fell country. Great Langdale, the Duddon, Eskdale, Wasdale and Borrowdale, all stake their claim as prime approaches into a wild, roadless hinterland.

An enormous amount of time and care has gone into the preparation of this guide, comprising fifty days of on-fell research, checking the existence and extent of paths, and the practicality of potential off-beat routes. The 2003 season has been exceptionally kind on the weather front. This book was surveyed during the period March to September with only six 'iffy' days of grey sky to spoil my quest for a well-rounded collection of truly representative photographic images. Each route is identified by a red number which links the diagrams and maps to the adjacent text. The routes themselves are depicted in three forms *(see preceding key)*: bold dashes for the principal trails; thin dashes for lesser paths liable to be intermittent or the old green tracks of shepherds' past, and lastly, dots, where there is no path on the ground, representing nothing more than my recommended route. Representation of a route, in whatever form, does not infer safe passage for all, at any time: the onus is on each individual to weigh up their own capabilities and the prevailing conditions. In fellwalking, as any mountain travel, retreat is often the greater valour. I have taken care to follow time-honoured routes and kept within bounds of access, yet cannot attest a right of way.

No two walkers follow the same tread, neither do they explore with the same plot, so what is revealed in this guide is a very personal expression of the potential route structure. Nonetheless, it is fundamentally reliable and for fellwalkers who love to explore, a rich source of entertaining route-planning ideas. A good guide should also be a revelation. Hence for each fell summit a full panorama is given, which alone should encourage readers to carry the tome to the top!

The guide may be formally structured to cover important matters such as the nature of the summit, safe lines of descent and the linking ridge routes, sprinkled with a few items of interpretation, but underlying it all is a desire to share the pleasure of exploration which is open to each one of us. Let us continue to love Lakeland and care for its future. May its magic remain an inspiration for each new generation.

The National Park have prepared a short advisory note for conscientious walkers :

Place your feet thoughtfully; every single footstep causes wear and tear on the environment. The slow-growing plants that can survive on mountains are particularly vulnerable.

Keep to the path surface; do not walk along the vegetation at the edge of the path.

Do not build or add to cairns - paths need stones more than cairns.

Do not take shortcuts - water will soon follow your tracks and an erosion scar will develop.

Remember, there may be only one of you, but there are another 12 million pairs of feet treading Lake District paths every year.

Walkers embarking on expeditions at the head of the Duddon valley will encounter a triple-stranded electric fence. This recent addition to the open fell was erected for a fixed five-year term to allow the National Trust's Herdwick flock to re-establish their instinctive heaf. While it may take a little longer to achieve this, the fence has its plus points. It is well supplied with stiles *(like this one at the head of Mosedale)* ensuring conventional walking routes are not hampered and in mist it is a sure guide to safe ground. One suspects other fences may yet feature on the high fell where it is thought possible to protect the delicate mountain flora from the tight bite of sheep. Such fencing need not interfere with the liberty of walkers, in fact we all ought to applaud such protection.

8

THE MID-WESTERN FELLS
four graphic projections of the range

FROM THE EAST

Langstrath · ROSTHWAITE FELL · Bessyboot · Woofgill Pike · Rosthwaite Cam · Comb Head · CLARAMARA · Skake Pass · merging into the CENTRAL FELLS · ALLEN CRAGS · Great Langdale · ROSSETT PIKE · GREAT END · Ill Crag · SCAFELL PIKE · SCAFELL · BOWFELL · Esk Hause · Eskdale · Long Green · LINGMOOR FELL · CRINKLE CRAGS · PIKE O'BLISCO · LITTLE STAND · Wrynose Pass · merging into the SOUTHERN FELLS

FROM THE SOUTH

Little Langdale · LINGMOOR FELL · Wrynose Pass · COLD PIKE · PIKE O'BLISCO · BOWFELL · CRINKLE CRAGS · LITTLE STAND · Esk Hause · Esk Pike · GREAT END · HARD KNOTT · Ill Crag · SCAFELL PIKE · Hardknott Pass · SCAFELL · SLIGHT SIDE · GREAT HOW · Boot · Boat How · ILLGILL HEAD · ESKDALE MOOR · WHIN RIGG · Esdale Green · Irton Pike

FROM THE NORTH

Irton Pike · WHIN RIGG · ILLGILL HEAD · Wastwater · Wasdale Head · SCAFELL · LINGMELL · SCAFELL PIKE · Styhead Pass · GREAT END · SEATHWAITE FELL · Seathwaite · Esk Hause · Esk Pike · ALLEN CRAGS · BOWFELL · CLARAMARA · ROSTHWAITE FELL · Bessyboot · Seatoller · COLD PIKE · Stonethwaite · PIKE O'BLISCO · Stake Pass · Side Pike · LINGMOOR FELL

FROM THE WEST

ROSTHWAITE FELL · Bessyboot · Thornythwaite Fell · Woofgill Pike · Rosthwaite Cam · Comb Head · CLARAMARA · SEATHWAITE FELL · LINGMELL · GREAT END · Broad Crag · SCAFELL PIKE · Micledore · SCAFELL · SLIGHT SIDE · CRINKLE CRAGS · merging into the SOUTHERN FELLS · Hardknott Pass · HARD KNOTT · LITTLE STAND · Wrynose Pass · Wastwater · Wasdale Head · Seathwaite · WHIN RIGG · ILLGILL HEAD · Boat How · Irton Pike

FELL MOSAIC

Chapter and page references to provide an overview of adjacent fell range mapping, inevitably fragmented within this guide, as an aid for planning your liberty on the fells.

(below) Great Gable from a pool high on the Corridor Route, beneath Broad Crag

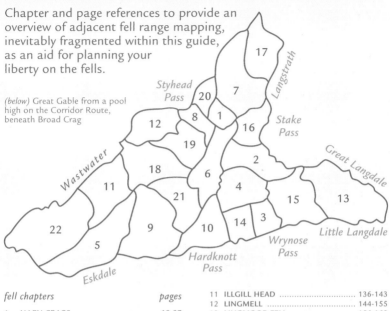

STARTING POINTS

	LOCATION	GRID REFERENCE	PARKING	BUS STOP
1	Seathwaite	235 123		
2	Seatoller (NT)	245 138	P	✳
3	Stonethwaite	261 139		✳
4	Old Dungeon Ghyll (NT)	286 061	P	✳
5	Langdale (NP)	295 063	P	✳
	Stickle Ghyll (NT)	294 063	P	✳
6	Elterwater (NP)	328 047	P	✳
7	Three Shires Inn, Little Langdale	316 034		
8	Blea Tarn (NT)	296 043	P	
9	Castle How	292 032		
10	Wrynose Pass	277 027		
11	Wrynose Bottom	266 023		
12	Cockley Beck Bridge	246 016		
13	Mosedale	242 016		
14	Hardknott Pass	231 015		
15	Roman Fort	220 014		
16	Brotherilkeld	210 012		
17	Taw House	202 009		
18	Wha House	200 009	P	
19	Woolpack Inn	190 010		
20	Dalegarth Station, Boot	173 007	P	
21	Eskdale Green	142 002	P	
22	Miterdale Forest	146 012	P	
23	Irton Pike	122 013	P	
24	Nether Wasdale	128 038		
25	Wastwater	148 048		
26	Wasdale Head (NT)	183 075	P	
27	Wasdale Head Village Green	186 085	P	

P - formal car parking facilities (some with coin meters) otherwise informal, limited lay-by parking
✳ - serviced bus stop close by

Public transport may be a problem elsewhere but here in the heart of Lakeland one may confidently plan a day around a reliable rural service, given a proper study of timetables. The Mountain Goat service is supplemented by regular Stagecoach services throughout the district. Pertinent to this guide is the Lakeslink 555 service which runs run along the A591 from Windermere via Ambleside and Grasmere, crossing Dunmail Raise bound for Keswick. This connects with the Langdale Rambler service 526 running via Elterwater to the Old Dungeon Ghyll Hotel and the Borrowdale Rambler service 79 from Keswick to Seatoller. On the west coast regular buses do not penetrate Wasdale, or Eskdale for that matter, though service 6 is useful. This runs from Whitehaven via Egremont to Ravenglass, thereby making a link with La'al Ratty.

For current advice contact:
TRAVELINE
public transport info
0870 608 2608

La'al Ratty 'turned tail' at Dalegarth Station

summit of Lingmell

THE MID-WESTERN FELLS

Legend:

- fell above 305m/1,000ft
- **27** parking text/map reference
- **22** Fell summit/chapter

Regions labelled:

- Central Fells
- Western Fells
- Southern Fells

Places and features:

- STONETHWAITE
- SEATOLLER
- SEATHWAITE
- Stake Pass
- Styhead Pass
- WASDALE HEAD
- Wastwater
- NETHER WASDALE
- SANTON BRIDGE
- ESKDALE GREEN
- BOOT
- Hardknott Pass
- Wrynose Pass
- LITTLE LANGDALE
- ELTERWATER

Scale:

miles 0 1 2 3 4 5

km 1 2 3 4 5

READY RECKONER *for route-planning*

GRADING: **A** *easy route-finding* **B** *some tricky ground* **C** *care in route-finding/mild scrambling*

start & route	text nos.	ascent *(feet)*	distance *(miles)*	grade
1 Allen Crags 8-27				
1 SEATHWAITE				
to Stockley Bridge	**1**	200	0.7	A
via Allen Gill	**2**	2,000	1.7	B
via Ruddy Gill	**3|5**	2,000	2.1	A
via west shoulder	**4**	2,050	2.2	A
3 STONETHWAITE				
via Langstrath	**6**	2,245	5.7	B
4 OLD DUNGEON GHYLL				
via Mickleden & Rossett Gill	**7**	2,255	4.1	A
2 Bowfell 28-43				
4 OLD DUNGEON GHYLL				
via The Band	**1**	2,650	3.1	A
via Climbers' Traverse	**2**	2,650	3.5	C
via Green Tongue	**3**	2,650	3.3	B
via Rossett Gill & Ore Gap	**4**	2,700	4.3	A
via Oxendale & Hell Gill	**5**	2,600	3.3	A
13 MOSEDALE				
via Mosedale & Ling Cove	**6**	2,240	3.6	A
15 BROTHERILKELD				
via Esk Gorge & Three Tarns	**7**	2,700	4.4	A
3 STONETHWAITE				
via Langstrath	**8|9**	2,650	6.0	A
via Rossett Pike	**8|10**	2,680	6.4	A
3 Cold Pike 44-51				
10 WRYNOSE PASS				
via south ridge	**1**	1,020	1.3	A
via Red Tarn	**2**	1,020	1.8	A
11 WRYNOSE BOTTOM				
via Wrynose Breast	**3**	1,350	1.1	B
4 Crinkle Crags 52-65				
4 OLD DUNGEON GHYLL				
via The Band	**1**	2,680	3.3	A
via Browney Gill	**2**	2,550	3.2	A
via Hell Gill	**4**	2,580	3.4	A
via Whorneyside	**5**	2,500	2.9	B

10 WRYNOSE PASS				
via Red Tarn	**3**	1,535	**2.6**	A
12 COCKLEY BECK BRIDGE				
via Little Stand	**6**	2,100	**2.8**	A
15 BROTHERILKELD				
via Esk Gorge	**7**	2,560	**5.1**	A
13 MOSEDALE				
via Mosedale	**8**	2,200	**4.0**	A
via Swinsty Gill	**9**	2,200	**2.8**	B
via Rest Gill	**10**	2,100	**3.2**	C
via Three Tarns	**11**	2,200	**4.0**	A

5 Eskdale Moor 66-77

18 BOOT				
via Burnmoor Tarn	**1**	940	**1.8**	A
via Brat's Moss	**2**	940	**1.6**	A
via Blea Tarn	**3**	950	**2.2**	A
20 MITERDALE				
via Miterdale	**4**	880	**4.3**	A
via Miterdale Forest	**5**	900	**3.1**	A
19 ESKDALE GREEN				
via Fell End	**6**	900	**4.0**	A

6 Esk Pike 78-89

15 BROTHERILKELD				
via south ridge	**1**	2,620	**5.3**	A
via Great Moss	**2**	2,600	**5.5**	A
via Cowcove zig-zags	**3**	2,650	**5.3**	A
via Ling Cove	**4**	2,600	**5.4**	A
1 SEATHWAITE				
via Ruddy Gill	**5**	2,520	**3.3**	A
3 STONETHWAITE				
via Langstrath & Ore Gap	**6**	2,590	**5.3**	B
4 OLD DUNGEON GHYLL				
via Rossett Gill	**7**	2,580	**3.8**	A

7 Glaramara 90-101

2 SEATOLLER				
via Thorneythwaite Fell	**1**	2,240	**2.6**	A
via Comb Gill	**2**	2,270	**2.8**	B
valley path to Seathwaite	**3**	100	**1.5**	A
1 SEATHWAITE				
via Hind Gill	**4**	2,230	**1.4**	B
3 STONETHWAITE				

via Langstrath *&* Sobby Gill	**5**	2,250	4.0	**B**

8   Great End 102-115

3   SEATHWAITE

via Grains Gill	**1|2**	2,590	3.0	**A**
via Styhead Pass	**3|4**	2,600	3.3	**C**
traverse above Skew Gill	**5**	150	0.3	**B**
via Lambfoot Dub	**6**	2,600	3.5	**B**

25   WASDALE HEAD

via Styhead Pass	**7**	2,720	3.1	**A**

9   Great How 116-125

18   WOOLPACK INN

to Eel Tarn	**1**	1,470	3.0	**B**
via Stony Tarn	**2**	1,470	2.9	**A**

18   BOOT

via Eel Tarn	**3**	1,660	3.2	**A**
via Lambford Bridge	**4**	1,680	4.2	**A**
via Oliver Gill	**5**	1,670	4.0	**B**

10 Hard Knott 126-135

14   HARDKNOTT PASS

direct route and Border End	**1**	550	0.7	**A**

13   MOSEDALE

via Dod Pike	**2**	1,020	1.2	**B**
via Mosedale	**3**	1,040	2.8	**A**

15   ROMAN FORT

via Border End *&* The Steeple	**4|5**	1,100	2.0	**B**

16 BROTHERILKELD

via Scar Gill	**6**	1,500	2.0	**B**

11 Illgill Head 136-143

26   WASDALE HEAD (NT)

direct route	**1**	1,750	2.4	**A**
balcony path to Miterdale	**2**	880	5.2	**A**

20   BOOT

via Burnmoor Tarn	**3**	1,820	4.2	**A**

12 Lingmell 144-155

27   WASDALE HEAD

via Piers Gill	**1**	2,400	3.3	**B**

26   WASDALE HEAD (NT)

via Lingmell Gill	**2**	2,440	2.9	**A**
via Goat Crags	**3**	2,400	2.7	**A**

13 Lingmoor Fell 156-169

6 ELTERWATER				
via Baysbrown Wood	**1**	1,330	**2.0**	A
valley path via Baysbrown Farm	**2**	120	**3.0**	A
valley path via Oak How	**3**	90	**2.3**	A
7 LITTLE LANGDALE				
via Bield Crag	**4**	1,200	**1.7**	A
8 BLEA TARN				
via Bleatarn House	**5**	860	**1.1**	A
via the west ridge	**6**	.1,020	**2.0**	A
via Birk Knott	**7**	875	**1.2**	A
traverse to Bield Crag	**8**	220	**0.9**	A
4 OLD DUNGEON GHYLL *&* 5 STICKLE GHYLL/LANGDALE				
to Side Pike	**9**	870	**0.5**	A
via Oak How Needle	**10**	1,250	**1.8**	A

14 Little Stand 170-175

12 COCKLEY BECK BRIDGE				
via Gaitscale Close	**1**	1,710	**1.3**	B
13 MOSEDALE				
via Mosedale	**2**	1,840	**3.2**	B

15 Pike o'Blisco 176-185

8 BLEA TARN				
via Blake Rigg	**1**	1,690	**2.8**	A
4 OLD DUNGEON GHYLL				
via Redacre Gill	**2**	2,000	**2.3**	A
via Skull Gill *&* Black Wars	**3**	2,000	**3.2**	B
via Browney Gill	**4**	2,000	**3.0**	A
10 WRYNOSE PASS				
via Red Tarn	**5**	1,030	**1.5**	A
via Black Crag	**6**	1,030	**1.3**	A
9 CASTLE HOW				
via Blake Rigg	**7**	1,690	**1.9**	B
via Wrynose Beck	**8**	1,680	**1.8**	A

16 Rossett Pike 186-193

4 OLD DUNGEON GHYLL				
via Mickleden *&* Rossett Gill	**1|2**	1,820	**3.1**	A
via Littlegill Head	**3**	1,810	**3.2**	A
via Stake Pass	**4**	1,830	**3.6**	A
3 STONETHWAITE				
via Stake Pass	**5**	1,820	**5.4**	A
via Angletarn Gill	**6**	1,820	**5.5**	A

17 Rosthwaite Fell 194-209

3   STONETHWAITE

via Stanger Gill	**1**	1,500	**1.6**	A
via Racomb Bands	**2**	1,540	**1.6**	A
via Tansey Gill	**3**	1,500	**3.0**	A
via Dry Gill	**4**	1,500	**1.8**	A
via Dovesnest Crag & W. Pike	**5**	1,740	**2.2**	B

18 Scafell 210-223

16   BROTHERILKELD   & 17 TAW HOUSE

via Cowcove zig-zags	**1**	1,020	**3.4**	A
via Esk Gorge	**2**	1,000	**3.8**	A
via Camspout Crag	**3|4**	1,880	**1.2**	B
via Foxes Tarn	**3|5**	1,880	**0.9**	A
26 WASDALE HEAD (NT)				
via Rakehead	**6**	2,960	**2.3**	A
via Hollow Gill	**7**	2,960	**2.5**	A
via Hard Rigg	**8**	2,960	**2.6**	A
via Lingmell Gill	**9**	3,200	**3.3**	B
via Lord's Rake *(serious rock-fall - out of bounds for forseeable future)*				
20 BOOT				
via Slight Side	**10**	2,980	**5.0**	A
via Hard Rigg	**11**	2,970	**4.7**	A

19 Scafell Pike 224-239

4   OLD DUNGEON GHYLL

via Rossett Gill & Esk Hause	**1**	3,130	**6.8**	B
1 SEATHWAITE				
via Corridor Route	**2**	2,800	**4.2**	B
via Esk Hause	**3**	3,000	**4.0**	B
27 WASDALE HEAD				
to Styhead Pass	**4**	1,330	**2.2**	A
via Broadcrag Col	**5**	1,630	**2.0**	B
via Hollow Stones	**6**	3,000	**2.7**	A
via Mickledore	**7**	3,000	**2.6**	B
16 BROTHERILKELD				
via Cam Spout & Mickledore	**8**	2,960	**5.2**	B
via Little Narrowcove *via* Pen	**9**	3,020	**5.4**	B
via Little Narrowcove *direct*	**10**	3,000	**5.6**	B

20 Seathwaite Fell 240-247

1   SEATHWAITE

via Aaron Crags *to* north top	**1**	1,560	**1.9**	B
via Styhead Pass *to* south top	**2**	1,660	**3.0**	A

via Taylorgill Force & south top	**3|4**	1,640	2.7	B
via Sprinkling Tarn & south top	**4|5**	1,680	3.0	A

21 Slight Side 248-257
20 BOOT
via Peelplace Noddle	**1**	2,300	3.8	B
18 WOOLPACK INN				
via Eel & Stony Tarns	**2|3**	2,200	3.0	A
18 WHA HOUSE				
via Terrace Route	**4**	2,200	3.0	A
17 TAW HOUSE & 16 BROTHERILKELD				
via Cowcove zig-zags	**5|6**	2,250	3.8	A

22 Whin Rigg 258-271
24 NETHER WASDALE
via Greathall Gill	**1**	1,580	1.9	A
via Latterbarrow	**2**	1,580	2.5	A
23 IRTON PIKE				
via Irton Pike & Fell	**3|4**	1,440	2.9	A
23 ESKDALE GREEN				
via Miterdale Forest	**5**	1,600	3.2	A
25 WASTWATER				
The Screes Footpath	**6|7**	150	4.7	C

Pulpit Rock on Scafell Pike, viewed in silhouette from Mickledore

ALLEN CRAGS

Defined by deep valleys and sustaining the two thousand foot contour for more than two miles, a wonderful ridge leads north from the saddle due north of Esk Hause, with Glaramara at its mid-point. Allen Crags forms its southernmost high point, the first rise on a perennially popular fell-top trek. A modest bag when set against the likes of neighbouring Great End, but a good objective for those all-too frequent days when the Scafells are scarified by mist. The best route climbs from the Grains Gill valley, from which aspect its rougher, and more characterful qualities are foremost. In truth, only from this side can the fell be considered a sole objective for a circular fellwalk. The greater ridge walk, via Glaramara and Rosthwaite Fell, launches north from the saddle below Esk Hause; crossing the summit on a circular expedition from Borrowdale, either by way of the long march up lonely Langstrath from Stonethwaite, or by Grains Gill or even Styhead Pass from Seathwaite. The ridge is occasionally used as a stirring mountain start to the northern approach to Scafell Pike. An even grander circular can be undertaken as a through-walk, linking Ambleside and Keswick by means of the Langdale and Borrowdale Rambler buses, neatly turning on Allen Crags, climbing out of the depths of Great Langdale via Rossett Gill and Angle Tarn.

784 metres   2,572 feet

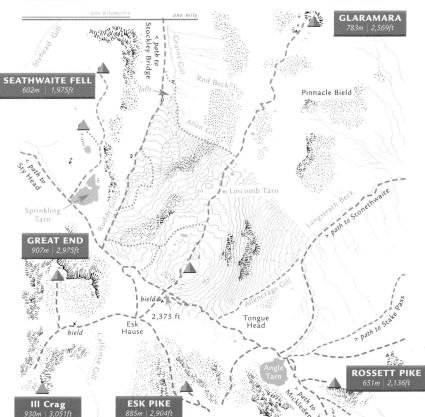

one kilometre　　　　one mile

GLARAMARA
783m | 2,569ft

Styhead Gill

Stockley Bridge

< path to

Grains Gill

Red Beck

Pinnacle Bield

SEATHWAITE FELL
602m | 1,975ft

falls

Allen Gill

< path to
Sty Head

Sprinkling
Tarn

Lincomb Tarn

Ruddy Gill

Langstrath Beck

> path to Stonethwaite

GREAT END
907m | 2,975ft

bield

2,375 ft

Esk
Hause

Allencrags Gill

> path to Stake Pass

bield

Tongue
Head

Calfcove Gill

Angle
Tarn

ROSSETT PIKE
651m | 2,136ft

Ill Crag
930m | 3,051ft

ESK PIKE
885m | 2,904ft

> path to
Mickleden

> path to
Mickleden

Allen Crags from Sprinkling Tarn on a glorious winter's day

NORTHERN APPROACHES

< path to BOWFELL

ESK PIKE

SCAFELL PIKE

Esk Hause

Angle Tarn

GREAT END

path from Mickleden **7**

The Band

slopes of ROSSETT PIKE

Sprinkling Tarn

5

4

6

H.House Tarn

3

Sty Head

path from Stonethwaite

Langstrath Beck

Ruddy Gill

GLARAMARA

Red Beck

2

SEATHWAITE FELL

slopes of GREAT GABLE

Styhead Tarn

Comb Head

Grains Gill

Styhead Gill

slopes of GREEN GABLE

Thorneythwaite Fell

slopes of BASE BROWN

bridle-track from Seathwaite

1

Taylorgill Force

ASCENT *from Seathwaite*

1 Follow the valley bridle-track through the farm via gates advancing to Stockley Bridge. After the hand-gate go left, beside the wall, on a path up Grains Gill: note the old out-gang walls below the path above the tree-shaded ravine. **2** Shortly after the next hand-gate, with path pitching apparent, bear half-left down to a broad wooden footbridge (pasture sharing passage for sheep). Head upstream, it is easier to stick at beck level initially. With the approach of the wooded gorge, bear up the bank to enjoy a grandstand view of the watersmeet fall of Ruddy Gill, little

Bowfell from High House Tarn

suspected from the main path above. Follow the moraine rigg. As Allen Gill comes close follow this on the rightbank, climbing steeply, keeping to the grass to its source, which meets up with the ridge path from Glaramara. Go right with High House Tarn an immediate embellishment to admire with the Langdale Pikes as a backdrop. More delightful is the tiny rock-girt Lincomb Tarn set among the outcropping just above (south) - reach for the camera. Follow the stony ridge path direct to the summit cairn.

3 The less taxing option is to stay with the sheltered Ruddy Gill path, scene of considerable pitching works in recent years. This path advances via a footbridge, where the gill begins to race dramatically down a gully and plunges into Allen Gill to form Grains Gill. While further upstream beautiful cascades are worth stepping aside to admire. Either stay with the modern hard trail, **4** or if a grass stair is preferred, you may find some respite in following an old path; bear half-left as a second tributary gill ford nears. A little used grass path leads up the bank near the gill. Pass a small flat outcrop, bear half-left (pathless) onto the narrow grassy moraine rigg. Rising easily to the skyline, bear right, cross two tiny gills. Mount onto the boiler-plate slab above the prominent outcrop to gain the broad marshy shelf. Skirt this to the right (west) passing a small cairn. Cross a further gill, then bear right, passing a small cairn to regain the modern path. The main trail rises with the constricting ravine close right. Just as the gill turns sharp left (east), one may climb onto the rock ridge (no path); follow this attractive, undulating slabby spine. With the craggy slope of Allen Crags ahead, bear half-left up the prominent grass ramp, traversing wet ground between outcropping to gain the ridge path south of the fell-top. Join the path and switch south onto the summit.

5 The normal course is to ford Ruddy Gill at the bend. Keeping beside the red-soiled ravine, ignore the right-hand branch path leading directly to Esk Hause. At the shallow saddle cross-paths, go left (north), up the loose trail, to the summit.

Sprinkling Tarn and Great Gable

ASCENT *from Stonethwaite*

6 It is a good five miles steady going from the hamlet to the summit. It's a sneaking up process among scenery that can let the mind wander too, in the 'getting away from it all' sense. Follow the main track from the hamlet, upon turning into the Langstrath valley choose between the bridle-path (east side), linked via the footbridge, and the footpath (west side); the former is better underfoot. All the really good scenery, there is plenty, is exhausted by the time one reaches the footbridge at the foot of Stake Beck. Cross the bridge, ignore the rising bridle-way, course of the Cumbria Way into Great Langdale. Keep to the narrow trod running along the base of Rossett Pike. The path copes well with the inevitable marsh. At the Angletarn and Allencrags Gills watersmeet, ford and follow Allencrags Gill on an intermittent path climbing to Tongue Head. Bearing up to the east/west saddle, setting sights on Allen Crag, the path winds north-east to the top.

ASCENT *from Great Langdale*

7 The summit lies four miles from the Old Dungeon Ghyll car park. Advance with the valley bridle-track in Mickleden to the footbridge where the Stake Pass and Rossett Gill paths fork. Go left, the old pony route is currently being greatly enhanced with sturdy pitching on the zig-zag beneath Bowfell's high buttresses. The path dips by the outflow of Angle Tarn and climbs Tongue Head to the Allen Crags hause saddle, often mistaken for Esk Hause by disoriented walkers in misty conditions. In the illustration below, note the cross-wall wind-shelter right foreground, a key distinguishing landmark to locate.

Ruddy Gill, the rich red soil giving the clue to the name

The Summit

One cairn on a small rock base marks this delightful top. The view is special, the Langdale Pikes, Bowfell, Esk Pike, Great End and Great Gable all feature large, a scene fit for a fresco.

Safe Descents

In deteriorating conditions set store on reaching the saddle in the connecting ridge (with a wind-shelter some 60 metres due S). It is located SW from the summit, a matter of eight minutes descent on a loose but obvious trail. Left (E) for Langstrath or, far better, Great Langdale 4 miles, right (W) for Borrowdale, holding company with Ruddy Gill 5 miles, or via Styhead Pass, Wasdale Head 4 miles.

Ridge Routes to...

ESK PIKE   DESCENT 200 ft ASCENT 530 ft   1 mile

Descend to the saddle SW, follow the clear path S passing by the wall shelter rising to the multi-cairned Esk Hause. Go left (SE), the path mounts onto the N ridge keeping basically on the W side, via rock bands. There is a cairn on the east top, though the summit is the bold bare outcrop to the right as you approach. Clamber up to the gap for either top, or come upon it more directly from the right.

GLARAMARA   DESCENT 600 ft ASCENT 440 ft   1.8 miles

This is one of those uncomplicated paths that never seems to get going, never clear of rock long enough to give the stride the freedom one really desires. The mid-point depression where lies a cluster of pools about High House Tarn is a place to dawdle. Beyond the ridge bulks further, via two intermediate tops separated by the depression at the head of Red Beck; cairns may lure left from the trail for the fine westward view, en route to the cairnless rock summit, with its snug wind-shelter.

GREAT END   DESCENT 200 ft ASCENT 640 ft   1.2 miles

Begin as to Esk Pike above; reaching Esk Hause, bear right (W), with its plethora of cairns. The popular trail leads up into the shallow hollow of Calf Cove, with a gill issuing from a marsh. Upon gaining the brow bear right (N), finding the stone-free mid-ridge to either of the cairned tops.

The Langdale Pikes from the path leading up to the summit from the south

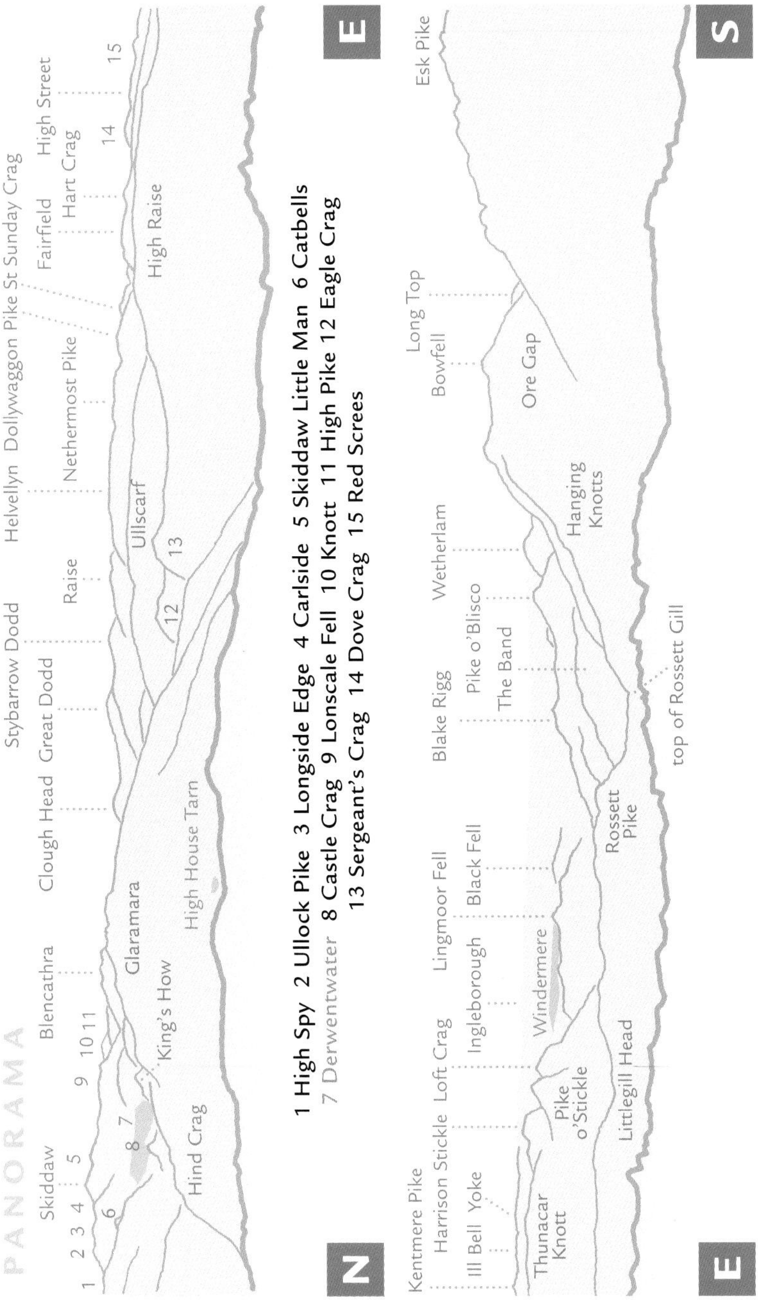

PANORAMA

E

S

N

E

1 High Spy 2 Ullock Pike 3 Longside Edge 4 Carlside 5 Skiddaw Little Man 6 Catbells
7 Derwentwater 8 Castle Crag 9 Lonscale Fell 10 Knott 11 High Pike 12 Eagle Crag
13 Sergeant's Crag 14 Dove Crag 15 Red Screes

Skiddaw · Blencathra · Clough Head · Great Dodd · Stybarrow Dodd · Helvellyn · Dollywaggon Pike · St Sunday Crag · Fairfield · High Street

Raise · Nethermost Pike · High Raise · Hart Crag

Glaramara · King's How · High House Tarn · Hind Crag · Ullscarf

Kentmere Pike · Ill Bell · Yoke · Harrison Stickle · Loft Crag · Lingmoor Fell · Blake Rigg · Wetherlam · Long Top · Esk Pike

Thunacar Knott · Pike o'Stickle · Littlegill Head · Ingleborough · Black Fell · Windermere · Rossett Pike · Pike o'Blisco · The Band · Hanging Knotts · Bowfell · Ore Gap

top of Rossett Gill

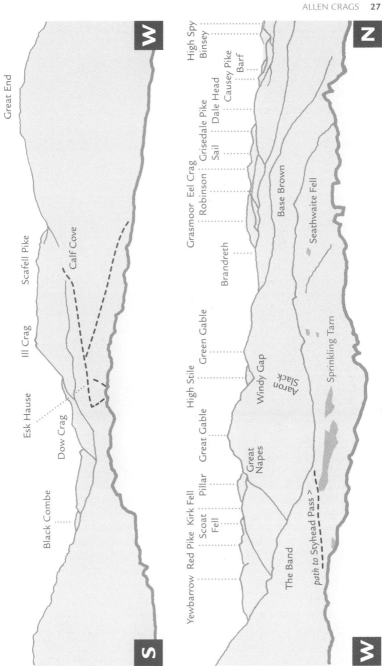

W

Great End

Scafell Pike

Ill Crag

Esk Hause

Dow Crag

Calf Cove

Black Combe

S

N

High Spy
Binsey
Causey Pike
Barf

Griesedale Pike
Dale Head
Sail

Grasmoor Eel Crag
Robinson

Base Brown

Seathwaite Fell

Brandreth

Green Gable

Windy Gap

Aaron Slack

Sprinkling Tarn

High Stile

Great Gable

Great Napes

Yewbarrow Red Pike Kirk Fell
Scoat Fell Pillar

The Band

path to Styhead Pass >

W

BOWFELL

For all the obvious appeal of the Langdale Pikes, they are like courtiers in the wings, deferring to the real overlord of Great Langdale. The summit, a monarch on his throne, the focus of longing attention from the Old Dungeon Ghyll. With the rough skyline of Crinkle Crags the heads of high officials, and lowly Rossett Pike the court jester, one just knows where the centre of power lies. Missing the magical 3,000 feet by a mere thirty-seven, Bowfell nevertheless, confirms its mountainhood by clearing the nine hundred metre threshold. Measurements alone don't make a mountain, and Bowfell makes a great impression whether viewed from Eskdale, Langstrath or Great Langdale. Three dales it contrives to command, though it is most associated, admired and climbed from Great Langdale.

The fell has two craggy aspects, the southern gullied wall of Bowfell Links *(see above)* and a more stern shadowed, upper eastern facade of crags, pre-eminently Bowfell Buttress, a famous proving ground for

903 metres   **2,963** feet

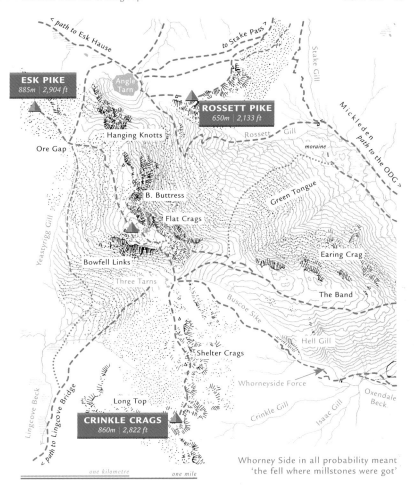

path to Esk Hause

to Stake Pass

Stake Gill

ESK PIKE
885m | 2,904 ft

Angle
Tarn

ROSSETT PIKE
650m | 2,133 ft

Hanging Knotts

Rossett Gill

moraine

Mickleden

path to the ODG

Ore Gap

B. Buttress

Green Tongue

Flat Crags

Earing Crag

Bowfell Links

Three Tarns

The Band

Buscoe Sike

Hell Gill

Shelter Crags

Whorneyside Force

Oxendale Beck

Long Top

CRINKLE CRAGS
860m | 2,822 ft

Crinkle Gill

Isaac Gill

Lingcove Beck

path to Lingcove Bridge

Yeastyrigg Gill

one kilometre   *one mile*

Whorney Side in all probability meant
'the fell where millstones were got'

climbers and the giant tilted slab-top of Flat Crags, the delight of the more adventurous fellwalker, though access to its base can be tricky in poor weather.

No fellwalk more typifies the gently, gently catch your mountain feeling than The Band, the east ridge approach via Stool End. It fits the bill superbly. The 2,600 foot ascent of Bowfell taken in nice steady stages climbing the spur ridge with ample opportunity to admire Pike o'Blisco, Crinkle Crags and the Langdale Pikes, particularly Gimmer Crag and Pike o'Stickle. A pleasing variant to the Three Tarns col leads by Oxendale to Whorneyside Force and Hell Gill. The longer, wilder Lingcove Beck approach can be the lead in to the upper Eskdale superhighway: an exhilarating skyline trek including Esk Pike, Scafell Pike,

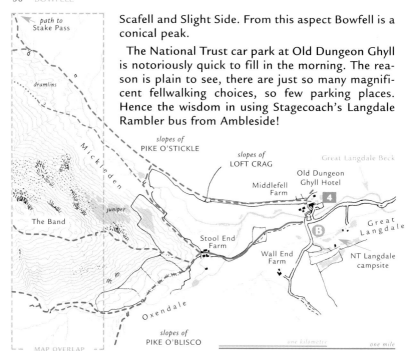

Scafell and Slight Side. From this aspect Bowfell is a conical peak.

The National Trust car park at Old Dungeon Ghyll is notoriously quick to fill in the morning. The reason is plain to see, there are just so many magnificent fellwalking choices, so few parking places. Hence the wisdom in using Stagecoach's Langdale Rambler bus from Ambleside!

ASCENT *from Great Langdale*

1 Either start from the Old Dungeon Ghyll car park or Langdale Rambler bus stop. Follow the approach road to Stool End Farm – the name might be analogous with The Band as the stool beneath the high table of Bowfell. Pass through the busy farmyard; rising from the gate take the repaired path right at the brow top. This leads up to a kissing-gate beside the Hamer memorial seat. This popular path has been extensively repaired of late and is bedecked with an over-abundance of casual cairns. Largely holding to a southern bias, at one point the path momentarily peers over Mickleden to admire Pike o'Stickle and Gimmer Crag, with extensive juniper thicket below. The path takes a side swipe, missing the top of The Band; there is merit in considering a detour to the brink of Earing Crag to look down upon Mickleden. From the subsequent shallow depression (GR 255062) the path forks. The right-hand completes a stony ascent to Three Tarns hause (GR 248061), although it is rare to find more than two pools. The ridges and gullies of Bowfell Links are well viewed from this point, as too across the south ridge of Esk Pike, the twin peaks of Scafell and Scafell Pike either side of Mickledore. A rough, stony path clambers up the southern flank of Bowfell, reaching the summit by the top of Flat Crags.

2 The confident walker, with a head for heights and well-adjusted mountain feet, may wish to consider following the Climbers' Traverse, branching innocently from the main route at the depression. Rising with the ridge, passing over to the shadowy northern side, the path is consistent but narrow. In some respects it is more exposed than Jack's Rake, so in wet, windy or icy conditions most walkers should leave it well alone! The traverse

keeps under the banded cliff-end of Flat Crags and, from a minor col, gains a handsome view of Bowfell Buttress, flanked by runs of scree, across the

Earing Crag, the name a reference to a former eyrie of golden eagles

The giant tilted slab-top of Flat Crags from the brink of Cambridge Crag

combe. Coming under the broken wall of Cambridge Crag, the path switches up left, onto the bouldery corner, running up the tilted slabs of Flat Crag. If the rock is dry you might find it more comfortable, and certainly more entertaining, to walk up the open slab itself - just watch your footing on any wet algae. The topmost outcropping exhibits well the banded nature of the bedrock. The path from Three Tarns appears at the top. There are three options from Mickleden: via **3** Green Tongue, a tough grass route (which demands walking poles in descent), **5** the popular Rossett Gill trail via Angle Tarn and Ore Gap, **6** a bruising pathless climb to Flat Crags veering off the Rossett Gill pony path zig-zags.

3 Follow the valley bridle-way from the Old Dungeon Ghyll; at first a lane, it opens beyond a sheep holding pen. The wall on the left ends, bear left, to cross the footbridge

The Climbers' Traverse, little more than a sheep trod on a perilous slope

Bowfell Buttress from Cambridge Crag

Bowfell from Bleatarn House

spanning Mickleden Beck. Go right, along the flat damp dale floor to join a shepherding drove-cum-quad bike trail, recently consolidated where it fords minor gills draining The Band. Shortly after passing an old fold, tucked down in a brackeny hollow, the drove slips right. Keep all the moraine to the right, contouring over damp ground, thus avoiding the bracken, until a rowan is spotted in a gill up to the left. Ascend the rigg beside the gill. Continue the steady, breathless climb, the compensation being the fine views of Rossett Gill and, as one gains height, the craggy

Pike o'Blisco from the point where Buscoe Sike enters the Hell Gill ravine

east face of Bowfell, a famous climbing ground. Higher still venture to the eastern edge to see Earing Crag on the north slope of The Band. Green Tongue crests above the shallow depression where The Band merges with Bowfell proper. Be warned: ignore the first path encountered – this leads to the Climbers' Traverse. Proceed further, slightly descending to join the main path to Three Tarns col and the popular path to the top.

4 The Oxendale route via Whorneyside Force. Often used as a novel descent alternative to The Band, serious erosion has mercifully been stemmed by exemplary pitching on the steep section at the foot of Hell Gill. The route leads into Oxendale from Stool End Farm; ignore the first footbridge, either keep to the river-bank path, which from the wall-end becomes narrow, or rise right, to contour easily on a good path to the second footbridge. The path now curves up the bank, with new pitching, though close to the mare's tail falls there is land slippage to be wary of. The small pool and waterfall with a large boulder at the top of Whorneyside Force give reason to idle. The path next fords the beck via boulders, passes under the embowered entrance to Hell Gill and mounts the new-made path. Take a look into Hell Gill as the slopes eases and, higher, admire the composition formed by Pike o'Blisco *(see left)*. The path pays little heed to Buscoe Sike, preferring to slant up the damp slope, passing a former small fenced area, latterly rising steeply to join The Band path just below the Three Tarns col.

Two further routes lead by Mickleden. 5 From the footbridge at the foot

Evening light streaming through Mickledore from Three Tarns

Evening sun highlights Hanging Knotts and reflected in the still waters of Angle Tarn

Cambridge Crag and Bowfell Buttress from the giant slab on top of Flat Crags

of Stake Gill follow the old pony path left, initially with Rossett Gill left, as it becomes excessively stony the path fords the Gill. (The old short-cut up the gill is a lost cause, just give it a miss!) The newly pitched trail veers away leftward, coping with rock outcropping via two zig-zags, the second the more extravagant.

6 At this point free-thinkers may motion diagonally off the path up the mightily rough slope, bee-lining to the foot of Cambridge Crag and thus step onto the base of Flat Crags, as an alternative approach to the Climbers' Traverse. The scree-run to the skyline left of Bowfell Buttress might also be tackled, but don't say I didn't warn you – it's a bruising trial going every inch of the way.

5 Fellwalkers paying into or receiving a pension will always choose to stay with the pony path cresting the top of Rossett Gill, sedately declining to the outflow of Angle Tarn *(see opposite)*. The tarn-name attests to its former piscean attributes, but it is no longer stocked for anglers. On the rise beyond take the left-hand fork in the path, which curves from west to south negotiating intermittent bouldery patches to gain the plain saddle at Ore Gap. Sharp-eyed prospectors must have christened it. Go left, with plenty of ankle-twisting boulders to test your sense of balance, the path trending slight east of south onto the ridge. Short of the final knoll go to the brink and look down the scree gully, with Bowfell Buttress down to the left. Just think, some folk entertain coming up this way. They must be mad and, yes, in the cause of testing everything for this guide the author must reveal himself in their number!

Whorneyside Force at the head of Oxendale from Black Wars

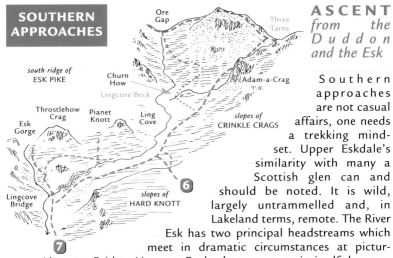

SOUTHERN APPROACHES

Ore Gap

Three Tarns

south ridge of ESK PIKE

Churn How

Lingcove Beck

Adam-a-Crag

Throstlehow Crag

Pianet Knott

Ling Cove

slopes of CRINKLE CRAGS

Esk Gorge

6

Lingcove Bridge

slopes of HARD KNOTT

7

ASCENT
from the Duddon and the Esk

Southern approaches are not casual affairs, one needs a trekking mind-set. Upper Eskdale's similarity with many a Scottish glen can and should be noted. It is wild, largely untrammelled and, in Lakeland terms, remote. The River Esk has two principal headstreams which meet in dramatic circumstances at pictur-esque Lingcove Bridge. Lingcove Beck, the eastern grain itself, has two prime points of issue, Ore Gap and Three Tarns, hauses that in turn define Bowfell to north and south, giving fellwalkers objectives on one or other approach march. **8** The swifter but duller approach tracks up Mosedale. The bridle-path, signposted off the open road west of Cockley Beck Bridge, squelches for 1.4 miles to the dale-head cross-rigg, passing via either a hand-gate or stile in the triple-stranded electric heaf fence. Both paths advance to Lingcove Beck and unite to trend right

Bowfell and Long Top from the herb-rich hay meadows of Brotherilkeld

(upstream). Passing well below the impressive Adam-a-Crag, western buttress of Long Top, slashed by a sinister gully, the path slants north-east up the moraine, then fords Rest Gill, named by exhausted travellers, no doubt. There is modest evidence of a path on the steady climb to the two tarns at Three Tarns.

9 The more impressive approach begins from Brotherilkeld accompanying the Esk to Lingcove Bridge. The path trends up right, short of the packhorse bridge, and climbs above Lingcove Beck into Ling Cove. The route to Ore Gap is less than obvious. There is little hint of a consistent path contouring round Churn How, ascending a rigg beneath the head-wall of Bowfell, well to the right of Yeastyrigg Gill. Slanting up left to a prominent skyline boulder, the path materialises underfoot now coming closer to the gill on the lead into to the pass. From Ore Gap (the red soil may explain the name, suggesting, if not producing, useful metal) go right towards the summit, on intermittently stony terrain.

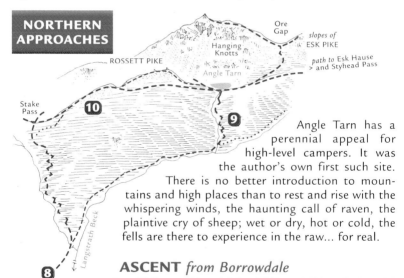

NORTHERN APPROACHES

Ore Gap

slopes of ESK PIKE

Hanging Knotts

ROSSETT PIKE

path to Esk Hause and Styhead Pass

Angle Tarn

Stake Pass

10

9

Angle Tarn has a perennial appeal for high-level campers. It was the author's own first such site. There is no better introduction to mountains and high places than to rest and rise with the whispering winds, the haunting call of raven, the plaintive cry of sheep; wet or dry, hot or cold, the fells are there to experience in the raw... for real.

Langstrath Beck

8

ASCENT *from Borrowdale*

Stonethwaite may seem a remote launch pad. However, as Bowfell does have a toe-hold in Borrowdale drainage, many fellwalkers reasonably contemplate including the summit in a through trek to Great Langdale; supercharged Cumbria Way hikers can elevate their expedition immeasurably by its inclusion. **10** Follow the bridle-track up the east side of Langstrath. From the footbridge at the foot of Stake Beck, 3 miles from Stonethwaite, keep to the dale path right, ford and follow Angletarn Gill to the tarn outflow. **11** Alternatively, reach this spot by following the Cumbria Way to the top of Stake Pass, take the ridge path, which may include the summit of Rossett Pike. Head up west, as if to Esk Hause, then take the first left fork. Rise easily to Ore Gap; the ridge path ignores the edge above Hanging Knotts, instead makes a bee-line to the summit.

The Summit

The ultimate ground is stone pure and simple, a mix of boulders and bedrock, a place of repose. Catch your breath and take in the marvellous all round view. No visit is complete if it ignores the eastern brink. Descent north-east to meet the path, traversing from Ore Gap to Three Tarns, cautiously wander to the edge of Cambridge Crag for the most sensational view of the Great Slab of Flat Crags and Bowfell Buttress. The view from the brink of Bowfell Links due south deserves a visit too.

Benchmarks were chiselled into rocks to fix height levels during original Ordnance Survey triangulation, set from a mean sea-level at the south pier tidal observatory at Newlyn

Ordnance Survey benchmark circa 1861

Safe Descents

With so much craggy ground beneath the summit, finding and abiding to an evident path is crucial. The path running diagonally just E of the summit pile should be used, NNW for Ore Gap and SE for Three Tarns.

Ridge Routes to...

CRINKLE CRAGS   DESCENT 600 ft   ASCENT 460 ft   1.4 miles

   A walk to sing about. Head E, joining the main ridge path leading by banded rocks close to the top of the Great Slab of Flat Crags. Leave the plateau SE on an often loose trail to Three Tarns, weave due S, visiting, or circumventing, successive craggy knotts. After Shelter Crags, Gunson Knott is the first true crinkle, the fourth crinkle is the summit.

ESK PIKE   DESCENT 370 ft   ASCENT 345 ft   1 mile

Head NNW to Ore Gap, then rise NW straight to the summit.

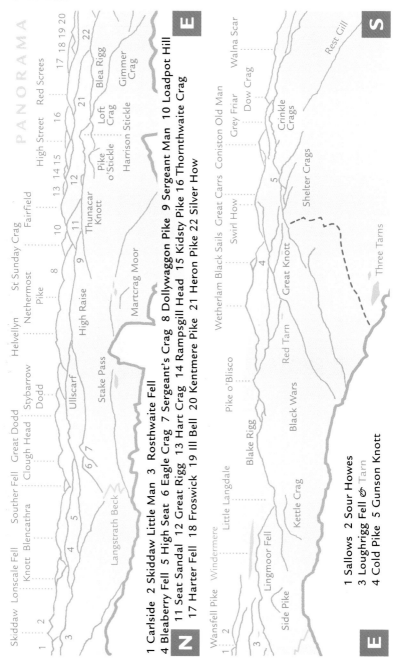

PANORAMA

E

Skiddaw   Lonscale Fell   Souther Fell   Great Dodd   Helvellyn   St Sunday Crag
Knott   Blencathra   Clough Head   Stybarrow   Nethermost   Fairfield   High Street   Red Screes
Dodd   Pike

N

1 Carlside 2 Skiddaw Little Man 3 Rosthwaite Fell
4 Bleaberry Fell 5 High Seat 6 Eagle Crag 7 Sergeant's Crag 8 Dollywaggon Pike 9 Sergeant Man 10 Loadpot Hill
11 Seat Sandal 12 Great Rigg 13 Hart Crag 14 Rampsgill Head 15 Kidsty Pike 16 Thornthwaite Crag
17 Harter Fell 18 Froswick 19 Ill Bell 20 Kentmere Pike 21 Heron Pike 22 Silver How

S

Wetherlam   Black Sails   Great Carrs   Coniston Old Man
Swirl How   Grey Friar   Dow Crag   Walna Scar

Wansfell Pike   Windermere
Little Langdale

E

1 Sallows 2 Sour Howes
3 Loughrigg Fell & Tarn
4 Cold Pike 5 Gunson Knott

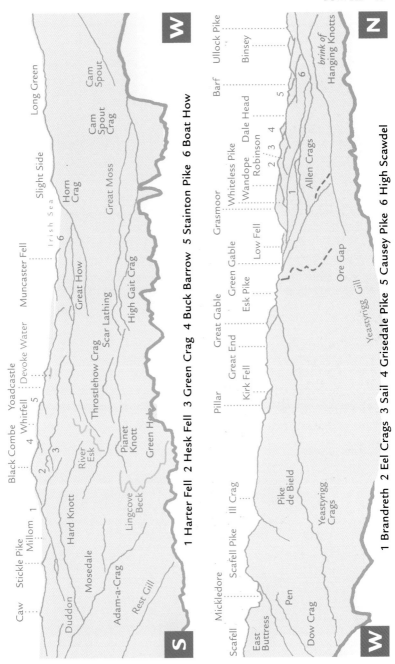

W

Long Green · Slight Side · Muncaster Fell · Devoke Water · Yoadcastle · Whitfell · Black Combe · Stickle Pike · Caw

Cam Spout · Cam Spout Crag · Horn Crag · Great Moss · Great How · Scar Lathing · Throstlehow Crag · High Gait Crag · Green Hole · Pianet Knott · River Esk · Lingcove Beck · Adam-a-Crag · Rest Gill · Hard Knott · Mosedale · Duddon · Millom

Irish Sea

1 · 2 · 3 · 4 · 5 · 6

S

1 Harter Fell 2 Hesk Fell 3 Green Crag 4 Buck Barrow 5 Stainton Pike 6 Boat How

N

Ullock Pike · Barf · Binsey · Grasmoor · Whiteless Pike · Wandope · Robinson · Dale Head · Green Gable · Low Fell · Pillar · Great Gable · Great End · Esk Pike · Kirk Fell

brink of Hanging Knotts · Allen Crags · Ore Gap · Yeastyrigg Gill

1 · 2 · 3 · 4 · 5 · 6

1 Brandreth 2 Eel Crags 3 Sail 4 Grisedale Pike 5 Causey Pike 6 High Scawdel

W

Mickledore · Scafell Pike · Ill Crag · Scafell · East Buttress · Pen · Dow Crag

Pike de Bield · Yeastyrigg Crags

COLD PIKE

Crinkle Crags has two projecting southern spur ridges, each ending in a flourish at outpost tops. Cold Pike is the more distinct eastern arm, an affiliated rebel crinkle. Across its northern flanks *(see above)* runs the ever popular path from Wrynose Pass via Red Tarn to Crinkle Crags, yet the fell deserves not to be cold shouldered. It makes a delightful quickly won objective from the top of the pass, its triple-piked summit is especially fun to explore, a place proliferating in easy scrambling ideas. As a viewpoint too its merits are manifest, the Langdale Pikes, Pike o'Blisco, and the Coniston group all hold attention.

From the start of the path at Wrynose Pass

701 metres   2,300 feet

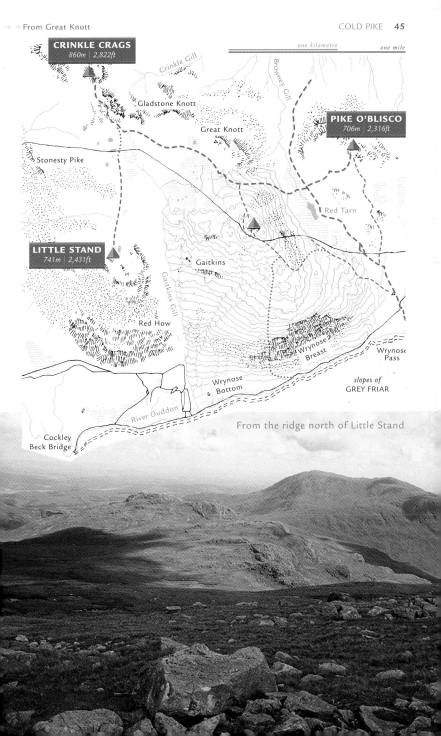

CRINKLE CRAGS
860m | 2,822ft

Crinkle Gill

Browney Gill

one kilometre   one mile

Gladstone Knott

Great Knott

PIKE O'BLISCO
706m | 2,316ft

Stonesty Pike

Red Tarn

LITTLE STAND
741m | 2,431ft

Gaitkins

Gaitkins Gill

Red How

Wrynose
Breast

Wrynose
Pass

slopes of
GREY FRIAR

Wrynose
Bottom

River Duddon

Cockley
Beck Bridge

From the ridge north of Little Stand

Thunacar Knott   Harrison Stickle
Pike   Loft
o'Stickle   Crag
                                      Pike o'Blisco

                                              Long Crag

                                      path to Wrynose Pass >

                              Red Tarn

ASCENT *from Wrynose Pass*

The Three Shire Stone is a Lancashire-only replica of a former genuine three shires stone, prior to 1974 the meeting point of Cumberland, Westmorland and Lancashire. **1** From the high point of the pass, a well-worn path strikes north, rising via a stile in the heaf fence; watch for a cairn indicating a half-left fork. Follow this lesser path. Fording gills rising onto the easy slopes of a moraine rigg, the path angles up to the prominent skyline knot due west *(viewpoint of scene above)*. Pass a banded outcrop with a large cairn to a tarn. Cross the fence, keep left of the first two outcrops to reach the summit. **2** A simpler route, with obvious paths all the way, keeps to the main path, crosses a second heaf fence stile, passing Red Tarn to the staggered path junction below Pike o'Blisco. Turn left (west), cross an exposure of iron oxide red soil. The path rises, giving a fine view down the Browney Gill valley towards the Langdale Pikes. Immediately prior to the first ford, as the path eases onto the moorland plateau, bear up left. A path soon materialises aiming direct for the summit.

Severed totem at top of the gully, and view down same to Wrynose Bottom

SOUTHERN APPROACHES

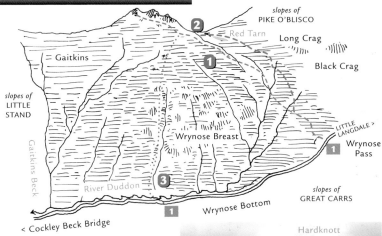

slopes of
PIKE O'BLISCO
Red Tarn
Long Crag
Gaitkins
Black Crag
slopes of
LITTLE
STAND
LITTLE
LANGDALE >
Wrynose Breast
Wrynose
Pass
Gaitkins Beck
River Duddon
slopes of
GREAT CARRS
Wrynose Bottom
< Cockley Beck Bridge

ASCENT
from Wrynose Bottom

Hardknott
Pass·
Harter Fell
Hard
Knott

3 The narrow, windy, open
road leads down from the pass,
the shapely form of Harter Fell
framed by the high fellsides of
the infant Duddon *(right)*. The
road soon levels accompanying
the stony beck. There's a footpath sign on the right with
verge parking in the vicinity. Across the ford is a stile in a brief fenced section of an otherwise largely walled enclosure line beside the river. Beyond
keep to the right slope; attention is immediately drawn to a large dark
square boulder with a bield wall *(below)*. Angle up the apron of grass
close by, the delta spill from a gill. This is the clue to an excellent steep
unorthodox ascent. The open gully of the gill harbours delicate flora to
intrigue the botanist and, being well endowed with grass, is never a problem in ascent. At the top note the small
outcrop to the left where a three metre
totem block stands perilously as a pinnacle waiting for the next shove of ice to
render the   illustration *(far left)* history.
The ground eases, three damp shelves are
crossed on the more sedate, pathless trek
up the slope to a tarn. Join the path from
Wrynose Pass at a tarn.

The Summit

The highest ground is without question the fell's finest moment. There are three pronounced rocky rises. Most visitors side-step the southern top and work through to the summit proper. Two cairns rest on opposing outcrops, the northern pile being the true summit, a splendid spot.

Safe Descents

With crags immediately east, the sensible choice in mist is NW. Meet up with the path from Crinkle Crags, go right, down to the cross-path saddle, then either left for Great Langdale, or right for the road at the top of the Wrynose Pass.

Summit benches

Bowfell   Great Knott

Glaramara

Crinkle Crags from the summit cairn

Black Sails
Coniston Old Man
Wetherlam
Swirl How
Great Carrs
Wetside Edge

The Coniston Fells from the middle top

Ridge Routes to...

CRINKLE CRAGS   DESCENT 280 ft   ASCENT 810 ft   1.25 miles
SEE THE PANORAMA FOR ROUTE NOTES

PIKE O'BLISCO   DESCENT 620 ft   ASCENT 630 ft   1.2 miles
Descend NW to join the popular trail, going right fording a gill in the saddle, heading E on a well-marked path which curves N to the summit.

The Langdale Pikes
Helvellyn
Fairfield
The Band
ODG

View down Browney Gill from the path to Crinkle Crags above Red Tarn

PANORAMA

E

S

N

E

1 Knott 2 Sergeant's Crag 3 High Seat 4 Blencathra 5 Thunacar Knott
6 Harrison Stickle 7 Nethermost Pike 8 Dollywaggon Pike 9 Hart Crag
10 Dove Crag 11 High Raise 12 Kidsty Pike 13 High Street
14 Harter Fell 15 Ill Bell 16 Kentmere Pike 17 Yoke

Red Screes 14 15 16 17 Loughrigg Fell

Lingmoor Fell

11 12 13

10

9

Pike o'Blisco

path to Wrynose Pass >

Red Tarn

Lonscale Fell

Pike o'Stickle   Great Dodd Helvellyn

High Raise

Seat Sandal   Fairfield

1 2 3   4

5   6

7   8

Martcrag Moor

Gimmer Crag

Great Langdale

The Band

Oxendale

Great Carrs

Swirl How

Hellgill Pike

Black Sails

Wetherlam

Wetside Edge

Bowland Fells AONB

Birk Fell

Windermere
(two sections)

Black Fell

Sallows

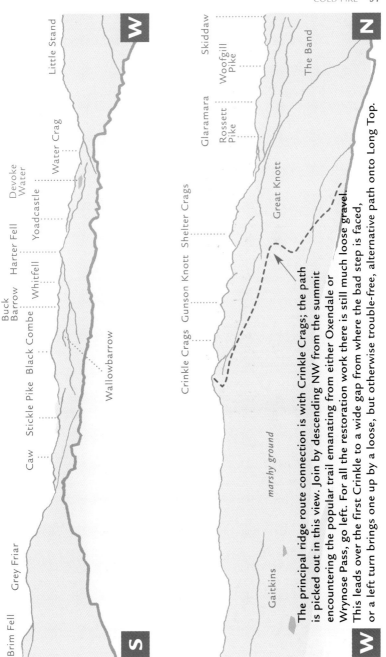

W Brim Fell | Grey Friar | Caw | Stickle Pike | Black Combe | Buck Barrow | Whitfell | Harter Fell | Yoadcastle | Devoke Water | Water Crag | Little Stand **W**

Wallowbarrow

N Glaramara | Rossett Pike | Skiddaw | Woofgill Pike | The Band **N**

Crinkle Crags | Gunson Knott | Shelter Crags | Great Knott

Gaitkins

marshy ground

W The principal ridge route connection is with Crinkle Crags; the path is picked out in this view. Join by descending NW from the summit encountering the popular trail emanating from either Oxendale or Wrynose Pass, go left. For all the restoration work there is still much loose gravel. This leads over the first Crinkle to a wide gap from where the bad step is faced, or a left turn brings one up by a loose, but otherwise trouble-free, alternative path onto Long Top. **W**

CRINKLE CRAGS

Seen from afar, notably from the south-west, it is easy to understand why Crinkle Crags is sometimes referred to as Long Top. Viewed from the east, particularly from Pike o'Blisco *(above)*, one is left in no doubt from where the popular name derived. Thus the fell belongs, in fellwalkers imagination, in the realm of Great Langdale. Witness a hunched-up huddled skyline mass of craggy ground, as if cringing from a shudder... try a bag of Crinkle Crags the rocky-ramblers favourite crisps! A deserved touch of levity in recognition of a much-loved fell.

The popular circuit heads up The Band from the ODG, trending south from Three Tarns. Walkers should be warned: this may appear the natural course, but the bad step, encountered on the southern descent from the main Crinkle, is more awkward than your average rock problem. It is better that the cautious novice avoids the wobbly by embarking anti-clockwise, tracking up Oxendale and above Browney Beck to meet the obstacle from below, when a sane decision can be made to take it on, or follow the left-hand variation onto Long Top, circumventing the problem altogether. The dale approach from Eskdale, via Lingcove Beck, enjoys handsome surroundings with an easy line to Three Tarns, a less conventional line via Adam-a-Cove and a challenging climb up the western bluff-end of Long Top from Rest Gill.

860 metres   2,822 feet

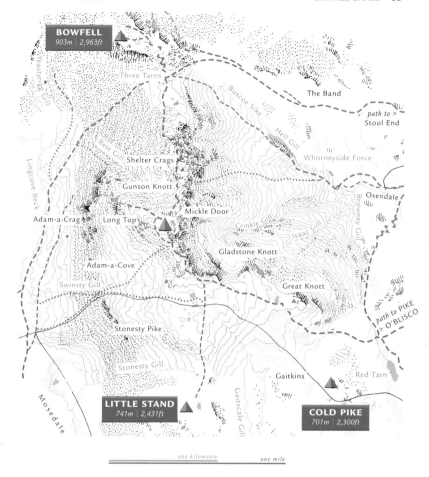

BOWFELL
903m | 2,963ft

Three Tarns

Buscoe Sike

The Band

Hell Gill

path to >
Stool End

Whorneyside Force

Shelter Crags

Red Gill

Gunson Knott

Mickle Door

Oxendale

Browney Gill

Adam-a-Crag

Long Top

Crinkle Gill

Isaac Gill

Lingcove Beck

Gladstone Knott

Adam-a-Cove

Swinsty Gill

Great Knott

path to PIKE
O'BLISCO

Stonesty Pike

Stonesty Gill

Gaitkins

Red Tarn

Gatescale Gill

Mosedale

LITTLE STAND
741m | 2,431ft

COLD PIKE
701m | 2,300ft

Yeastyrigg Gill

one kilometre   *one mile*

Wall End Farm and Oxendale with the Crinkles cosseted in a mantle of cloud

Looking down Crinkle Gill to Oxendale and Great Langdale from Mickle Door

ASCENT *from Great Langdale*

From the ODG the irregular skyline has obvious appeal, an inviting coconut shy of craggy tops waiting to knocked off. **1** The obvious route follows the Stool End farm-road; pass through the busy farmyard via a gate, take the clear branch right onto the foot of the ridge. Rising to a hand-gate by the Hamer seat, passing through, the path climbs steadily. At one point it ventures to peer at the mighty face of Gimmer Crag and Pike o'Stickle across the great gulf of Mickleden, otherwise Kettle Crag and the elegant peak of Pike o'Blisco rising above Oxendale have sway during the climb. Thankfully the path has been consolidated of late, the pitching giving firm footing where previously a loose unsightly trail had existed. As the path avoids the actual crest, some walkers may be tempted to wander onto the higher ground above Earing Crag: the name alluding to a former nesting site of golden eagle. The main path roughens underfoot as it reaches up to the Three Tarns col. Don't waste too much time searching for a trio of tarns, there are seldom more than two, though in turning south a delightful pool can be found to the left, over peaty ground, jammed tightly in a rock crevice. The path avoids the first minor cairned knot in mounting Shelter Crags; there are several paths, but no one true way. Higher up a reedy pool is passed en route to the gap below Gunson Knot, the goal of the direct ascent from Oxendale. Attention is focused on the sequence of little knots, all of

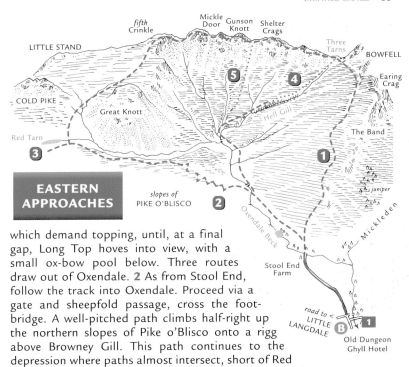

LITTLE STAND

fifth Crinkle

Mickle Door

Gunson Knott

Shelter Crags

Three Tarns

BOWFELL

Earing Crag

COLD PIKE

Great Knott

5

4

Hell Gill

The Band

Red Tarn

3

1

juniper

EASTERN APPROACHES

slopes of PIKE O'BLISCO

2

Oxendale Beck

Mickleden

which demand topping, until, at a final gap, Long Top hoves into view, with a small ox-bow pool below. Three routes draw out of Oxendale. **2** As from Stool End, follow the track into Oxendale. Proceed via a gate and sheepfold passage, cross the foot-bridge. A well-pitched path climbs half-right up the northern slopes of Pike o'Blisco onto a rigg above Browney Gill. This path continues to the depression where paths almost intersect, short of Red

Stool End Farm

road to < LITTLE LANGDALE **B**

1

Old Dungeon Ghyll Hotel

Tarn. **3** This point is popularly visited from the top of the Wrynose Pass, crossing the heaf fence twice en route to Red Tarn. Turn west, ford the gill and cross a patch of iron oxide-rich soil. Walkers will notice that numerous ridge-top saddles have a patch of red soil, Ore Gap an obvious example. Such deposits were formerly used for sheep marking purposes. Upon reaching the moor, ford a gill, the way wends on at an easy gradient. The path has recently been ushered into a tighter line by stones, the net result a less than comfortable loose gravelly trail. Great Knott is ignored by the path, but walkers should not assume this prominent top

is without virtue as a viewpoint. The first Crinkle gained with much relief, firm ground at last! Cross over into the grassy gap with its view back down Great Cove towards Oxendale. For a sure, unfettered ascent, trend half-left; a simple path mounts onto the western end of Long Top. More earnest walkers will see the bad step as merely another straightforward scramble to deal with, though it is not just a matter of putting the right foot first, whether or not it is the right foot, the arms and a steady head have to be right too!

direct scramble

The bad step

The fifth Crinkle from Long Top, the Coniston Fells forming the backdrop

3 The eastern combe attracts more than the occasional walker. Several gills drain into this amphitheatre, though Crinkle Gill is not so appealing as may be thought; however, Hell Gill is another matter. Follow the path beyond the footbridge, bearing right at the wall-end, and rise onto a contouring path, thus avoiding the awkward path along the edge of the beck. Across the footbridge, the path, with a few pitched sections, rises diagonally; on approaching the handsome mare's tail of Whorneyside Force, gingerly cross a landslip to visit the upper fall and pool with its big boulder. Whorneyside meant 'the wren's fell pasture'.

Ford the beck at the foot of the Hell Gill ravine - no entry! Mount the left-hand bank, path-works here have made the path so much sweeter to tread, eradicating a scar too. As the ground eases, look into the ravine and back to Pike o'Blisco: a delightful subject for the camera. Buscoe Sike drains into Hell Gill, though the path drifts slightly leftwards, passing an old fenced area. It only comes near the gill higher up, advancing towards Three Tarns.

4 From the footbridge below Whorneyside Force, wander up the main path only as far as the top of the first paved section, find a bracken-light line up the rigg. Escaping the bracken's clutches, climb the grassy moor with eyes intent on the high gap between the craggy mass of Gunson Knott and Shelter Crags. Inevitably the ground steepens, but a sure and largely scree-free line can be found. Having tested this route in descent I found walking poles eliminated any need for the use of grasping hands. For all the lack of a path the ground is good and firm; nonetheless, this is not a route to consider in poor conditions.

Three Tarns and Shelter Crags sunlit from the brink of Bowfell Links

ASCENT *from the Duddon and the Esk*

A superb nine mile outing takes in the whole ridge from Little Stand to Esk Pike, returning via Pike de Bield and the south ridge fording Lingcove Beck below Pianet Knott, 'the magpies rocks', to enter Mosedale. **6** This would start from Cockley Beck Bridge (*See* LITTLE STAND (GR246017) *page 172*) . The summit of Little Stand gives a hint to the attractions of the

SOUTH-WESTERN APPROACHES

Crinkles, though the intermediate ridge is quite tame, advancing via the heaf fence stile to the southernmost crinkle. **7** The longest approach begins from the foot of Hardknott Pass in Eskdale (GR212012). Follow the farm track to Brotherilkeld and the subsequent waymarkedpath, initially tight by the Esk. Leaving the shelter of trees traverse enclosures, via gates, onto a regular path where the dale hems in approaching Lingcove Bridge. The path to follow keeps up right, just before the sheepfold which presages the elegant footbridge. Clamber up on the stony path

The summit stack from the fifth Crinkle

above the delightful Lingcove Beck gorge. Notice the existence of heather clinging to the fringes of the gorge beyond the reach of sheep. One wonders how long since heather held sway in this dale, as it mercifully still does on Harter Fell. Enter the open, wilder aspect of Ling Cove.

8 A damp bridle-path leads off from the bottom of the Hardknott Pass road (GR243017) threading through Mosedale to meet up with this path, via the heaf fence in the dale-head moraine rigg. Note: this path splits just short of the rigg-top, leading either by a hand-gate or stile set some thirty yards apart; the two paths only come together close above Lingcove Beck. The main valley path keeps reasonably near to the beck leading upstream, though a higher path exists which runs up under Adam-a-Crag. Warning – this is used by adventurous souls who ascend a challenging gully on the north side of the crag. Having taken one look at it, I retreated. On a previous occasion I had descended west off Long Top and discovered the path leading up from the top of this awful cleft. Give it a

Swinsty Gill

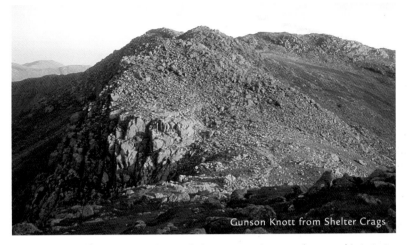

Gunson Knott from Shelter Crags

miss if you value the fair face of the mountain... and your skin! **9** As Lingcove Beck bends north, Swinsty Gill enters from the right; this may be followed, no path, keeping up to the right; and not within its ravine. The mid-section is suitable for competent scramblers only, as anyone who chances to descend close to the beck will discover: that there is a path at all in the mid-rigg is the result of descending walkers' partial descents and expedient retreats! A sane alternative is to follow the heft fence from the head of Mosedale, keeping close company up the steep grassy fellside, glancing by the out-cropping of Stonesty Pike to gain the ridge, latterly skirting a cluster of pools. **10** Follow the path slip-ping over Churn How to reach the stony delta of Rest Gill. Strong walkers might like to gain Long Top from this point; don't ford, instead keep up on the right slope, and cer-tainly not in the ravine. The steep

The Langdale Pikes from Three Tarns

ground is unrelenting but presents no difficulty in fair weather. Angle up under the outcrops above the ravine. As these abate, go right over boul-ders below a crag with, for the first time, faint evidence of a path; cross over the knott to find a clear path in the grass coming in left from the gill, traverse a few boulders to join the worn path coming up from the gully in Adam-a-Crag mentioned earlier. Now scramble in relatively easy steps up the broken western bluff-end of Long Top, the path never in doubt. **11** For an easy life, having forded Rest Gill, keep with the old path which continues to Three Tarns.

First cairned knott, south of Three Tarns

Summit cairn on Great Knott, looking to Cold Pike and the misty Coniston Fells

Crinkle and Shelter Crags from Oxendale Beck

The Summit

The Scafells from the fifth Crinkle

For all its girth, Crinkle Crags is known and adored for its fascinating north to south ridge. One conclusive top after another, each having attracted cairn-builders, each a fine excuse to pause and contemplate the next stage in the exciting crescendo. However, there is no doubting the actual summit. The characteristic Long Top runs east to west, with the principal cairn elevated towards the eastern end. Rock and rough ground is everywhere. The view does justice to the setting. It is particularly attractive looking east down Crinkle Gill to Oxendale, westward to the Scafells and, most handsome, Bowfell due north. This is God's own country... be it revelation or just plain elation, you'll know the feeling!

Safe Descents

It is imperative to know that tiered cliffs fall east and a mass of steep ground falls south, elsewhere is but rough ground. For those new to the

A pool on Shelter Crags

fell two points are of real concern. The bad step takes its annual casualty, from reckless or feckless folk who rush down and take a tumble. There is no problem as long as you take it steadily

Bowfell from the summit

and methodically. The other issue is the line of cairns chasing off the western bluff-end of Long Top, apparently bound for the Lingcove Beck valley. They are so consistent and the path so worn that one would be excused for thinking it was a safe line of descent. This is not the case. In fair or foul weather the safe ways are only to be found by sticking to the ridge proper, north to Three Tarns, turning right for Great Langdale, or south, following the prominent path down towards Red Tarn, there choosing between left for Oxendale and the ODG or right to Wrynose Pass, the quickest way to a motor road.

Ridge Routes to...

BOWFELL   DESCENT 460 ft   ASCENT 400 ft   1.4 miles

The delightful vagaries of the ridge ensure a thoroughly engrossing time N, en route to the Three Tarns hause. A worn trail mounts to the easier ground above Flat Crags and beyond to the summit pyramid.

LITTLE STAND   DESCENT 450 ft   ASCENT 60 ft   1.1 miles

Either via the bad step, immediately down to the left, or the evasive route, off the top starting W of the summit cairn. Traverse the fifth Crinkle, break right from the popular path, head due S via the heaf fence stile, with some intervening broken ground on the ridge.

COLD PIKE   DESCENT 750 ft   ASCENT 300 ft   1.5 miles

From the fifth Crinkle follow the popular path SE until, upon fording a gill at the edge of the moor, branch up right to the prominent top.

PANORAMA

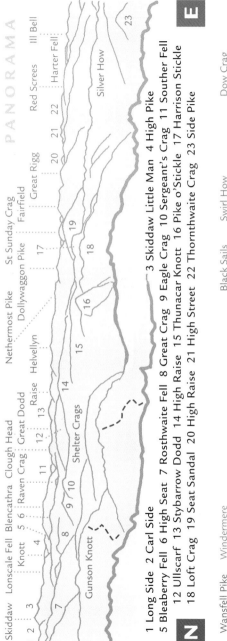
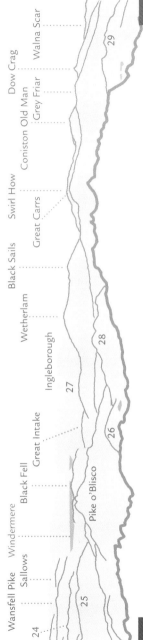

E

N

Skiddaw Lonscale Fell Blencathra Clough Head
Knott Raven Crag Great Dodd
Nethermost Pike St Sunday Crag
Dollywaggon Pike Fairfield
Great Rigg Red Screes Ill Bell
Raise Helvellyn
Harter Fell
Silver How
Shelter Crags
Gunson Knott

1 Long Side 2 Carl Side
3 Skiddaw Little Man 4 High Pike
5 Bleaberry Fell 6 High Seat 7 Rosthwaite Fell 8 Great Crag 9 Eagle Crag 10 Sergeant's Crag 11 Souther Fell
12 Ullscarf 13 Stybarrow Dodd 14 High Raise 15 Thunacar Knott 16 Pike o'Stickle 17 Harrison Stickle
18 Loft Crag 19 Seat Sandal 20 High Raise 21 High Street 22 Thornthwaite Crag 23 Side Pike

S

E

Wansfell Pike Windermere
Sallows
Black Fell
Great Intake
Black Fell
Pike o'Blisco
Ingleborough
Wetherlam
Great Carrs
Black Sails
Swirl How
Coniston Old Man
Grey Friar
Dow Crag
Walna Scar

24 Loughrigg Fell 25 Lingmoor Fell 26 Great Knott 27 Birk Fell 28 Cold Pike 29 Little Stand

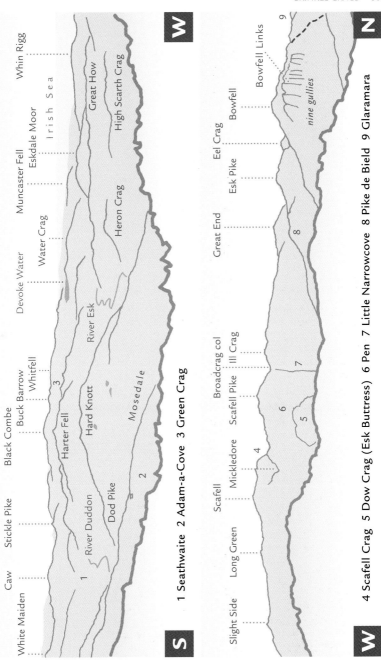

W

N

Whin Rigg

Bowfell Links

Irish Sea

9

Eskdale Moor

Bowfell

Great How

Muncaster Fell

Eel Crag

High Scarch Crag

Esk Pike

nine gullies

Water Crag

Heron Crag

Great End

Devoke Water

8

River Esk

Broadcrag col

Buck Barrow

Ill Crag

Black Combe

Whitfell

3

Scafell Pike

7

Harter Fell

Hard Knott

Mosedale

6

Stickle Pike

5

Scafell

Caw

River Duddon

Dod Pike

2

Mickledore

4

White Maiden

1

Long Green

Slight Side

S

1 Seathwaite 2 Adam-a-Cove 3 Green Crag

W

4 Scafell Crag 5 Dow Crag (Esk Buttress) 6 Pen 7 Little Narrowcove 8 Pike de Bield 9 Glaramara

ESKDALE MOOR

But for La'al Ratty and the motoring test of the Hardknott Pass, Eskdale might have remained a lost valley. Even with these inducements, only discerning tourists make it into the gorgeous valley with its long tradition of welcome for the walker and camper. Fringed to the south by the heather-clad slopes of Harter Fell and Green Crag, with the rugged foothills of the Scafell massif immediately north, there can be no denying the scenic pleasures it offers the free-minded explorer. Viewed from along these edges the valley is a joyous mix of pasture and woodland, the interplay of light on crags, on verdant slopes and meadows delighting the eye from so many angles.

The triangular wedge of Eskdale Moor is the perfect place to explore when all the old favourite fell-tops are blanketed in mist, for all one tends to have in mind the image of an old-timer trudging up the foothills Wainwright conjured up on the cover of his *Outlying Fells* guide. This more than modest fell is dignified by Bronze Age antiquities, indicative of the importance held by this tract of country before the Romans entered, stage left. A long shank of fell runs south-west from Burnmoor Tarn to be chiselled to a point above Eskdale Green by Miterdale. In its upper reaches, this shy valley is itself quite unique, being more akin to the narrow mountain limestone valleys characteristic of the Derbyshire Dales and the Yorkshire Three Peaks.

A word about boo-tiful Boot, the name appropriate for a place to walk, though the derivation has no connection with sturdy footwear, meaning either a humble dwelling or bend in the river. The narrow-gauge railway came into being in service of a haematite mine above the village. This closed just prior to the First World War. Mercifully the

337 metres   1,105 feet

track-bed survived and the toy-town trains continue as the
centre-piece of Eskdale tourism, their distinctive
hauntingly dry 'hoot' a familiar sound from many
points in the locality. Ratty deports visitors
from Ravenglass in regular batches at the
Dalegarth Station with its superb
view of Scafell (not the Pike
as often cited) to
patronise

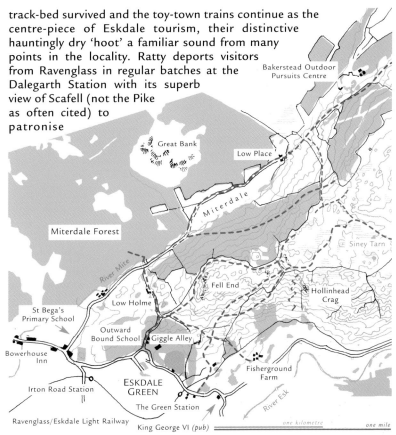

Bakerstead Outdoor
Pursuits Centre

Great Bank

Low Place

Miterdale

Miterdale Forest

Siney Tarn

River Mite

Fell End

Hollinhead
Crag

Low Holme

St Bega's
Primary School

Outward
Bound School   Giggle Alley

Bowerhouse
Inn

Fisherground
Farm

Irton Road Station

**ESKDALE
GREEN**

The Green Station

River Esk

Ravenglass/Eskdale Light Railway

King George VI *(pub)*

one kilometre   one mile

three hostelries in the vicinity, Brook House, Burnmoor and the
Woolpack Inns. It is a delightful sojourn for the casual visitor, with the
rustic delights of Eskdale Mill marking the end of the tiny street. Only a
fraction of these happy travellers venture up the track to the peat
houses and then seek out the real bounty of the area, namely the cluster
of stone circles and cairns on Brat's Moss, the wild moorland setting
being quite magical, a real druids cathedral. Burnmoor Tarn too has an
air of its own, the placid waters lapping close to the boarded-up
Burnmoor Lodge, an old fisherman's retreat keeping silent vigil. The few
specimen trees recently planted in its paddock indicate the one component the landscape most dearly needs – more trees please! There are further tarns to discover, encouraging one to rove over this rambling little
hill; Blea, Siney and Blind Tarns situated on the narrowing well-defended ridge above Beckfoot. Plus the bonus of an excellent minor viewpoint
in Fell End, surveying Muncaster Fell and the Irish Sea. Boo-tiful indeed!

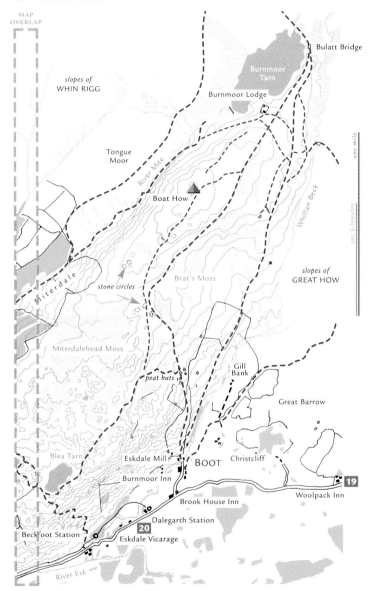

MAP
OVERLAP

slopes of
WHIN RIGG

Bulatt Bridge

Burnmoor
Tarn

Burnmoor Lodge

Tongue
Moor

River Mite

Boat How

one mile

one kilometre

Whillan Beck

Miterdale

stone circles

Brat's Moss

slopes of
GREAT HOW

Miterdalehead Moss

peat huts

Gill
Bank

Great Barrow

Blea Tarn

Eskdale Mill

BOOT

Christcliff

Burnmoor Inn

19

Woolpack Inn

Brook House Inn

20

Dalegarth Station

Beck Foot Station

Eskdale Vicarage

River Esk

ASCENT *from Boot (car parking at Dalegarth Station)*

1 The Burnmoor Tarn route: Follow the brief village street through to cross the single-arch bridge to reach the charming Eskdale Mill.

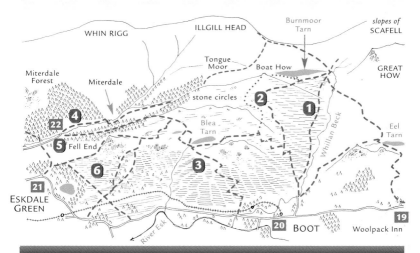

SOUTHERN & WESTERN APPROACHES

My most recent visit coincided with the cutting of a new mill-wheel shaft. From the gate a track leads up the slope of Boot Bank - not the last resting place of discarded boots! Soon after passing through this first gate watch for the fork in the way. The bridle-path to Wasdale Head bears half-right via a sequence of enclosure gates rising gently above the Whillan Beck valley to Burnmoor Tarn, a little over two miles distant. After gazing across the tarn to the less than flattering flank of Illgill Head, turn to admire Scafell - north-east not its best side either, and the bold escarpment of Great How, definitely its best side! At the plank footbridge known as Bulatt Bridge, switch back on yourself to follow the green track slanting onto the shoulder of Eskdale Moor. One may visit the environs of Burnmoor Lodge and take a confident trod that bee-lines to Boat How from the top of the brow. Otherwise a faint path (not indicated by a cairn, unfortunately) can be found, bearing off half-right from the main green track at its highest point, into the tough moor grass. Brushing your boots through the prairie with the distinctive summit of Boat How as target, from this angle the upturned hull shape is unmistakable.

2 The Brat's Moss route: Keep to the track with the wall to the right rising to the group of six former eighteenth-century peat huts. Some have retained their roofs, others are ruined walls, their purpose to store and dry peat cut on Miterdale Moss for winter fuel. An upland more associated with midges than mites! The path forks in their midst. The cairned left-hand way leads unerringly gently onto Bleatarn Hill and Blea Tarn. The right-hand branch leads to Brat's Moss, naughty ragamuffins not

Stone circle at GR 173 024 looking to Whin Rigg

One of five stone circles above Brat's Moss

implied: brat a dialect word for 'an apron'. Watch out for the tell-tale sign of stone to the left, there are three obvious sites in harmony, the first a double ring. To think they have been so configured for over three thousand years is quite staggering. How much water has sluggishly drained from this moor in that time, enough to fill the Irish Sea? The plain track curves north-east but the ridge path takes a slightly more westerly line via a cairn. Two further circles of lesser moment on Low Longrigg can be visited, though the ridge path should be adhered to for the more comfortable walking. Passing a low wall, clamber up a shallow slope and advance to the broken bank of Boat How, with a tiny fold in its lap.

3 The Beckfoot zig-zags to Blea Tarn: From Beckfoot Halt cross the railway to a gate. Find the footpath winding up the bracken bank; a slow plod does the trick, the view down upon Boot and across the broader Eskdale valley is worth every bead of sweat.

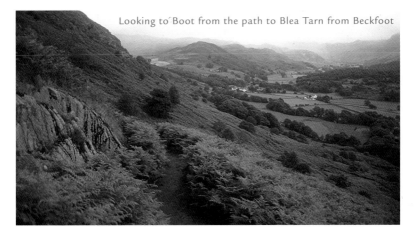

Looking to Boot from the path to Blea Tarn from Beckfoot

Great Bank and Whin Rigg from Fell End

ASCENT *from Miterdale*

The Miterdale Forest picnic area and open space car park (GR 146012) secreted up the unsignposted lane by St Bega's Primary School in Eskdale Green provides the ideal starting point for a quiet exploration of Miterdale and Eskdale Moor. Three routes present themselves for consideration. **4** Miterdale - the valley route via Burnmoor Tarn, with Scafell a distant focus of attention all the way up the dale: leave the open space crossing the broad bridge, follow the farm-track to Low Place. Pass between the farmhouse and the traditional barn, go right via the gate, curving round left with the wall. Notice the wooden board *(see below)* set into the wall. The farmer employed Cumbrian dialect, his wry humour prompted by frequent requests for directions from walkers. 'HOD REET FUR ESHDEL' speeds them on their way down the valley. Occasionally one spots similar touches elsewhere advising travellers to watch out for red squirrels, ewes and lambs etc. It would be nice to see more signs of this nature to raise a chuckle and show that real people live and, importantly, work among the fells. Twenty metres after the ford find and cross the footbridge lurking in the bushes. Follow the rough open track

leading via a gateway and subsequent gate into a lane. Ignore the green-way left to Bakerstead (used as a variation of Outward Bound by a school in Egremont). Instead advance on a path to a stile at the corner of the plantation. The path next fords a gill, crossing a marshy patch, continues up the valley with conifers up to the left. At a ladder-stile and gate by a sheep handling pen the open but very narrow upper section of the dale is entered. There are two options at this point, the natural valley route or the balcony path, the latter useful as a dry-shod path to Wasdale Head and to survey the greater surround of fells. The balcony path strictly belongs to Illgill Head, though some walkers will deem it a neat variation to Eskdale Moor on their return after following the Miterdale valley to the tarn, either by switching up west from the little amphitheatre at its head, or followed direct. In which case ford the beck and follow the steep path beside the plantation, at the top of the rise, ushered right by the enclosure fence/wall, soon to bear off into the bracken contouring above Miterdale. The natural valley path keeps down by the south bank, though there is some trace of a path on the immediate north bank. In summer the mid-section runs in subterranean silence, so reminiscent of a White Peak valley *(see below)*. The amphitheatre at the valley head is a curious feature; either enter to climb out on the south side, or bypass just prior. From the north a waterfall spills into the rocky combe, giving scope for photographers. Ignore the continuing path which only grapples with the marsh to the west of Burnmoor Tarn. Boat How can be reached more sedately by bearing half-right bound for Burnmoor Lodge, where switch back onto the brow, or make an abrupt turn sharp right up the steep bank, crossing sheep trods for a direct approach.

Upper Miterdale - summer dry beck

'Stanley' at Eskdale Mill - puss in Boot!

5 To visit Siney and Blea Tarns, ahead of the main mass of the fell, two routes can be used: the footpath branching up from the track beyond Low Place is the inferior option. Better go via the forest track directly from the picnic site; cross the stile right of the broad forest gate. Gently rising to exit at a gate, ignore the advancing track connecting to the next block of forestry. Go immediately up right, on the footpath mentioned earlier, quickly reaching the moorland. Bear left on a pronounced path, watch for the right fork which leads to a further fork, right for Fell End, left to Siney Tarn. First impressions may cause one to say 'no signey tarn'. Skirt the broad marsh, which eventually reveals several sheets of water; advance either straight on, or skirt half-right by Siney and Blind Tarns to reach Blea Tarn, cross the outflow. The path from Beckfoot converges at this point. Keep left along the shore to ascend an unusual rocky dry valley to a prodigiously large cairn. The path winds on, nicely cairned (using old walling as a source), passing a fenced mine shaft - be ye ever so careful! At this point either continue down to the peat houses, or contour with sheep trods, directly to the Bronze Age stone circles.

Peat hut looking to Great Barrow

ASCENT *from Eskdale Green*

Paths lead onto the ridge from Hollin How, Fisherground and Giggle Alley. **6** Giggle Alley (a more youthful variant on Lover's Lane one might deduce!) can be considered the more efficient approach, rising directly from the village street in Eskdale Green. At the top of the wooded lane branch right into the narrow path leading to a hand-gate; thereon either hold to the left-hand wall, skirting under the craggy brow of Fell End (worth clambering to the top for the superb view it offers) or slip down to the cross-paths, bearing left via gates, climbing through the undergrowth and outcropping to a fence to join the aforementioned path. Wind on eastward, skirting Sineytarn Moss, and link up with the path from Miterdale Forest **5** leading to Blea Tarn.

The Summit

Mindful of the Bronze Age monuments in the vicinity, it might be thought the summit a man-made mound. From many angles this looks plausible. 'How' wrong you can be, when close at hand the outcropping bedrock promptly dispels any such notion. Boat How *(in view above, from Hardrigg across Burnmoor Tarn with Miterdale right)* is aptly named from its likeness to the upturned hull of a rowing-boat perched in a sea of grass. There may or may not be a few stones gathered cairn-wise. Sheep sit here with great regularity, you'll have noticed this characteristic of ewes: find a high spot and look down on the world, their rueful expressions betraying a woolly branch of philosophy! They inevitably deposit the spoils of their grazing which can attract monster midges. In fact the sultry evening I chose to obtain the panorama, midges were in swarming residence, terrorising my bid to obtain a steady string of shots and, would you guess it, I had to change films mid-flow! To offer advice on safe descents and ridge routes would be to insult the intelligence of my readership.

Scafell from Boat How

PANORAMA

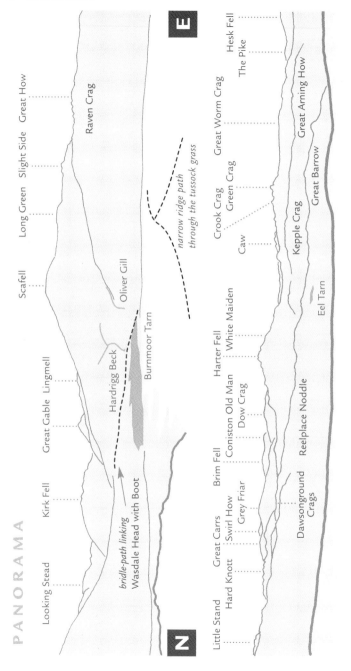

E

Looking Stead   Kirk Fell   Great Gable   Lingmell   Scafell   Long Green   Slight Side   Great How

Raven Crag

Oliver Gill

Hardrigg Beck

Burnmoor Tarn

bridle-path linking
Wasdale Head with Boot

narrow ridge path
through the tussock grass

N

S

Little Stand   Great Carrs   Brim Fell   Harter Fell   Crook Crag   Great Worm Crag   Hesk Fell
Hard Knott   Swirl How   Coniston Old Man   White Maiden   Green Crag   The Pike
Grey Friar   Dow Crag   Caw

Dawsonground
Crags

Reelplace Noddle   Kepple Crag   Great Arning How

Eel Tarn   Great Barrow

E

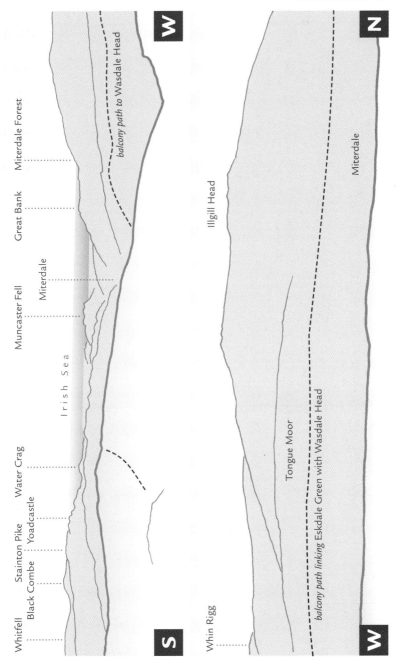

Whitfell   Stainton Pike   Water Crag   Muncaster Fell   Great Bank   Miterdale Forest

Black Combe   Yoadcastle

Miterdale

Irish Sea

S

W

balcony path to Wasdale Head

Whin Rigg   Tongue Moor   Illgill Head   Miterdale

balcony path linking Eskdale Green with Wasdale Head

W

N

ESK PIKE

A deceptively extensive fell. For all it is nipped off to the north beneath Tongue Head, the south ridge reaching right down to Throstle Garth is quite the meat and matter of good fellwalking. From the confluence of Lingcove Beck with the juvenile Esk at Lingcove Bridge a staggered sequence of rocky headlands draws up the fell, giving intermediate breaks to this focal ridge. The path side steps all the rocky action, bread and butter walking keeping to grass until Yeastyrigg Crags. Can a name be more domestic in origin, Yeastyrigg, 'the ridge that rises like baking dough'!

The ultimate mass of fell is flanked by two notable high passes, Ore Gap and Esk Hause, the latter renowned for confusing walkers in mist, especially those who have only made a cursory reference to their map. Many wander up from either Ruddy Gill or Angle Tarn, cross over the lower east/west Allen Crags hause, only to realise their folly when the purpose of the walk is too remote to contemplate the effort of back-tracking. Walkers hell bent on Scafell Pike will have registered the actual Esk Hause as a key point on their journey, the attendant fell ignored on ascent, then dismissed on descent... but not by everyone. Smart campaigners, who know a good thing when they see it, embrace the fell-top between Esk Hause and Ore Gap and are blessed with a bonus viewpoint with minimal extra effort.

885 metres   2,904 feet

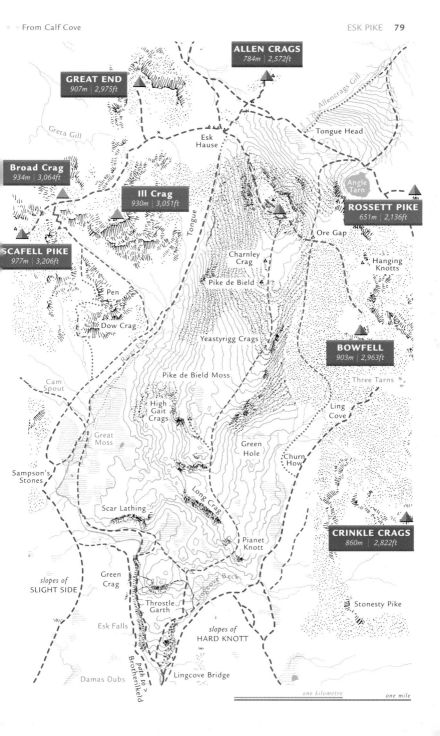

High Gait Crags languish some distance from the normal passage of walkers up or, more like as not, down the south ridge. Acute eyes will note a cairn on the headland. The reason for the cairn? To mark the most magnificent viewpoint for the Scafells. Make the effort, wander over to this delectable spot and delight in the scene. In suitable weather climbers may be seen (and heard) on Esk Buttress.

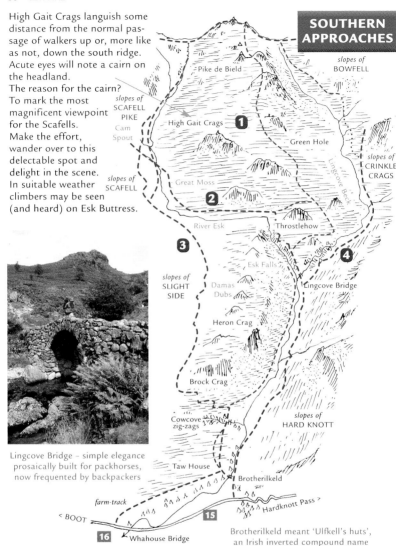

SOUTHERN APPROACHES

slopes of BOWFELL

Pike de Bield

slopes of SCAFELL PIKE

Cam Spout

High Gait Crags **1**

Green Hole

slopes of CRINKLE CRAGS

Lingcove Beck

slopes of SCAFELL

Great Moss

2

River Esk

Throstlehow

3

Esk Falls

4

slopes of SLIGHT SIDE

Damas Dubs

Lingcove Bridge

Heron Crag

Brock Crag

Cowcove zig-zags

slopes of HARD KNOTT

Taw House

Brotherilkeld

farm-track

< BOOT

15

16   Whahouse Bridge

< Hardknott Pass >

Lingcove Bridge – simple elegance prosaically built for packhorses, now frequented by backpackers

Brotherilkeld meant 'Ulfkell's huts', an Irish inverted compound name

ASCENT *from Brotherilkeld*

1 A walk of longing in every respect, both for pleasure and exercise. Just to set foot on the south ridge requires a two mile approach march to Lingcove Bridge, followed by a three mile climb. The summit seems to take an eternity to arrive, but there is blessing in that. Few fellwalking aficionados will begrudge the effort, the scenery – total fell immersion; but

Ill Crag

Great End

Pike de Bield

Yeastyrigg Crags

South-eastern aspect from Rest Gill on Crinkle Crags

for aircraft overhead one can forget the trappings of modern life. Use the special lay-by parking, follow the farm-road to Brotherilkeld from the red telephone kiosk. Even in this age of mobile phones, the existence of such facilities is of enduring value for beleaguered walkers and bedraggled drivers stuck upon the infamous Hardknott hair-pins. A permissive path, neatly avoiding the farmyard, wanders tight by the beautifully embowered river. Notice several exposed tree roots indicating, how, on occasion, the Esk runs wild. From a hand-gate, the path traverses pasture upon an open track, via gates, to enter the more confined section of the valley. Crags loom, soon the river booms, rushing through Pillar Pot and Tongue Pot, this latter a popular plunge pool in high summer for shriek-

Scafell Pike and Ill Crag from the remains of the Throstle Garth deer-wall

ing bravado dives! A sheepfold, originally used during sheep-washing, heralds Lingcove Bridge, restored to serve many more generations at this crucial crossing. Upstream, Lingcove Beck fights through a series of narrow, stepped rocky channels, finishing at a delightful fall *(see right)* in view from the bridge. Follow the main path leading north from the bridge, take the right-hand fork nearing the brow, a tangible path weaving through the bracken above the lower outcrop of Throstle Garth. The path comes close to Lingcove Beck. Watch for the smart diversion half-left, onto the fell, rising over the grassy rigg to pass through the low, broken wall that

once defined Throstle Garth, 'Frostildr's deer fence'. The ridge path is picked out no greater than a sheep path, so a keen eye is needed to keep it underfoot. Otherwise the rising grassy ridge, with dips and delves, is accompanied over the shoulder between Long Crag and Pianet Knott. It slants ever upward above Greenhole and Yeastyrigg Crags. Outcropping makes it difficult to adhere to a consistent path. Clambering onto the higher ridge, divert left to the prominent cairn on the neat peak of Pike de Bield. The endeavour now eases. Another larger cairn is found above Charnley Crag before advancing to the spine of the fell; bear up left to the summit.

Esk Pike and Bowfell from Long Crag

Scafell Pike and Ill Crag from Pike de Bield Moss

There are two dale routes to consider. **2** The more appealing travels with the Esk, on the popular path for Cam Spout. If the river is down, one may ford at Great Moss, walking upstream on the true west bank to mount the rigg and thread the ravine of Tongue Gill *(below)* to Esk Hause.

3 In notably wetter conditions use the Cowcove zig-zag route, passing by the upland marsh of Damas Dubs to the sheepfold complex beneath Cam Crag. Skirt the marsh below Cam Spout, Dow Crag and Little Narrowcove in order to reach the foot of Tongue and climb dry shod. The ravine section half-way up may be awash, causing evasive action up to the left. **4** Accompany Lingcove Beck from Lingcove Bridge, rough at first, a narrow path 'comes round the mountain'

to enter the combe over the saddle from Mosedale and soon beneath Adam-a-Crag. Divert from the well-marked path bound for Three Tarns. As it shapes to cross Churn How, contour into the bowl of Ling Cove directly beneath Bowfell. *'Where has all the ling gone? Long time passing, Grazed by those Herdy sheep every one'*… no, not quite true, niftily heather persists, notable in the Lingcove gorge, forming frilly edges beyond the reach of those naughty nibblers. The path avoids the lower section of Yeastyrigg Gill, which is far too stony. It ascends the rigg in the midriff of Bowfell then, curving left over the brow, keeps above a prominent erratic boulder, then comes close to the gill by stony hops to reach Ore Gap.

ASCENT *from Borrowdale*

Straddling the headwaters of the Esk and Langstrath Beck, the summit holds a certain remote magic. Few walkers set sail with Esk Pike a prime objective from Borrowdale. One suspects it is visited more on a whim when close at hand, a wise whim for all that. **5** The more direct route begins from Seathwaite. Follow the tread of a million soles to Stockley Bridge, turn south climbing via Grains and Ruddy Gills to join the path rising from Styhead. Take the right-hand fork to reach Esk Hause, with the north-west ridge path onto Esk Pike beckoning. **6** From Stonethwaite and the best excuse yet to explore Langstrath to its ultimate extent, keep to the west side path to the Tray Dub footbridge, cross the footbridge at the foot of Stake Beck, follow Langstrath Beck, with the high fellsides progressively hemming the path. Ford Angletarn Gill: when the beck is in spate this can be easier said than done. The subsequent fellside, running up the headstream of Allencrags Gill, is rough, with just the hint of a path on the steep ground rising to Tongue Head. The popular path joined, with some relief, go right, to the cross-wall wind shelter. Slant up leftward to Esk Hause onto the north-west ridge.

ASCENT *from Great Langdale*

7 The regular path climbs out of Mickleden via Rossett Gill, on a solidly pitched double zig-zag trail bringing walkers to Angle Tarn with Bowfell or Scafell Pike their principal objectives. For a little extra effort why not include Esk Pike in your journey?

For the former, continue to the saddle south of Allen Crags. Turn by the cross-wall wind shelter *(see above)*, rising to Esk Hause, there stepping up the inviting north-west ridge upon the well-marked rocky path. Scafell Pike puts demands on most walkers they little suspect, so Esk Pike is best considered on the return, when energies are ascertained, again traverse to Ore Gap from Esk Hause. Though, should the cloud suggest that higher brethren will be shrouded out, Esk Pike might be thought a good walk-saving substitution. Follow the path west from Angle Tarn, branch first left on the rise, curving up to Ore Gap.

Summit, north cairn

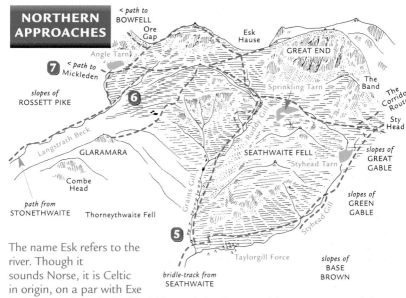

NORTHERN APPROACHES

< path to BOWFELL
Ore Gap
Esk Hause
< path to Mickleden
7
6
Angle Tarn
GREAT END
Sprinkling Tarn
The Band
The Corridor Route
Sty Head
slopes of ROSSETT PIKE
Langstrath Beck
GLARAMARA
SEATHWAITE FELL
Ruddy Gill
Styhead Tarn
slopes of GREAT GABLE
Combe Head
Grains Gill
slopes of GREEN GABLE
path from STONETHWAITE
Thorneythwaite Fell
5
Styhead Gill
Taylorgill Force
slopes of BASE BROWN
bridle-track from SEATHWAITE

The name Esk refers to the river. Though it sounds Norse, it is Celtic in origin, on a par with Exe in Devon and Axe in Staffordshire and simply meant 'the source-stream', in recognition of Esk Pike's pivotal position on the Esk watershed.

From Allen Crags

Hanging Knotts

Bowfell

The Summit

The south top is fundamentally rock, the north top a looser affiliation, surmounted by a more concerted cairn. The eye-catching pale rock, which from a distance has the appearance of chalk, is most prevalent on the south side; on close inspection it proves to be a thin flaky surface glaze. The central situation on the main ridge, encircling the great wilderness of upper Eskdale and high above upper Langstrath, lends the summit special qualities as a viewpoint. There are several subsidiary vantages either side of the summit worth finding. Descend north a matter of 150 metres. Peering down a gully into upper Langstrath yields a view of Glaramara. While on the other side of the summit find the bird's-eye view down the same scarp to Angle Tarn backed by Rossett Pike and the Langdale Pikes. Pike de Bield at the top of the south ridge is the better stance for upper Eskdale.

Looking north

Safe Descents

The best objective is Ore Gap. Follow the ridge path SE from the summit. At the Ore Gap depression turn left, N, down a rough but plain path. Join the path from Esk Hause winding on down to the outflow of Angle Tarn. Ford and continue SE bound for Rossett Gill, with its newly pitched zig-zags, and Mickleden for the shelter of Great Langdale. NNW from the summit, the ridge path descends to Esk Hause, a notoriously confusing place in mist. Bear right to find the cross-wall shelter, a key landmark hereabouts.

Ridge Routes to....

ALLEN CRAGS   DESCENT 550 ft   ASCENT 225 ft   1 mile

To embark upon the Glaramara ridge, descend the NW ridge to Esk Hause, slant right, passing down by the cross-wall to the saddle. Continuing on the stony trail, easily climbing NE to the summit.

BOWFELL   DESCENT 330 ft   ASCENT 400 ft   1 mile

Descend the SE ridge to Ore Gap. Continue on an oft stony trail which mounts steadily S, only really getting onto the ridge proper at the brink of the scree gully between Bowfell Buttress and Cambridge Crag: an impressive moment to survey Mickleden and the Langdale Pikes. The final rocky crest of the fell ensues; step up SW, veering off the line of the diagonal shelf path. This is a proper fell-top, plenty of stony seats for that all important breather.

GREAT END   DESCENT 410 ft   ASCENT 530 ft   1.3 miles

Descend the NW ridge to Esk Hause. A string of pointless cairns guide to the all too apparent path across the broad depression into Calf Cove. The excessively boulder-ridden W slope of Great End should be given short shrift. Slant up left beyond the bield wall with this the popular path to Scafell Pike. Take a right-hand turn due N. Where the stony ground eases follow the gently rising broad ridge to the summit, almost devoid of rough ground, which will have seemed a wildly ambitious concept when down in Esk Hause.

Glaramara from the northern scarp

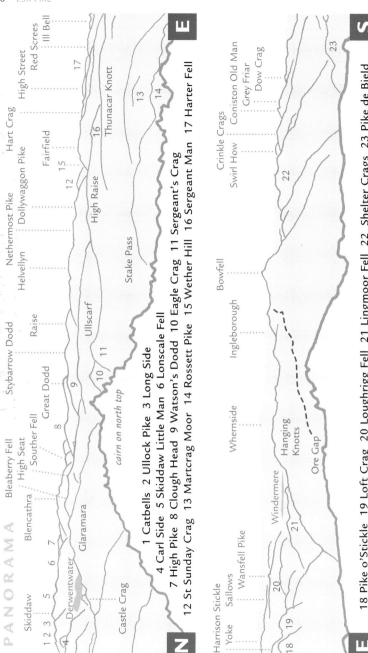

PANORAMA

Skiddaw · Bleaberry Fell · Stybarrow Dodd · Nethermost Pike · Hart Crag · High Street

Blencathra · High Seat · Souther Fell · Helvellyn · Dollywaggon Pike · Fairfield · Red Screes · Ill Bell

Derwentwater · Glaramara · Great Dodd · Raise · Ullscarf · High Raise · Thunacar Knott

Castle Crag · Stake Pass

cairn on north top

N **E**

1 Catbells 2 Ullock Pike 3 Long Side
4 Carl Side 5 Skiddaw Little Man 6 Lonscale Fell
7 High Pike 8 Clough Head 9 Watson's Dodd 10 Eagle Crag 11 Sergeant's Crag
12 St Sunday Crag 13 Martcrag Moor 14 Rossett Pike 15 Wether Hill 16 Sergeant Man 17 Harter Fell

Harrison Stickle
Yoke · Sallows · Whernside · Ingleborough · Bowfell · Swirl How · Coniston Old Man · Grey Friar · Dow Crag

Wansfell Pike · Windermere · Hanging Knotts · Crinkle Crags

Ore Gap

E **S**

18 Pike o'Stickle 19 Loft Crag 20 Loughrigg Fell 21 Lingmoor Fell 22 Shelter Crags 23 Pike de Bield

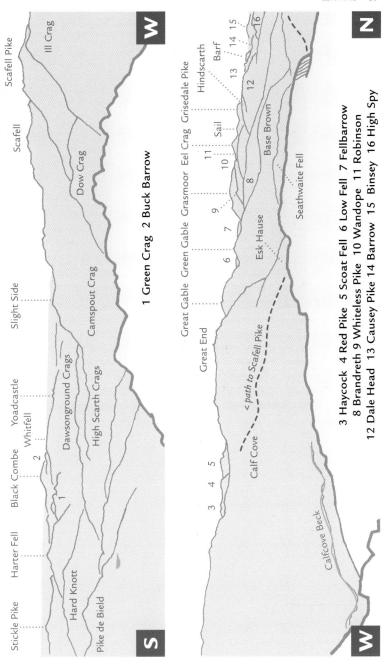

W / **S**

Scafell Pike   Scafell   Slight Side   Yoadcastle   Whitfell   Black Combe   Harter Fell   Stickle Pike

Ill Crag   Dow Crag   Camspout Crag   Dawsonground Crags   High Scarth Crags   Hard Knott   Pike de Bield

1 Green Crag   2 Buck Barrow

N / **W**

Grisedale Pike   Hindscarth   Barf   Sail   Eel Crag   Grasmoor   Green Gable   Great Gable   Great End

Base Brown   Seathwaite Fell   Esk Hause   Calf Cove   < path to Scafell Pike   Calfcove Beck

3 Haycock 4 Red Pike 5 Scoat Fell 6 Low Fell 7 Fellbarrow
8 Brandreth 9 Whiteless Pike 10 Wandope 11 Robinson
12 Dale Head 13 Causey Pike 14 Barrow 15 Binsey 16 High Spy

GLARAMARA

Cumbria is blessed with a generous helping of the most delightfully lyrical fell-names. Glaramara is a favourite of many, one may almost sense it to have a hint of the Blarney. The earliest record shows it as 'Houedgleuermerhe', meaning 'headland of the shieling by the chasms', which like Comb Head only referred to the summit. Understandably the 'Houed' was severed from archaic speech when the original summer-farmstead was lost. Thus at a stroke the name was transferred in its entirety to the fell: strictly the name Glaramara belongs to the summit bastion, not the broader fell. The elevated central setting gives it esteem over and above the lovely name. Indeed, if any fell can be called the Borrowdale fell, then this is it, especially when coupled with its more prominent components, Thorneythwaite Fell and Comb Head.

The fell makes a wonderful objective from either Stonethwaite, Seatoller or Seathwaite. Not truly on a par with Scafell Pike of course, but being so nucleated to the Borrowdale scene there is a certain wholeness in the climb. The summit is also part of a greater mass of fell, the principal northern spur of the Scafell massif, being the mid-point of a ridge rising smartly from Stonethwaite, climbing in rough steps over Rosthwaite Fell and initially culminating above Comb Gill at Comb Head. This ridge is defined and thoroughly isolated by deep dales, the headstreams of Borrowdale to the west and lonely roadless Langstrath to the east. The quickest way to the top is by Hind Gill, but the best way, by far, is by handsomely curved and craggy Thorneythwaite Fell ridge.

783 metres   2,569 feet

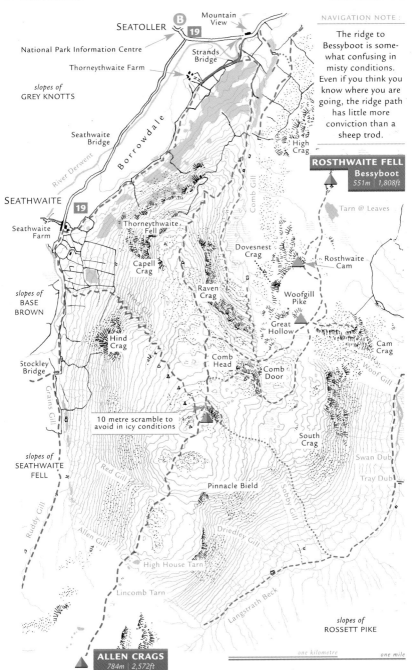

SEATOLLER ⓑ
19

NAVIGATION NOTE :

The ridge to
Bessyboot is some-
what confusing in
misty conditions.
Even if you think you
know where you are
going, the ridge path
has little more
conviction than a
sheep trod.

Mountain
View

National Park Information Centre

Strands
Bridge

Thorneythwaite Farm

slopes of
GREY KNOTTS

Seathwaite
Bridge

High
Crag

Comb Gill

ROSTHWAITE FELL
Bessyboot
551m | 1,808ft

Tarn @ Leaves

SEATHWAITE
19

Seathwaite
Farm

Thorneythwaite
Fell

Dovesnest
Crag

Rosthwaite
Cam

Capell
Crag

Raven
Crag

Woofgill
Pike

slopes of
BASE
BROWN

Great
Hollow

Cam
Crag

Hind
Crag

Woof Gill

Stockley
Bridge

Comb
Head

Comb
Door

South
Crag

Swan Dub

Grains Gill

Sosby Gill

Tray Dub

slopes of
SEATHWAITE
FELL

10 metre scramble to
avoid in icy conditions

Red Gill

Pinnacle Bield

Ruddy Gill

Driedley Gill

Allen Gill

High House Tarn

Lincomb Tarn

Langstrath Beck

slopes of
ROSSETT PIKE

one kilometre   one mile

ALLEN CRAGS
784m | 2,572ft

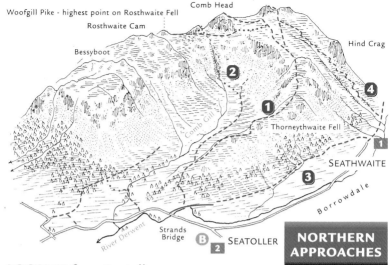

Woofgill Pike - highest point on Rosthwaite Fell
Rosthwaite Cam
Comb Head
Bessyboot
Hind Crag
Thorneythwaite Fell
SEATHWAITE
Comb Gill
Borrowdale
River Derwent
Strands Bridge
SEATOLLER

NORTHERN APPROACHES

ASCENT *from Seatoller*

1 The royal road to the top. The Thorneythwaite Fell ridge obviates the need to climb Rosthwaite Fell. Begin from the National Trust car park in Seatoller. Follow the verge past the appropriately named Glaramara holiday centre. At Stands Bridge, beside the terrace of gabled cottages known as Mountain View, go right, with the Thorneythwaite Farm access lane. Watch for the kissing-gate left after 70 metres. Pass through and follow the rough track which becomes a grooved path rising up the lightly wooded ridge to a further kissing-gate in the intake wall. Without wavering, keep to the obvious path climbing the north ridge, making one pronounced switch up right onto a craggy step. There is a fine view into the inner recesses of the lost valley of Comb Gill to Dovesnest and Raven Crags, facing each other across the dale-head. The climb gives ample opportunity to survey the handsome fell surround of Honister Pass, the growing majesty of Great Gable looming above Base Brown. As height is gained one may drift onto the edge above the Comb Gill valley for splendid views, then climb onto Comb Head. This is a handsome place to stand, better than Glaramara, in terms of the northern view. Alternatively, keep assiduously to the trail, which steps over marshy ground before coping with the headstream of Hind Gill, to confront Glaramara proper. The fell path turns rock ramble in tackling a six metre scramble; being prone to shadow this can be slippery when wet or icy, for good measure the rocks are awkwardly rounded too! If this is a bit more than you can take then, no worries, either skirt to left or, easier still, to the right, rounding the main outcrop to complete the climb as from the south or west.

Thorneythwaite Fell and the Comb Gill valley from Comb Head

2 The Comb Gill valley gives a different perspective, the sturdy qualities of the fell constantly impressed upon the route. The use of the Old English term 'comb' for an deep upland valley is interesting. It was an early loan from the old Celtic Cumbrian language; elsewhere in the district 'cove', another variant, is evident, which really does echo of links with Cornish cousins. The Vikings brought 'gill' with them, though this found specific application for tight ravines, hence the only mildly tautological, Comb Gill.

Branch from the Thorneythwaite Fell route shortly after passing through the intake gate. A fine waterfall in Comb Gill holds attention short of the path fork, which is marked by a cairn. A clear trod leads by the curious remains of an oval fold, set on a slope. A holding pen for a sheep-wash perhaps? The path leads into the moraine-fringed hollow at the heart of the combe. No trace of a tarn, this will have drained away centuries ago. The path is most commonly used by climbers heading for Raven Crag, the severity of the routes intensified by the lack of sun. Dovesnest Crag on the opposing fellside beneath Rosthwaite Cam is, by comparison, quite balmy. The ancient judder that made the lower portion of the crag a place for brave speleologists, a cause to visit on another occasion. Departing from the path aiming for the sheepfold, you may make your choice between Dovesnest or Comb Gill. Keeping to plan A, follow the gill due south; at the mouth of the ravine, site of a fox earth,

clamber onto the right-hand bank. The ground may be steep, but an occasional cairn and the faint traces of a zig-zagging path, as height is gained, will embolden your stride. The ravine climbs straight out of the comb to a shelf directly below Comb Door. The regular ridge path from Rosthwaite Fell contours this shelf and may be followed to the right. Alternatively, clamber on up to Comb Door *(see above)*, the view back to Rosthwaite Fell, the Jaws of Borrowdale and Derwentwater ample justification. Passing through the gap, past the shaded tarn, take one of two paths mounting onto Comb Head up to the right, the second, furthest, climbing onto an all too brief slab, rising up the edge north-westward to the Comb Head cairn. Glaramara lies across the damp hollow to the south.

3 The two miles of valley path from Strands Bridge to Seathwaite has been adopted by the Allerdale Ramble. This lovely track gives walkers relief from the inevitable traffic on the Seatoller to Seathwaite road. Follow the farm-lane guided left, as it turns towards the farm, along a fenced passage to a hand-gate; now with a wall right, advance on a basically level track below the rugged wooded slopes of Thorneythwaite Fell, with a couple of gates taken, latterly becoming a path, en route to the Seathwaite Farm.

Thorneythwaite Fell across the Comb Gill valley from Dovesnest Crag

Glaramara from Comb Head

ASCENT *from Seathwaite*

4 Hind Gill is more often than not incorporated into route plans late as a quick retreat from the tops, though many will appreciate it as an equally nifty ascent. If the pitching of paths has any credence then the steep section of this path certainly deserves attention, if for no other reason than to heal the growing scar! Follow the regulation valley path from the farm; after the second gate bear left via a gate fording the several bouldery strands of Hind Gill. Ascend the pasture via a broken wall to a hand-gate in the intake wall. The path winds up the right-hand side of the gill. Dispel thoughts of following the gill itself. Hind Crag is not particularly obvious from the path. Cairns litter the path, several may be found on the spacious open fell above, leading to the summit. The best approach to the summit is from the south. Incidentally, a hind is a female red deer, a rarity in this quarter of Lakeland today.

The awkward step onto the summit; prone to shadow, it is particularly difficult when frozen

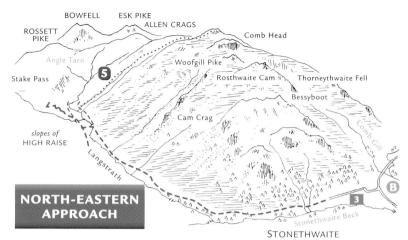

ROSSETT PIKE
BOWFELL
ESK PIKE
ALLEN CRAGS
Comb Head
Angle Tarn
Woofgill Pike
Rosthwaite Cam
Thorneythwaite Fell
Stake Pass
Bessyboot
5
slopes of HIGH RAISE
Cam Crag
Langstrath
B
NORTH-EASTERN APPROACH
3
Comb Gill
Stonethwaite Beck
STONETHWAITE

ASCENT *from Stonethwaite*

Regular paths can wear thin after a while and some fellwalkers yearn for something a little different, to catch their fells unaware. Glaramara forms a considerable proportion of the upper reaches of Langstrath so an ascent that combines the fullest enjoyment of that valley with a sneaky line beside an attractive ravine can be contemplated with enthusiasm. Sobby Gill 'flowing like tears' (Ribby Gills on Ordnance Survey maps) is one of two adjacent watercourses spilling from the high eastern shoulder of Glaramara. Despite the steepness of the ground, there is no fellside outcropping, a major inhibition to routes elsewhere on this flank of the valley. I can attest that Woof Gill, for instance, is no place to wander, the point of entry particularly well defended by bracken and boulders, though scramblers find pleasure in mounting the Cam Crag ridge, as well as dubious shelter among Woof Stones. Woof is a contraction from the 'call of a wolf', as I'm sure you've already guessed. The Stones were a likely last hold out for a pack, as too the labyrinthine clefts of Dovesnest Caves directly over the ridge... and maybe one day a home again: the fashionable trend for re-introduction of native species may extend to the Lakeland fells 'wolf call'?

5 The route to Sobby Gill is straightforward. Keeping to the west side track up Langstrath, ignore the Tray Dub footbridge. Stay with the valley beck close left to minimise contact with the ubiquitous bracken, though the ground is quite marshy: the name Langstrath means 'the long marsh'. With a broken wall and sheepfold in view, some 150 metres ahead, take a bold turn right as a notable gill enters the beck. Hold to the left-hand gill where it forks, this is Sobby Gill. The bracken relents as the slope steepens. There is no evidence of a path but, no matter, the going is easy enough and the views to Bowfell and Esk Pike compensatory. A pinnacle is passed as the upper grains draw up to a rocky arete, beyond which the gill melds into the pasture to a red scarred birth. Climb on to ascend either Comb Head, or take the direct line to Glaramara – the choice, as ever, is yours.

Rossett Pike
Bowfell
Esk Pike

Knobby pinnacle in Sobby Gill
(*right*) A grain feeding into Sobby Gill

The Summit

The name Glaramara strictly belongs to the summit. Which summit you ask? Well the more northerly. The southern top has a cairn on a more permanent basis and a sumptuous prospect to Great End and Gable. A cairn seldom lasts long on the main top. In fact on three of my four visits in 2003 there was no cairn to be found. How's that for transitory? A small wall shelter lies tucked into the rocks adjacent on this splendid high platform.

Safe Descents

One tends to refer to safety in terms of the general descent. However, there is 'a nasty' lurking close at hand that has the potential for grief.

In icy conditions I too shied from this six metre bad step. The 'event' is situated on the main path on the north side of the summit outcrop; the rocks are rounded and the steps down long. The problem is no problem. Leave the summit, stepping down south into a shallow depression and go right; this puts easy ground underfoot at a stroke. Wandering north, follow Hind Gill and bear off NW; as a quickie descent to Seathwaite it's fine. But 'green' walkers will not wish to exacerbate its erosion, preferring to go down the Thorneythwaite Fell ridge. So continue north along a clear path which quickly materialises across the headstream of Hind Gill. The ridge path brings the walker down to Strands Bridge, a short stride from Seatoller... *and that lovely little tearoom!*

Looking south from the summit

Ridge Routes to...

ALLEN CRAGS   DESCENT 440 ft   ASCENT 520 ft   1.7 miles

How a ridge can change. Glaramara marks the point of transition on the greater ridge, as well as in the fortunes of walkers. The joyous roller-coaster journey south is not interrupted by obstacles. The ridge path avoids the second summit, heading SSW across a stony plateau to a marshy depression. Further stony ground, peppered with tiny pools, ensues before the dip to High House Tarn. Make a point of drifting left at the next rise to find the exquisite Lincomb Tarn, spell-bindingly beautiful, held in the grip of outcrops *(see facing page)*: Lincomb means 'flax-valley'. The ground gradually rises, with further small pools adding to interest until the summit cairn is at hand. All that ascent and still only a stride higher than Glaramara, one metre to be precise!

Bowfell from Lincomb Tarn

ROSTHWAITE FELL   DESCENT 280 ft   ASCENT 200 ft   1.9 miles

Be aware, Rosthwaite Fell is intricate and confusing in mist. There are two crucial early options, neither is preferable, both are entertaining given suitable weather. Follow the northern path heading for Thorneythwaite Fell - mindful of the rock step off Glaramara. Curve right, under the scarp of Comb Head along a terrace, the path only becoming apparent as the shelf narrows beneath Comb Door and above the deep cleft of Comb Gill. Contour to dip into the marshy bowl of Great Hollow. Traverse to cross a short length of wall *(see below)*, keep to the right of the crest of Woofgill Pike (a viewpoint not to be ignored). The path holds to an eastern drift, avoiding Rosthwaite Cam, winding down towards Tarn at Leaves; keep up on the minor ridge to its west before climbing the final cone of Bessyboot. The alternative route slants right, from the foot of the rock step, across the marshy hollow skirting around the eastern flank of Comb Head, then weaves along the eastern edge to the broken wall below Woofgill Pike. A further route option slips through a breach in the Comb Head scarp, descending west through Comb Door to join up with the terrace path above Comb Gill. Good luck and have fun!

Comb Head
across the Great Hollow

PANORAMA

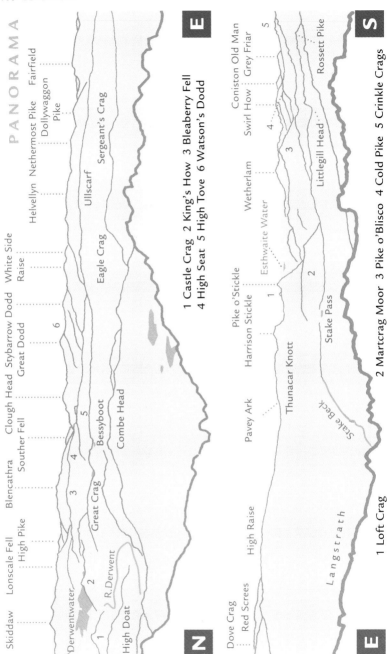

E

Skiddaw · Lonscale Fell · Clough Head · Stybarrow Dodd · White Side · Helvellyn · Nethermost Pike · Fairfield · Dollywaggon Pike

High Pike · Blencathra · Souther Fell · Great Dodd · Raise

Ullscarf · Sergeant's Crag

Eagle Crag

6

5

Bessyboot

4

3

Great Crag

Combe Head

2

Derwentwater

1

R.Derwent

High Doat

N

1 Castle Crag 2 King's How 3 Bleaberry Fell
4 High Seat 5 High Tove 6 Watson's Dodd

S

Coniston Old Man · Swirl How · Grey Friar

5

Wetherlam · Littlegill Head · Rossett Pike

4

3

Esthwaite Water

2

Pike o'Stickle · Harrison Stickle

Pavey Ark · Thunacar Knott

Stake Pass

1

Stake Beck

Dove Crag · Red Screes

High Raise

Langstrath

E

1 Loft Crag

2 Martcrag Moor 3 Pike o'Blisco 4 Cold Pike 5 Crinkle Crags

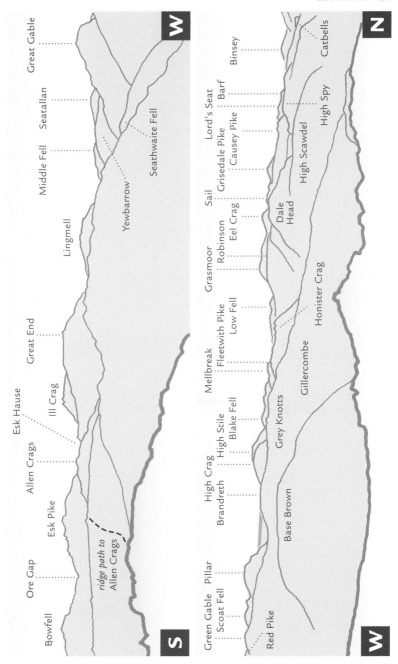

Great Gable

Seatallan

Middle Fell

Lingmell

Yewbarrow

Seathwaite Fell

Great End

Esk Hause

Ill Crag

Allen Crags

Esk Pike

Ore Gap

ridge path to Allen Crags

Bowfell

W

S

Binsey

Catbells

Lord's Seat   Barf

High Spy

Sail   Griesdale Pike   Causey Pike

High Scawdel

Robinson   Eel Crag

Dale Head

Grasmoor

Fleetwith Pike   Low Fell

Honister Crag

Mellbreak

Gillercombe

High Crag   High Stile   Blake Fell

Grey Knotts

Brandreth

Base Brown

Green Gable   Pillar

Scoat Fell

Red Pike

N

W

GREAT END

The Great End of the Scafells: what could be more expressive? Whether viewed from Wasdale Head or Borrowdale, observe this as the abrupt termination to the high plateau. Broad Crag and Ill Crag by long convention are treated as component parts of Scafell Pike, though on shaky grounds. For in truth they are separated by a deep col which brings them more in harmony with Great End. The ambiguity is such that this guide accepts the status quo, but reluctantly. Neither Broad Crag nor Ill Crag can claim regular 'stand-alone' ascents which, at the end of the day, must approximate to a definition of individuality.

Great End is a firm, out on a limb, objective gifted with the most sumptuous, uninhibited northward prospect. Stand at the brink of the north-facing cliff, invariably you'll be alone with your ecstacy, charged with a scene-induced good feeling that lingers long after the day. From Sprinkling Tarn, this shadow-darkened face, etched with gullies and renown for its winter ice climbs, is seen to perfection.

907 metres   2,976 feet

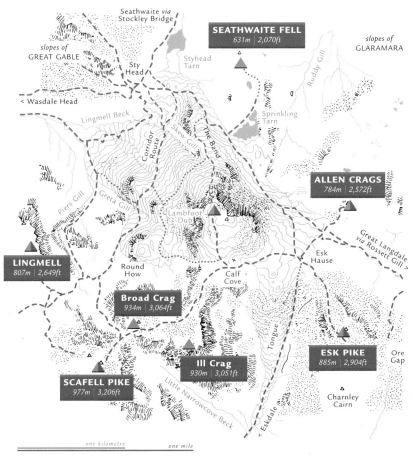

SEATHWAITE FELL
631m | 2,070ft

Seathwaite via
Stockley Bridge

slopes of
GREAT GABLE

Sty
Head

Styhead
Tarn

slopes of
GLARAMARA

< Wasdale Head

Lingmell Beck

Sprinkling
Tarn

Corridor
Route

The Band

Ruddy Gill

ALLEN CRAGS
784m | 2,572ft

Piers Gill

Greta Gill

Lambfoot
Dub

Great Langdale
via Rossett Gill >

LINGMELL
807m | 2,649ft

Round
How

Calf
Cove

Esk
Hause

Esk Hause

Broad Crag
934m | 3,064ft

Tongue

ESK PIKE
885m | 2,904ft

Ore
Gap

Ill Crag
930m | 3,051ft

SCAFELL PIKE
977m | 3,206ft

Little Narrowcove Beck

Charnley
Cairn

< Eskdale

one kilometre   one mile

Great End and Broad Crag from Lingmell - a really rugged mountain prospect

Round How

path to Broad Crag col

Corridor Route

The walker should not be intimidated by the fell's outward ferocity, for there are wonderful ways to discover that bring the very best of the rugged ground safely underfoot, and at least one 'easy peasy' ascent for those of a nervous disposition. Great End is often added to expeditions from Great Langdale, conveniently bolted onto the journeys to and from Scafell Pike. The primary lines of ascent, however, stem from Wasdale Head and Seathwaite, as described here.

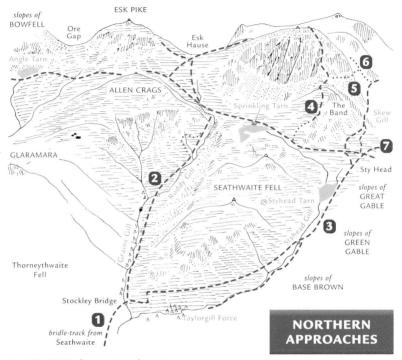

NORTHERN APPROACHES

ASCENT *from Seathwaite*

1 The linch-pin for ascents from Borrowdale is Stockley Bridge. The valley track leads from the farm, via gates, to this beautiful single span packhorse bridge, constructed stoutly, but elegantly upon bare rocks, where Grains Gill forces through a modest but quite beautiful ravine. The place attracts visitors' lingering admiration, entranced by the hydrodynamics of water, especially exciting when in spate. The gate on the west side is the point where two dale routes divide.

2 Via Grains and Ruddy Gills. Without question this is the easiest route to the top. The path, more popular of recent years, and has secured its future as the high-road to Esk Hause thanks to intensive pitching works. The path crosses a footbridge as Ruddy Gill makes its final flight down a

Skew Gill from the path south from Styhead

Great End from Sprinkling Tarn

cleft to a secretive fall and a fuming watersmeet with Allen Gill, career-
ing on as Grains Gill. Those of a certain age will know what's coming...
graded grains make finer falls! At the second minor gill crossing one may
drift up the rigg half-left onto the prominent shelf; this is the older
packhorse route, retired with the ponies, which nonetheless makes an
interesting soft staircase variation to the hard pitching; skirt the marshy
ground on the shelf to the west side, then link back to the modern trail.
The upper section of Ruddy Gill runs through a deep ravine with some
tree growth indicative of what could grow up here if it were not for them-
there herdy-wickers! The Scafell massif should be fenced-off from the
impoverishment of sheep and the delicate mountain flora given a new
lease of life.

  Ford the gill to join the path ascending from Sprinkling Tarn, taking the
right-hand fork to reach Esk Hause above the cross-wall shelter. Leading
into the shallow combe of Calf Cove, a ceaseless flow of walkers ensures
a palpable path with a superfluity of cairns to boot and a few of them
deserve to be booted too! As the ground eases above this damp hollow,

branch right heading north up the broad semi-pasture ridge, thereby completely side-stepping the boulder-infested east slope.

3 Via Styhead Pass. There is a palpable antiquity about this route. The setting itself, beneath the massive slopes leading up to Great Gable and the Scafell massif is quite stirring, climbing above Taylorgill Force by Styhead Tarn to the Pass from where travellers of yore wended down the scree shelf to Wasdale Head. How many walkers in the modern age have traipsed this way from Borrowdale to partake of a pint of Cumberland Ale or Black Sheep at the Wasdale Head Inn, then backtracked in the dense stumbling darkness of night? What we do for fun!

The path winds up from the gate beyond Stockley Bridge, via a rock step to a gate in the intake wall below Black Waugh, a broad, ice-smoothed grim-looking rock-face. The name actually interprets as 'the dark stranger': the native Celts were termed 'woffs' by Norse folk who saw the indigenous people as the misfits! The path continues, gradually easing in gradient though not necessarily in its roughness. Crossing a footbridge, advance to glance by the western shore of Styhead Tarn – a popular high-level campsite. Arrive at the Mountain Rescue stretcher box at Styhead Pass, a natural rendezvous: the name refers to the sty or 'steep path' climbing from Spouthead Gill. Go left, setting course for Esk Hause. The path, never in doubt, crosses the outflow of Sprinkling Tarn; crossing over a low saddle, join the path by Ruddy Gill.

4 The Band, no we're not on Bowfell this time, is boldly centre-stage when viewed from Styhead Tarn. This ridge is nowhere near as intimidating a climb as might be thought at first sight. Before Sprinkling Tarn

Skew Gill from the Corridor Route

Great Gable from the foot of Cust's Gully

leave the route to Esk Hause, more precisely when abreast outcropping on the slopes of Seathwaite Fell to the left. Climb to a small col, as a grassy trod winds on up the ridge. The impressive Spout Head scarp close to the right gives magnificent views to Lingmell. A shallow gully marks the top of Skew Gil, a point of further divide. The direct, mild scramble continues upward with a certain inevitable vagueness. Never fear, there is a simple line which draws up to a gully providing a fine view to Cust's Gully *(see facing page)*, identified by its huge chockstone, best seen from above. This gully, itself a demanding scramble, is not recommended, so take my advice, give it a miss unless you have the necessary climbing skills, i.e. a competence level well above my own, for I usually tramp alone and avoid too much dare-devilry... my family like to see my cheery face of an evening! A bouldery slope ensues, giving a rock-hopping conclusion to the climb. Make a point of skirting the cliff edge to see the top of Central and Cust's Gully with its dramatic fell arena below.

5 From the top of Skew Gil a contouring line can be crafted. Good weather is of course essential; duck and weave by outcropping to reach Lambfoot Dub, where it is possible to link with route **6**.

6 Begins from the Styhead Pass stretcher box, starting along the Victorian guides' route, long known as the Corridor Route. This heads up the Esk Hause path onto the first rise, branches right, crossing the vestige of a short wall, dips and contours to the mouth of the Skew Gill ravine. Alternatively, follow a short-cut across the head of Spouthead Gill, arriving at the same place. At Skew Gill, frequently a dry jumble of stones, mount the opposing slope, climb on, slipping through a short rock cutting. Plenty of new pitching confirms the hard staircase. When a round-headed knoll is spotted high above, branch off the trail. Clamber up the predominantly grassy slope, slipping behind the knoll to find Lambfoot Dub, a peaceful pool *(see below)*: the tiny limb extension north must be the lamb's foot, though imagination

Cust's Gully

needs to be vigorously applied. The pool is surprisingly clear and deep, a lovely spot to rest alone, blissfully gazing across to Great Gable, well above the chattering trekkers on the Corridor. Traverse into the nameless combe behind Round How, joining the headstream of Greta Gill which curves up left to its source at the natural weakness in the scarp. This gives steep, but simple, access to the saddle above and thereby the summit up to the left (north).

Great End from Lingmell Beck

ASCENT *from Wasdale Head*

7 To Styhead Pass: Great End captivates one's attention on the walk up Lingmell Beck from Burnthwaite, the high, rugged skyline a tempting call to arms – I think I mean to legs! Leave the village green car park, following the lane to Burnthwaite. Pass to the left of the farm buildings to a gate. Keep right, the obvious way heads on between varying walls, via a gate, to cross a footbridge spanning Gable Beck. Soon a choice of routes may be considered, both are equally sound routes to Sty Head. The normal route just sticks religiously to the rising path which passes through a hand-gate before taking on the scree section. The passage of several hundred years has ensured a well-defined shelf has been padded down and, but for one brief stumbly section, and a good deal of ball-bearing gravel, the path delivers the walker with minimal fuss. However, the smart card route lies up the valley. Either bear off as bracken begins to encroach or wait a further hundred metres to find a clear path slanting down to the hand-gate near the foot of the descending wall. Keep alongside Lingmell Beck, fording the stream just after the confluence with Piers Gill. A clear green trail winds up the rigg, then fords to the left a gill that might have tenuous flow links with Lambfoot Dub. Slant across the next rigg to ford Spouthead Gill, then zig-zag up to Styhead Pass. Visitors with only modest walking ambition ascend by the Gable scree path and descend by the valley route, appreciating this as a 'taster' outing in a very tasty setting!

Sprinkling Tarn and the watery plateau of Seathwaite Fell from high on The Band

The Band, evening sun casting the shadow of Great Gable across Styhead Tarn

The Summit

Two tops vie for pre-eminence, for the difference in height must be slight. The north-west cairn is selected simply out of personal preference. Being further forward it better commands the northern prospect, though the Langdale Pikes and Lingmoor Fell are thus hidden. A cairn and wind-shelter provide the foreground focus.

The summit cairn, the north-west top

The top of the cliff looking to Rossett Pike

chockstone

View down Cust's Gully

Safe Descents

Take the road most travelled. Walk south to the depression, a little over a quarter of a mile distant, to meet up with the path from Scafell Pike. Switch sharp left in the company of this popular trail descending Calf Cove to Esk Hause. Whatever you do, do not walk south from this point. You'll give yourself endless walking down Eskdale and the logistical dilemma of getting back to Langdale, Borrowdale or Wasdale and all the excuses under the sun won't wash with the Mountain Rescue! Find the cross-wall – this is the best clue to progress, for it is only a short stride S to Allen Crags hause; this saddle is the 'false' Esk Hause, a place of confusion in mist.

Crossing the saddle E/W, a regular path leads to safety: E to Angle Tarn and Rossett Gill for Great Langdale and W for Ruddy Gill and Borrowdale, or further to Styhead Pass for Wasdale Head.

Stockley Bridge, the parting of the ways from Seathwaite

Ridge Routes to...

ESK PIKE   DESCENT 490 ft   ASCENT 425 ft   1.25 miles

Descend S to the depression, with minimal hindrance from rocks or boulders. Join the path from Scafell Pike switching left, NE. Descend Calf Cove following the line of cairns to Esk Hause. Cross straight over, mounting the well-marked path up the NW ridge.

SCAFELL PIKE   DESCENT 330 ft   ASCENT 600 ft   1.4 miles

Descend S to the depression to join the path emerging from Calf Cove. Continue SW, soon encountering an awkward and unavoidable section of boulders. The ridge, narrows succeeded by a mild interval of gravelly trail slipping into the dip between Ill Crag and Broad Crag, though, in mounting over the E shoulder of the latter, boulder-hopping resumes with a vengeance! Descend to Broadcrag Col and climb the facing narrow greatly hammered ridge, loose stones in abundance. Eventually matters ease and the walled summit stand hoves into view. With wind and rain the norm, choose from several stone shelters for relief from the storms; the best shelters are to be found on the E side, over to the left as you reach the plateau.

PANORAMA

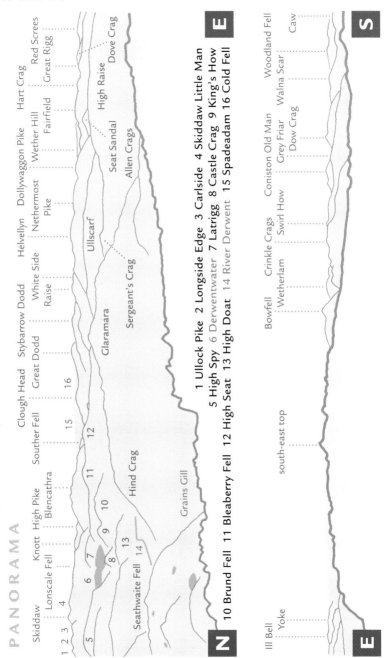

N

E

Skiddaw Lonscale Fell Knott High Pike Blencathra Clough Head Souther Fell Great Dodd White Side Raise Stybarrow Dodd Helvellyn Dollywaggon Pike Nethermost Pike Wether Hill Fairfield Hart Crag Red Screes Great Rigg

Glaramara Sergeant's Crag Ullscarf Seat Sandal Allen Crags High Raise Dove Crag

Seathwaite Fell Hind Crag Grains Gill

1 Ullock Pike 2 Longside Edge 3 Carlside 4 Skiddaw Little Man
5 High Spy 6 Derwentwater 7 Latrigg 8 Castle Crag 9 King's How
10 Brund Fell 11 Bleaberry Fell 12 High Seat 13 High Doat 14 River Derwent 15 Spadeadam 16 Cold Fell

S

Ill Bell Yoke Bowfell Crinkle Crags Coniston Old Man Woodland Fell
Wetherlam Swirl How Grey Friar Walna Scar
Dow Crag Caw

south-east top

E

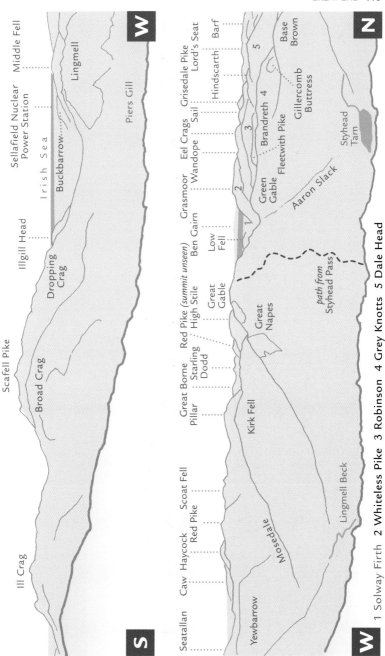

W

Middle Fell

Lingmell

Sellafield Nuclear Power Station

Irish Sea

Buckbarrow

Illgill Head

Dropping Crag

Piers Gill

Scafell Pike

Broad Crag

Ill Crag

S

N

Griesdale Pike
Lord's Seat
Barf

Hindscarth

Base Brown

Sail

Eel Crags

5

Grasmoor
Wandope

Brandreth 4

Gillercomb Buttress

Green Gable

Fleetwith Pike

3

Ben Gairn

Low Fell

2

Aaron Slack

Styhead Tarn

Red Pike (summit unseen)
High Stile

Great Gable

1

Great Borne
Starling Dodd

Great Napes

path from Styhead Pass

Pillar

Kirk Fell

Scoat Fell

Haycock
Red Pike

Caw

Mosedale

Lingmell Beck

Seatallan

Yewbarrow

W

W   1 Solway Firth 2 Whiteless Pike 3 Robinson 4 Grey Knotts 5 Dale Head

GREAT HOW

The 'Great How and Where' might be the more appropriate name. Few walkers have cared to know this fell and why should they? Its broad slopes perform little more than the lead in to Slight Side, either by the Woolpack Inn path or the Terrace Route. Need one say more! Well, yes, it has all the noble characteristics solitary fellwalkers adore. Set apart, its scarp has great bearing upon Burnmoor Tarn and, but for the monster pile of Scafell, as pile it is from this western aspect, it would indeed be seen as a prime objective for expeditions from Boot.

There is a real sense of space about this rambling height, the approach slopes from Eskdale are fascinatingly rough and reward a quiet afternoon's meandrous rambling. Bracken and bog may abound, but so do many fine stretches of waving grass prairie and ice-sculpted slabs. There are several small pools near the summit, though the special jewels lie closer to Boot. Stony Tarn has a certain austerity, but Eel Tarn is divine, resplendent with bobbing water-lily rings, a fringe of reed within a surround of varied mosses and a backdrop of Great How, overtopped by Scafell *(see above)*.

When the higher fells are in doubt, perhaps lost in cloud, and a good walk is sought, Great How comes into its own. Not that having the view is not an important ingredient, for its setting lends it a special place to survey the rugged fells sweeping round the southern arc from Bowfell to the sea, with Burnmoor Tarn glistening in late afternoon sunlight. From the Eskdale slopes Harter Fell and Green Crag form shapely backdrops too. The fell is defined by Whillan Beck and the upper Esk branched to Cowcove Beck. Rough, irregular slopes lead north to a scarped spur running south-west from Slight Side, separated by the peat moss of Quagrigg Moss, its hags quite benign, in fact quite Pennine!

523 metres   1,716 feet

For navigational
clarity contours
are shown to the
Eskdale Moor ridge
even though it is
not an integral
part of Great How

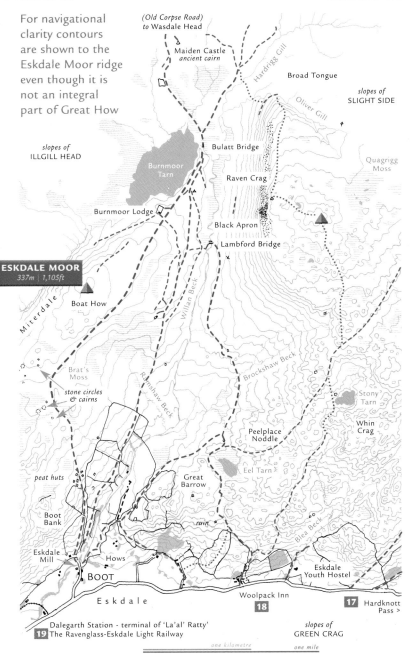

(Old Corpse Road)
to Wasdale Head

Maiden Castle
ancient cairn

Hardrigg Gill

Broad Tongue

Oliver Gill

slopes of
SLIGHT SIDE

slopes of
ILLGILL HEAD

Burnmoor
Tarn

Bulatt Bridge

Raven Crag

Quagrigg
Moss

Burnmoor Lodge

Black Apron

Lambford Bridge

ESKDALE MOOR
337m | 1,105ft

Miterdale

Boat How

Willan Beck

Brockshaw Beck

Brat's
Moss

stone circles
& cairns

Ramshaw Beck

Stony
Tarn

Whin
Crag

Peelplace
Noddle

Eel Tarn

Great
Barrow

peat huts

Boot
Bank

Blea Beck

ruin

Eskdale
Mill

Hows

BOOT

Eskdale
Youth Hostel

E s k d a l e

Woolpack Inn

18

17 Hardknott
Pass >

Dalegarth Station - terminal of 'La'al' Ratty'
19 The Ravenglass-Eskdale Light Railway

slopes of
GREEN CRAG

one kilometre

one mile

Woolpack Inn

ASCENT *from Eskdale*

The two principal routes spring from the Woolpack Inn, a fresh place to start and a refreshing place to end any walk. **1** The more regular path leads by Eel Tarn. Follow the lane signed from the road left of the Inn 'Burnmoor and Wasdale Head'. This leads up behind the inn to a gate, rising to an obvious path divide with bracken looming. Go left with the enclosure wall, this path rises close by a roofless stone bothy *(see page 120)* over the brow to encounter Eel Tarn. This Norse tarn-name means 'dangerous bog', and it is true one should be circumspect and not walk too close, though I tested my luck in a drought and survived! The path skirts the blanket bog to the left, keeping to firmer ground. Watch for the branch right that effectively swings on round the tarn to head east into the irregular area of craggy knolls known by the surreal name Peelplace Noddle. Goodness knows what this means. Is it indeed a pub joke that found its way onto maps? Your guess is probably better than mine. The path trends up the ridge, negotiating marshy ground and keeps up to the left of Stony Tarn. Watch you don't get lured into following it, as this path has a higher intent, being the bee-line for Slight Side.

2 The second approach reaches this vicinity by branching right above the inn. This path rises naturally, in secretive spongy terrain, to come above the open marshy bowl of Blea Beck. Keep just to the left of the beck, into its upper amphitheatre. Ford the beck with small falls to the left. Climb a steeper bracken bank, with next to no evidence of a path, keep to the firmer ground in contouring to the natural dam rigg, drop to the outflow of Stony Tarn. The tarn, backed by the craggy rim of Dawsonground Crags, has black plastic piping drawing water from its

Harter Fell

Eel Tarn

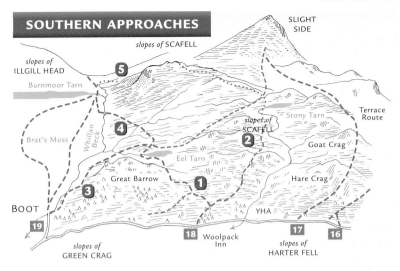

SOUTHERN APPROACHES

SLIGHT SIDE

slopes of SCAFELL

slopes of ILLGILL HEAD

Burnmoor Tarn

5

4

Brat's Moss

Whillan Beck

Eel Tarn

3

Great Barrow

1

slopes of SCAFELL

2

Stony Tarn

Terrace Route

Goat Crag

Hare Crag

BOOT

19

YHA

slopes of GREEN CRAG

18 Woolpack Inn

17

slopes of HARTER FELL

16

The Great How escarpment from Hardrigg Gill

outflow. Cross the outflow heading north by the sheepfold; climb onto the flat ridge to meet up with the path from Eel Tarn. **3** Follow this only so far as it stays on the ridge, as it veers right, to contour, head left onto the undulating ridge. Drift slightly left of north to the summit outcrop and cairn.

4 The other main line of ascent, from the north via Oliver Gill, can begin from Wasdale Head, using the bridle-path to Burnmoor Tarn from Brackenclose, this can also be a novel precursor to Scafell. For ease of crossing this involves fording Hardrigg Gill and Oliver Gill immediately prior to their confluence to form Whillan Beck.

This point may also be reached from the opposite end of the bridle-path in Boot, by crossing the Burnmoor Tarn outflow plank bridge. But the more coherent line is actually from Eel Tarn. Begin as with route **1**, continuing from Eel Tarn on this well-used a path that was once consistently marked by white crosses daubed on stones *(see above)*. I only found two, though the bracken was high. See one just before it curves down to Lambford Bridge. Cross Lambford Bridge, switching left and right to avoid the marshy patch beyond, the path angling up to join the main path from Boot and crossing the sleeper bridge at the outflow of Burnmoor Tarn.

Forking half-right on the low path traversing the sheepfold at the foot of Hardrigg, veer right to ford Hardrigg and Oliver Gills, climbing the south bank by the prominent waterfall: a huge rock block topped by a garden of heather. Keep up the rigg to the right of the gill, thus avoiding the loose scree within the actual gill. Grass predominates, soon easier ground is found. Ascend south on a gently rising scarp edge to the cairn above Raven Crag. From the cairn go east, passing two lovely sheets of water; aim for the left of three outcrops, mounting to find the summit cairn.

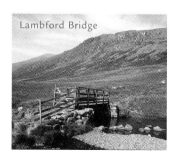

Lambford Bridge

The Summit

The highest ground is defined by a solid outcrop with a smaller pike of comparable height to the south-west; visitors have not deigned to give it a cairn, which is understandable. From here, Scafell looks like a massively boring heap, the white flecked peak of Slight Side has the greater visual impact. The only named tarn in view is Eel Tarn, Burnmoor coming into frame from the cairn 300 metres due west above the Raven Crag scarp. Between Illgill Head and the sleek slopes of Scafell *(see above)* there is a window into the Western Fells over Yewbarrow, the grander skyline sweep being the southern arc from Bowfell right round to Ravenglass.

Tarn west of the summit outcropping

Waterfall in Oliver Gill... a feature garden transposed from Chelsea Flower Show!

Little and Great Barrow above Christcliff

Bulatt Bridge at the outflow of Burnmoor Tarn, looking to Raven Crag

Safe Descents

The sense of isolation is emphasised by the total lack of paths in the upper reaches. The one cause for concern is the western scarp, the one course to avoid east across Quagrigg Moss. For ease of progress aim SE, watching for the several minor outcrops en route to join the flimsy trail running S for Eel Tarn and the Woolpack Inn or, slightly better, cross and continue down the slope to join the more certain Terrace Route path in Catcove Beck, again heading S.

Ridge Route to...

SLIGHT SIDE   DESCENT 150 ft   ASCENT 935 ft   1.4 miles

To minimise bog trotting across Quagrigg Moss, leave the summit aiming SE on line with Hard Knott, thereby joining the path from Boot. Switch acutely NE (left); as the grassy slope intensifies the Terrace Route path joins from the right. The way is obvious, higher up the path is embroiled in loose stones. Keep right, onto the ridge; it is easier to climb onto the rocky summit ridge from the N side. It is simply superb.

Great How seen across Quagrigg Moss during the ascent of Slight Side

PANORAMA

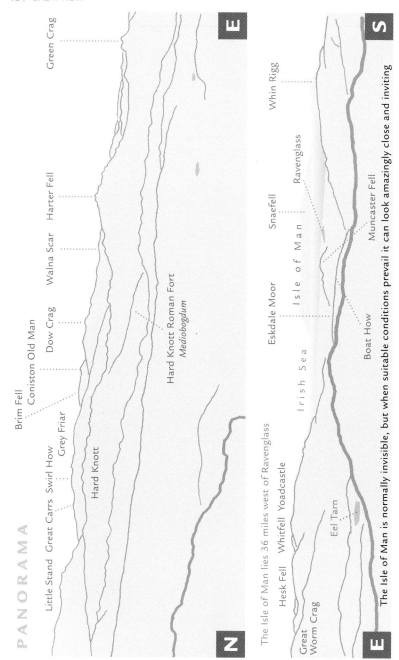

E

Green Crag

Harter Fell

Walna Scar

Dow Crag

Coniston Old Man

Brim Fell

Grey Friar

Swirl How

Great Carrs

Little Stand

Hard Knott Roman Fort
Mediobogdum

Hard Knott

N

The Isle of Man lies 36 miles west of Ravenglass

Hesk Fell   Whitfell   Yoadcastle

Great
Worm Crag

Eel Tarn

S

Whin Rigg

Ravenglass

Snaefell

Eskdale Moor   I s l e   o f   M a n

I r i s h   S e a

Muncaster Fell

Boat How

E

The Isle of Man is normally invisible, but when suitable conditions prevail it can look amazingly close and inviting

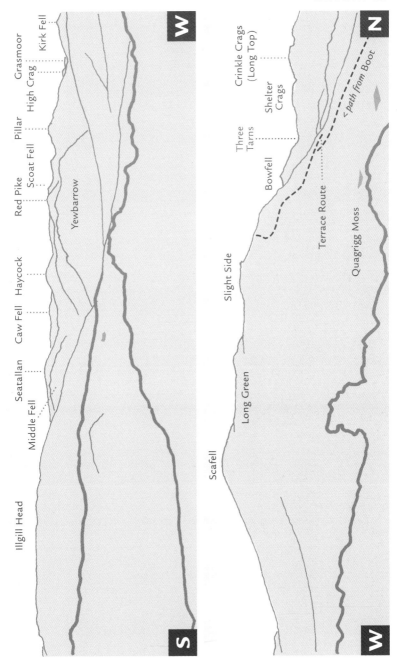

HARD KNOTT

The fell is almost an island in terms of the Mid-Western Fells, a low saddle at the head of Mosedale giving connection with the Crinkle Crags massif. Its real ally is Harter Fell, which is firmly rooted in the Southern Fell domain, these two fells are often climbed together. The fell-name must derive from an Eskdale perspective; climb the Hardknott Pass from Brotherilkeld and, boy, doesn't Border End loom, a hard nut to crack indeed. In fact Hard Knott is not that hard at all, it's all a tough front! The western scarp is steep and rimmed with crags, with little succour for man or beast. Though standing tall amidst this broken frontage, The Steeple or Eskdale Needle gives inquisitive walkers cause to explore. An exquisite piece of natural architecture, it takes on the appearance of a Roman 'thumbs-up', save the Christian... throw the gladiator to the lion instead! The fell has two tops of note, both deserving to be visited as special viewpoints: Border End, for its excellent bird's eye view on lower Eskdale and, most specifically, the Roman Fort, displayed on the flat ridge directly below; the main summit, for the grand parade of fells encircling the head of Eskdale. Motorists know the name of the pass as a high bridge between the Duddon and Eskdale, bringing out the macho in even the gentlest of characters. Surely it must always have been so, demanding horse-power throughout the ages.

552 metres   1,811 feet

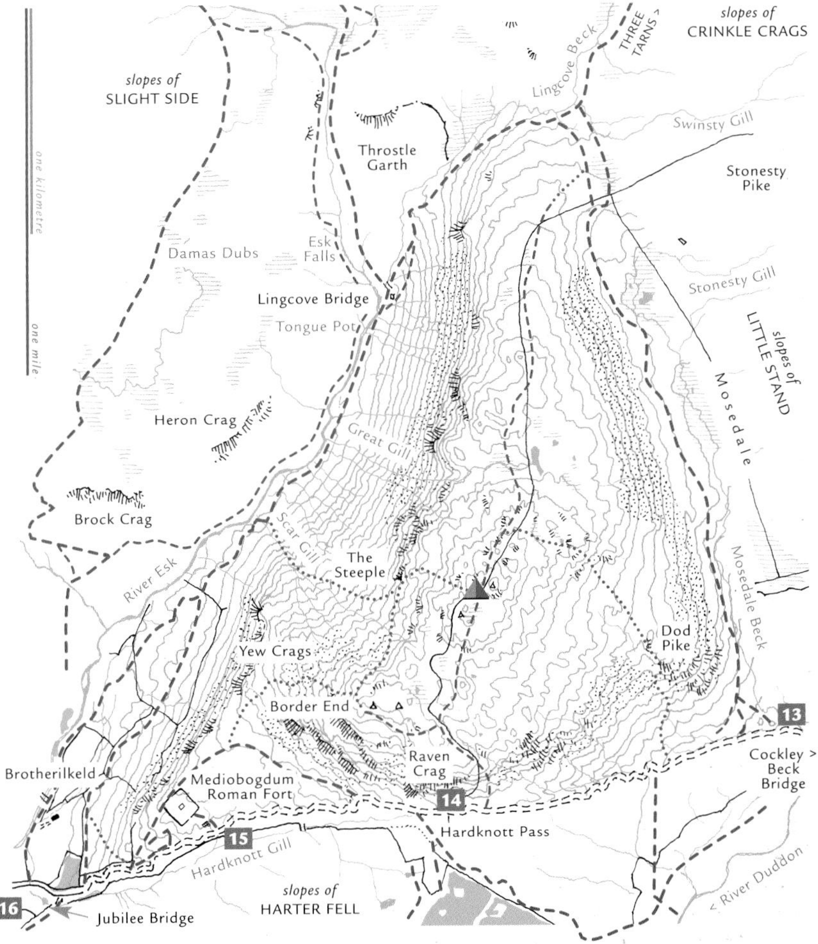

slopes of
CRINKLE CRAGS

slopes of
SLIGHT SIDE

Lingcove Beck

THREE TARNS

Throstle
Garth

Swinsty Gill

Stonesty
Pike

Damas Dubs

Esk
Falls

Stonesty Gill

Lingcove Bridge

Tongue Pot

slopes of
LITTLE STAND

Heron Crag

Great Gill

Mosedale

Brock Crag

Scar Gill

River Esk

The
Steeple

Mosedale Beck

Yew Crags

Dod
Pike

Border End

13

Raven
Crag

Cockley >
Beck
Bridge

Brotherilkeld

Mediobogdum
Roman Fort

14

15

Hardknott Pass

Hardknott Gill

River Duddon

16

Jubilee Bridge

slopes of
HARTER FELL

Slight Side　　Scafell　　　　　Scafell Pike　　Ill Crag　Great End
　　　　　　　　　　　　　　Broad Crag

The Scafells from Border End

Devoke Water

Muncaster Fell

slopes of
GREEN CRAG

Woolpack Inn

Wha House

slopes of
HARTER FELL

River Esk

Taw House

FORT

Brotherilkeld

BATH-HOUSE

PARADE GROUND

COMMAND PLATFORM

MEDIOBOGDUM

The fell has a most unusual treasure further enhancing its mystique, for perched on the south-west spur ridge *(seen above from Border End)* is a fully-fledged Roman Fort. Contemporary with the construction of Hadrian's Wall, it was part of the native Celt-calming infrastructure of the time. Known to the Romans as *Mediobogdum, medio* being 'in the middle of' while *Bogdum* was the pre-existing British name for the locality... bogs and sandals spells wet feet, clearly not a popular posting!

One wonders what these Dalmatian conscripts called the Scafells which were, after all, the constant focus of their daily lives. For the Roman legionaries this posting must have been considered a trial; fellwalking was not all the rage at that time and as the fort apparently did not attract a civil settlement they must have felt right out-on-a-limb.

The typical playing-card plan curtain wall has been restored sufficiently high to give a real sense of the structure, the outline of the key internal buildings revealed, the headquarters at the centre, flanked by the commandant's house and granaries. Man cannot live by bread alone... well up here the recruits had to make a stab at it! Closer to the road lies a bath-house in three-roomed format, a *calderium* to open the skin's pores (sadly the bee-hive-shaped furnace was vandalised only as recently as the 1930s), a *tepidarium*, the warm room for scraping the grime from the skin and a *frigidarium* to cool off. When the fort was vacated it is thought that this was adapted and found use for a considerable period as a wayside hostelry, much as the Woolpack Inn is today. The Roman road from the port of *Clanoventa* (Ravenglass) to *Galava* (Ambleside) will have remained an active highway throughout succeeding centuries.

To the east of the fort is a large level parade ground. The Romans cleared the stones, no doubt tipping them over the nearby scarp. That scarp will have been something of a focus for them, the north gate giving out directly onto it. One could imagine the auxiliaries testing their nerve on the little pinnacle immediately beyond. An inscribed stone, discovered in 1964 near the SE gate, recorded that the fort was erected 'for the Emperor Caesar Trajan Hadrian Augustus' by the Fourth Cohort of Dalmatians. Coin finds suggest the fort was occupied AD120-138 and again AD160-197.

The setting for contemporary eyes is quite magnificent. One's imagination can run riot - sense the place when in active occupation, hear the strident note of the brass horn out on the parade ground and the creak of metal hinges at the south gateway as an ox-cart draws in delivering stores, and the strange voices of men from a far-back mid-European culture. These are among the many sensations that can help bridge the lost centuries and lend romance to one's all too fleeting visit.

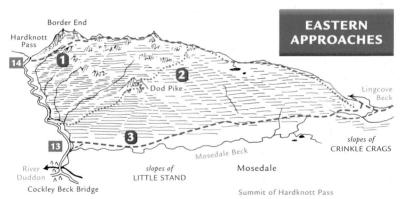

Summit of Hardknott Pass

ASCENT *from Hardknott Pass*

1 There is less scope for casual parking at the top of Hardknott than there is on Wrynose Pass. From the one good lay-by, east of the cattle grid and summit cairn, you can make a swift, unhindered start to a climb. Currently an electric heaf fence runs up beside the

path and right along the ridge, which might be thought useful in mist, though there are some boggy hollows that the fence doesn't always miss! Rise upon an easy grass trod, crossing a fence stile en route to the boggy ridge-top hollow, resplendent with cotton grass. Another stile is encountered, paths branch to left and right. A left turn puts one on course for a cairned top from which a further cairn is espied. Advance 150 metres to reach this, the actual summit of Border End. What a superb viewpoint: Harter Fell is seen top to toe. The verdant strath of Eskdale too, is so pleasing and, yes, I had to mention it, the majestic mountain sanctuary of upper Eskdale excites eyes and hearts. A scene that is played out consistently during a traverse of the fell. Backtrack to the stile and cross.

Pool at the top of the ascent via Dod Pike

Broad Crag

Ill Crag

Great End

Esk Pike

Bowfell

Long Top

ASCENT *from Mosedale*

2 Motorists find the final steep incline at the foot of the Hardknott Pass road quite a problem, particularly in descent; to wit, the amazing wheel-scored tread-marks up the opposing slope, just where a bridle-path is signed to Black Hall. A matter of a forty metres further down the road and a short rough track (used to feed supplements to sheep) indicates a suitable point to embark on the ascent of Dod Pike. The slope, dogged by bracken, is soon beaten. En route inspect the striking rock-wall corner in the lowest outcrop clamber up and round to top the main outcrop for a novel view of the Duddon valley, with Little Stand and Grey Friar prominent. Traverse the moorland ridge aiming north-west; several steps are taken to reach a large pool on a broad shelf, with specimen peat groughs close by. Continue to reach the electric heaf fence, turning back south to reach the summit.

3 A bridle-path is signposted into Mosedale off the open road (GR244017), though some walkers start a hundred metres further east; both ford a small gill. The bridle-way shows evidence of old pitching where it runs close to the beck. Within Mosedale proper soggy ground has to be tackled. Well the name should have warned you at the 'middle of Bogdum'! Having plodded this way on half a dozen occasions during the research for this guide, the fear of wet feet was overcome by knowing where load-bearing stones lay! Two old cairns are passed en route to the hand-gate in the heaf fence, situated on the transverse watershed rigg. Pass through and follow the fence up left, there are two stiles on the first stage, then the path drifts right of the fence dipping to traverse a damp hollow - the fence runs through a real mire - and rises to further stile. The outcropping in this vicinity is rather impressive, the tilted slabs providing tempting camera angles for the Scafells.

The Steeple or Eskdale Needle backed by Slight Side and Scafell

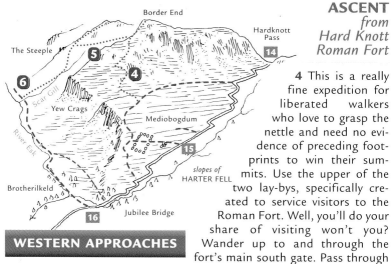

Border End
Hardknott Pass
The Steeple
Scar Gill
Yew Crags
Mediobogdum
River Esk
slopes of HARTER FELL
Brotherilkeld
Jubilee Bridge

WESTERN APPROACHES

ASCENT
from
Hard Knott
Roman Fort

4 This is a really fine expedition for liberated walkers who love to grasp the nettle and need no evidence of preceding footprints to win their summits. Use the upper of the two lay-bys, specifically created to service visitors to the Roman Fort. Well, you'll do your share of visiting won't you? Wander up to and through the fort's main south gate. Pass through to the north gate, turn right, following the path clinging to the scarp, thus avoiding the parade ground. This footpath makes an exaggerated sweep up the fell, ultimately joining an upper hair-pin of the modern road. But the more exciting action lies in weaving up the irregular west ridge, dexterously avoiding rocks to achieve the cairn on Border End. You should take time to soak up the stunning view before heading off. **5** There are two options. The more natural inclination is to make a simple circular walk by aiming for the top of Hardknott Pass. A path underfoot guides to the adjacent cairned top and eastward to a cotton-grass filled hollow divided by the heaf fence. Turn right down by the infant Hardknott Gill, then via a stile down to the summit of the Pass. Cross the cattle-grid and follow the road down or better still use the footpath under Border End to complete a circuit. Option two continues the theme of quest. The Steeple, otherwise known as Eskdale Needle, merits a visit. This is achieved by descending north from the top of Border End. Grassy ground can easily be found as one drifts down and across the slope, keeping an eye out for the handsome pinnacle. The Steeple makes a superb foreground for a view on the Scafells. Inspect from both sides, then aim directly up the fell to cross the heaf fence, as you find convenient, onto the summit knoll.

ASCENT *from Brotherilkeld*

6 It is unusual to contemplate climbing Hard Knott from the west, but on a direct ascent to the summit there is a sound easy line which can include The Steeple. This follows Scar Gill, clearly identifiable beyond the intake wall gate as the rough re-entrant ford situated opposite Heron

Crag, on the popular path beside the Esk from Brotherilkeld to Lingcove Bridge. Bracken and rough ground are not an issue and, being pathless, route-finding is a only matter of personal choice, the ascent linking with route **5** in the vicinity of The Steeple.

Summit cairn, with the Scafells as the backdrop

The Summit

Marked by a small cairn set upon a rock. A marvellous place to enjoy the great circle of fells about the head of Eskdale. A word on the triple-stranded electric fence which weaves along the spine of the fell. Stiles have been placed where the ridge path conventionally crosses, but no concession has been allowed for anyone interested in visiting The Steeple. The fence was installed by the National Trust immediately after the outbreak of Foot & Mouth Disease in 2001 wiped out their heafed flocks of Duddon Herdwick. The plan is to keep the fence up for a temporary period of five years, though common sense will rule at least ten years necessary to achieve the stated goal of restoring the sense of heft in the breeding ewes. I will be surprised if it is removed before the next edition of this guide. Which explains why the fence is shown on the attendant maps.

Safe Descents

In fog the fence becomes a real bonus, head south in its company. There are two marshy hollows where path and fence take differing lines before coming together at the third hollow. At this point cross the stile and bear left. Cross the fence twice more to reach the road at the top of Harknott Pass, head down west for Eskdale and the nearest phone box/hostelry.

PANORAMA

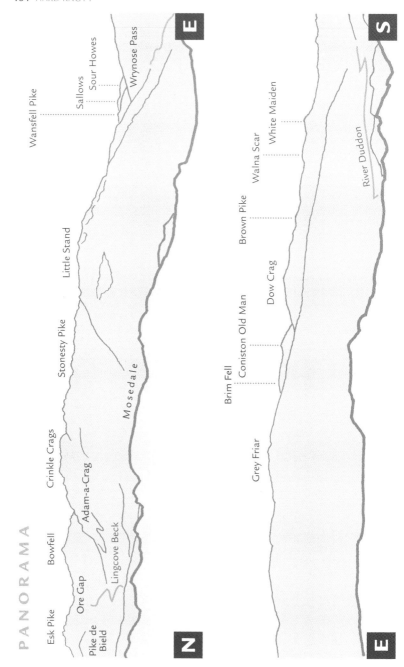

N

Esk Pike
Ore Gap
Pike de Bield
Bowfell
Adam-a-Crag
Lingcove Beck
Crinkle Crags
Stonesty Pike
Mosedale
Little Stand
Wansfell Pike
Sallows
Sour Howes
Wrynose Pass

E

E

Grey Friar
Brim Fell
Coniston Old Man
Dow Crag
Brown Pike
Walna Scar
White Maiden
River Duddon

S

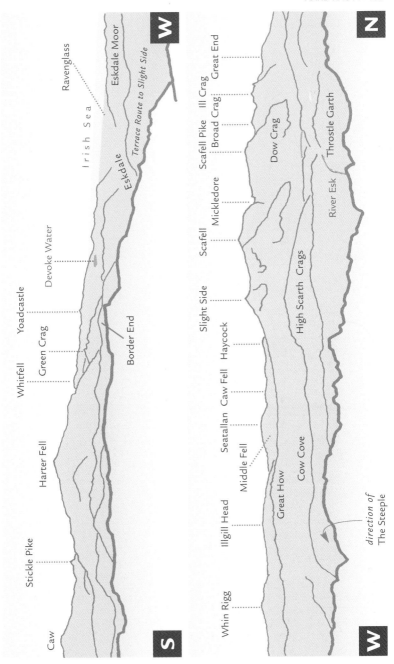

W

Ravenglass

Eskdale Moor

Terrace Route to Slight Side

Eskdale

Irish Sea

Devoke Water

Yoadcastle

Green Crag

Whitfell

Border End

Harter Fell

Stickle Pike

Caw

S

N

Scafell Pike   Ill Crag   Great End

Broad Crag

Dow Crag

Throstle Garth

River Esk

Mickledore

Scafell

High Scarth Crags

Slight Side

Haycock

Caw Fell

Seatallan

Middle Fell

Cow Cove

Great How

Illgill Head

direction of
The Steeple

Whin Rigg

W

ILLGILL HEAD

Illgill Head and Whin Rigg, a theatrical double act, share custodianship of the majestic Wastwater Screes. An arresting mural of rock and scree, a stunning showcase, an unrivalled exhibition, the delight of all tourists. Motorists find irresistible the urge to pull up along the open lakeside road leading to Wasdale Head, mesmerised by this awesome display, a combination of volcanic might and glacial nudity.

The fell is the higher, northern culmination of a great ridge born on Irton Pike above Santon Bridge. The two summits are separated by a broad pool-filled saddle *(see above)*. The two sides of the ridge could not be more different. So much so that an observer at the outflow of Burnmoor Tarn, unaware of The Screes, would dismiss the ridge as of no interest. Mind you, they would have little good to say about Scafell from that angle too and might wander onto the scarp of Great How for solace! Search in vain, maps show no hint to the identity of the actual Ill Gill, though one suspects it to be the dry gully plummeting from the edge thirty metres from the west top cairn. Ill-tidings for anyone who attempts to climb by such a course from the Wastwater shoreline path. The rough scarp is no place for the likes of us; a flora-rich environment that needs leaving well alone. Heather abounds on these higher northern slopes, a joy to behold during August, especially when flooded by the golden light of a late afternoon sun.

Like Slight Side, this is a fell with one natural line of ascent, with two strands of approach off the old corpse road which linked Wasdale Head with consecrated ground in Eskdale. Illgill Head has more than equal share of the Screes Footpath, albeit a basically shoreline travail. There is nothing like it elsewhere in Lakeland, though the worst section

609 metres **1,998** feet

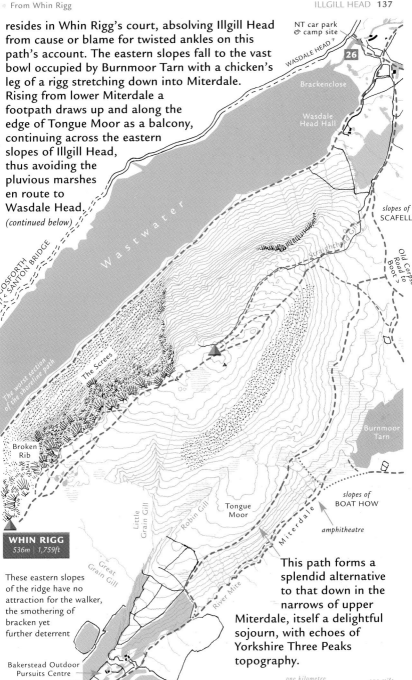

resides in Whin Rigg's court, absolving Illgill Head
from cause or blame for twisted ankles on this
path's account. The eastern slopes fall to the vast
bowl occupied by Burnmoor Tarn with a chicken's
leg of a rigg stretching down into Miterdale.
Rising from lower Miterdale a
footpath draws up and along the
edge of Tongue Moor as a balcony,
continuing across the eastern
slopes of Illgill Head,
thus avoiding the
pluvious marshes
en route to
Wasdale Head.
(continued below)

NT car park
& camp site

WASDALE HEAD

26

Brackenclose

Wasdale
Head Hall

slopes of
SCAFELL

Old Corpse
Road to
Boot

GOSFORTH
SANTON BRIDGE

Wastwater

Straighthead Gill

The worst section
of the shoreline path

The Screes

Burnmoor
Tarn

Broken
Rib

Little
Grain Gill

Robin Gill

Tongue
Moor

Miterdale

slopes of
BOAT HOW

amphitheatre

WHIN RIGG
536m | 1,759ft

Great
Grain Gill

River Mite

These eastern slopes
of the ridge have no
attraction for the walker,
the smothering of
bracken yet
further deterrent

This path forms a
splendid alternative
to that down in the
narrows of upper
Miterdale, itself a delightful
sojourn, with echoes of
Yorkshire Three Peaks
topography.

Bakerstead Outdoor
Pursuits Centre

one kilometre   one mile

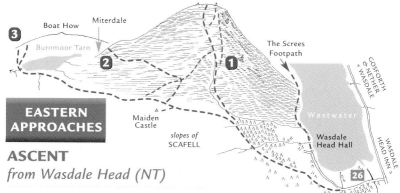

EASTERN APPROACHES

ASCENT
from Wasdale Head (NT)

1 Leave the car park, follow the trackway left to cross the broad farm-bridge spanning Lingmell Gill. Bear left, flanked by gorse, wend upstream to a fork in the way at Brackenclose: a Lakeland Fell and Rock Club property. Follow the path right, signposted 'Eskdale'. The track passes through three gates, rises over the fairy tale twin-arched bridge, where Hollow and Groove Gills converge. Pass a group of ruined eighteenth-century peat huts, and, shortly after the conifers end, the path forks, cairns indicating the old corpse road up to the saddle. However, keep right to ford Straighthead Gill and begin the climb in earnest. Soon the wall draws close to the path left; higher up the main path crosses it and continues unshackled; one may choose to keep by the wall in misty conditions, but its ultimate fate is the top of a crag, not the fell! Nearing the prominent shoulder brow the path splits again, the regular path taking the ridge head-on by a cairn leading irrevocably to the shelter-cairned east summit.

2 The balcony traverse to Miterdale: a through route of exceptional merit in the context of Illgill Head, which serves the valuable function of forming a key connection for a ten mile grand girdle of The Screes massif, when combined with the bridle-path over Irton Fell. Follow the old corpse road to the crest of the broad depression (GR 183057). A clear path diverges right. As the slope begins to steepen a strong path enters from the left; follow this contouring south, thus keeping well above the marshy ground. Being in regular use, the path and, by implication, your legs, are not troubled by bracken and it is a fine parade for Burnmoor Tarn. Crossing the feeder gills spilling into the amphitheatre at the top of Miterdale, it mounts onto the shoulder of Tongue Moor, sweeping easily through the bracken at balcony level, with a novel view on Boat How, backed by Harter Fell and Green Crag. The path emerges onto a declining shoulder with a wall/fence right, and is forced steeply down the bank beside the plantation to ford the infant Mite (might that be a dear little mite!). Join the dale-bottom path which continues via a stile and gate to cross a footbridge approaching Low Place Farm.

Illgill Head bathed in late evening sunlight, in view from the west ridge of Lingmell

Looking down the Broken Rib gully into a gloriously surreal aquamarine Wastwater

The head of Wastwater from the wall below the east top

Seatallan and Middle Fell from the scarp brink near the west top

ASCENT *from Boot*

3 Though somewhat estranged from Eskdale, walkers have every good reason to bring this summit into their travels. Branch off the old corpse road, to revel in its situation as a prime viewpoint for the Western Fells and the fabulous array of shapely fells encircling Wasdale Head. Park at Dalegarth Station. Leave the head of the village street at the gate beyond Eskdale Mill. Follow the green track branching right via gates up the steadily rising path onto Eskdale Moor parallel with Whillan Beck. Cross the plank footbridge at the outflow of Burnmoor Tarn, continuing level for a time, then, mounting a short rise, branch half-left at the top. An evident path leads through a shallow depression, rising diagonally NNW up the easy slope crossing the balcony path from Miterdale, now tackling steeper ground to join the popular path at the top of Straighthead Gill.

East top shelter cairn

The Summit

Surveyors have fixed the highest point to be on the swelling plateau, south from the shelter cairn. However, walkers have not deigned to erect a significant cairn, preferring instead a less momentous spot some 100 metres to the south, a point that at least gives a good view towards the Eskdale fells and the more distant Black Combe. Nevertheless, quite the majority of visitors are more than satisfied to rest at the shelter cairn at GR 168050, prizing its priceless view of the head of Wastwater. The large cairn on the western top appears more elevated, a fact/illusion intensified because Whin Rigg is completely blocked out. Visit this western cairn and stride thirty bold paces north, holding your breath at the brink of the scarp... now you know the real thrill of The Scree!

Wasdale Head from the broken wall

Solitary cairn south of the summit

Ridge Route to...

Safe Descents

The proximity of a wall *(see above)* is always good news, especially one that acts as a certain guide to a good valley base of the calibre of Wasdale Head. Leave the summit cairn NE, the wall quickly coming into view. This leads down by Straighthead Gill to meet up with the N/S orientated bridle-path, continue N, via gates, to the shelter of Wasdale Head.

WHIN RIGG   DESCENT 440 ft   ASCENT 240 ft   1.4 miles

A clear path leads along the broad plateau to the west top, the ground falls steadily into the wide depression. There is a every good reason to follow the lead of sheep; adopt their narrow trod along the very brink of The Screes escarpment. Trend right, off the common ridge path, to reach the obvious edge. Excitement must be tempered by the severity of the fall and attention given to its nuances. There are sections where the continual process of slippage is revealed in fracture slumps; note how even the sheep show due caution and keep to the firmer ground. There are several places where aretes permit one to venture onto spurs, allowing a more dramatic involvement in the fierce slope, offering views of the deep dark waters of Wastwater from on high. The main ridge path, which has two winding variants, passes a pair of tarns before ascending to the shelter cairn (both fell-tops now have a wind-break cairns) on the slightly more certain summit knoll, on the north side of the path.

PANORAMA

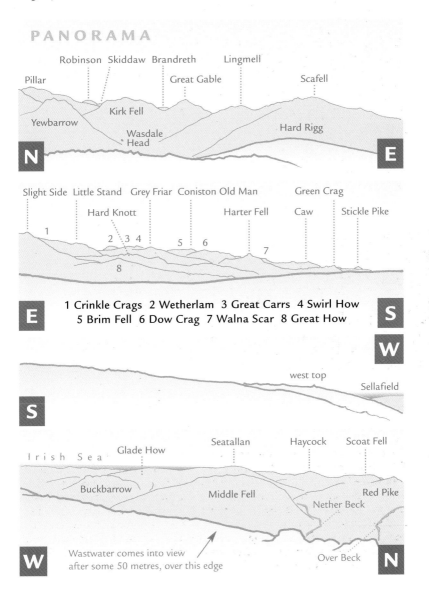

1 Crinkle Crags 2 Wetherlam 3 Great Carrs 4 Swirl How
5 Brim Fell 6 Dow Crag 7 Walna Scar 8 Great How

LINGMELL

Side show, not a bit of it, star performer, with a trick or two up its not inconsiderable sleeve, to entertain any fellwalking day. Many an ascent of Scafell Pike has been given zest by the inclusion of this handsome height. Yet an expedition that makes Lingmell the sole player is truly worthy of any season. The circuit from Wasdale Head, climbing via Piers Gill to Lingmell Col and descending the west ridge, is pure magic from start to finish. The rise over the fell-top from the high col is absolutely stunning, revealing the most exciting aspect of Great Gable, the sheer gullies leading down into the dizzy depths of Piers Gill, and the course of the Corridor Route from Styhead, overtopped by Great End and Broad Crag. While during the traverse of southern slopes Pikes and Scafell Crags are seen to their very best effect too.

The fell has two personalities, smooth and debonnaire to the south and west, rough, tough and mean to the north and east. While Lingmell Gill gathers debris from the high Scafells and runs of scree from the fell's south slope, the greatest monument to the ravages of ice and rain is the mighty gash of Piers Gill, torn into the north-eastern flank of the fell in alpine proportions. The ferocity of storms has, down the millennia, brought boulders in profusion into Lingmell Beck, constantly shuffling towards the lake. In the vicinity of the National Trust campsite in times

807 metres   2,649 feet

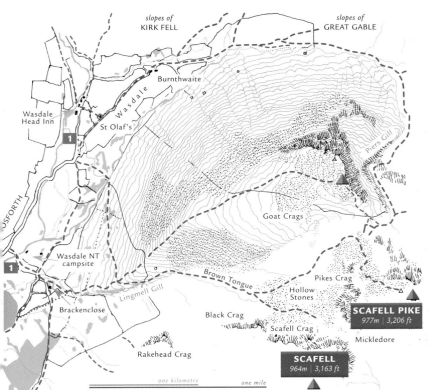

of drought the beck flows in subterranean silence, but in normal inclemency the surging water fills and spills from its wide channel, frequently making progress along the footpath to the Village Green car park and Wasdale Head Inn impractical.

The fell-name confirms a certain expectancy for heather, not well evidenced today; while mell, the Celtic for 'a bald hill', indicates that it was at one time different from surrounding fells in not having a good tree cover. This begs the question, when, and to what extent, were the neighbouring fells wooded? Thorn bushes do persist along its flanks and the slopes of Scafell below Rakehead. It would be an asset to the scene if deciduous trees were planted in blocks among them. Suitably fenced to exclude sheep, they would add immeasurably to the bio-diversity of this far-famed and much revered mountain sanctuary.

A slender cairn on a lower tier of the north ridge

Looking down Piers Gill from the Corridor Route.
Don't be lured by the loose scree tumbling innocently into the gully to think that
you can do the same and follow the ravine down to Lingmell Beck. In degrees of
sanity its well below zero, as too your chances of survival!

(right) Perpendicular! Great Gable from the top of the Piers Gill gully on Lingmell

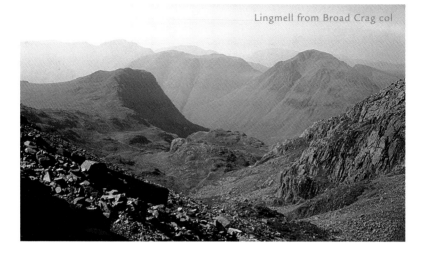

Lingmell from Broad Crag col

ASCENT *from the Village Green, Wasdale Head*

1 Follow the farm lane from the Village Green car parking area, leading by the yew-tree shaded St Olaf's Church directly to Burnthwaite Farm. The path is ushered left of the farm-buildings to a gate. Go through and bear right, passing through a gate en route to a footbridge spanning Gable Beck. Take one of two optional paths right at dale-floor level, leading to a hand-gate in a descending wall. The crags of Great Napes pierce the sky above the massive scree bank up to the left, with the dark shaded bulk of Lingmell overbearing to the right. At the confluence with Spouthead Gill the path fords, a clear zig-zagging path continuing up the rigg. Watch for the branching path right, keeping company with the lower ravine of Piers Gill. Ford the stony foot of Greta Gill, continuing with ever heightening excitement beside Piers Gill. The path climbs to a nine metre rock step, which might be considered a problem for descending walkers. But the hand- and foot-holds are very sharply angled, making it a straightforward exercise in ascent at least. Above this, the path comes close to the deepest section of Piers Gill. You may be tempted to peer over the edge at the right-angle bend; immense care is needed. There is a curious white solution spilling from the facing gully, beneath a crag capped by an apron of scree, while a little further look up the ravine, thrilling at the view towards Dropping Crag on Scafell Pike. Advancing to meet up with the Corridor Route, the path passes a second exceptional viewpoint of the same subject *(see page 231)*. Go right, fording the gill near the lip of the ravine *(see page 146)* and traverse up to the broken wall on the saddle of Lingmell Col. The fell-top is easily gained. Make a point of keeping right to note, half-way up, the stupendous view down Piers Gill and across to Great Gable *(see page 147)*.

SOUTHERN APPROACH

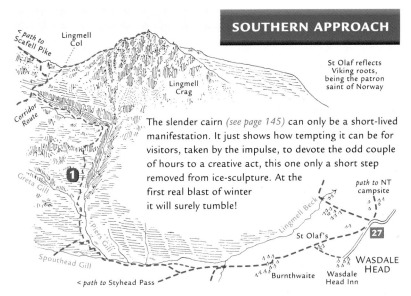

path to
Scafell Pike

Lingmell
Col

Lingmell
Crag

St Olaf reflects
Viking roots,
being the patron
saint of Norway

Corridor
Route

Greta Gill

The slender cairn *(see page 145)* can only be a short-lived manifestation. It just shows how tempting it can be for visitors, taken by the impulse, to devote the odd couple of hours to a creative act, this one only a short step removed from ice-sculpture. At the first real blast of winter it will surely tumble!

path to NT
campsite

Lingmell Beck

St Olaf's

27

Piers Gill

Spouthead Gill

St Olaf's

Burnthwaite

Wasdale
Head Inn

**WASDALE
HEAD**

< path to Styhead Pass

Lingmell dominated by Piers Gill from the Spout Head scarp edge of The Band on Great End

(above) Scafell has two particularly handsome aspects, the eastern crags, as viewed from Hard Knott *(see page 131)* and this magnificent northern perspective on Scafell Crag from the west ridge path, the golden light of evening drenching this late-summer scene to perfection

(opposite) The Wastwater Screes are the 'Everyman's Edition' of this scene: fellwalkers lie in bed dreaming of this view and long for many happy returns: Great Napes, Westmorland Crags and the summit of Great Gable from a little over half-way up the south-east ridge of Lingmell.

(below) The sleek, scree-streaked west ridge from Rakehead Crag overlooking Lingmell Gill

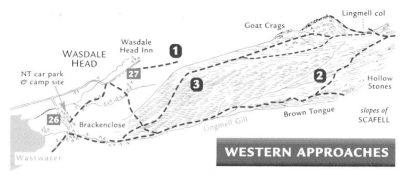

ASCENT *from Wasdale Head (The National Trust car park)*

2 Start out along the farm-track, cross the broad bridge spanning Lingmell Gill. Follow upstream to the gated footbridge, cross the bridge, keep up the valley via two hand-gates, the path pitched throughout much of its course, quite simply because of its inevitable popularity as a primary route to Scafell Pike. The path climbs onto the green rigg of Brown Tongue. Watch keenly for the left branch of the path which draws up Hollow Stones. As the path bends right to address the broad north-west ridge of Scafell Pike, bear off towards the easy saddle of Lingmell Col, identified by its wall. The first two routes are very much the way up, route three is the natural descent. **3** Early in the ascent of Lingmell Gill with the footbridge just crossed, rise to the next hand-gate in a fence (NT collection box close by). Leave the gill path slanting up left onto the rising rigg, cross over the path swinging over the ridge from Wasdale Head bound for Lingmell Gill (which it joins at the top hand-gate). Ahead sweat and toil on the steep climb mounting the prow of the west ridge. Near the top the inevitable loose gravel adds to the effort; once topped, ahead is an ocean of grass on a gentle gradient. The path either crosses over the broken outcropped subsidiary top of Goat Crags, or takes the earlier half-right branch bypassing on the south side to join and follow the wall to Lingmell Col. The former is the direct option; it comes up to the broken wall. At an erratic integrated into the wall, quaintly topped with a crown of walling stones *(see right, looking to Pulpit Rock, Pikes and Scafell Crags)*, leave the wall heading due north.

Traverse the western slopes, reaching the north ridge at the lower scarp brink and follow the edge up, via several steps and cairned tops, above the spectacular Lingmell Crag.

The Summit

The cairn an edifice of pride, befitting of a noble vantage point. The summit is a personal favourite, running a close second to Great End in the Mid-Western Fell group, with Scafell chasing up in third place. The view is dominated by the almost perpendicular aspect of Great Gable. While from the cairnless south top witness a peerless view of Scafell.

Safe Descents

The first concern is to avoid Lingmell Crag which plummets from the northern edge. By walking generally S from the summit you will encounter a wall. If you go precisely SE from the summit it is easy enough to reach Lingmell Col and link up with the path descending from Scafell Pike into Hollow Stones and, by this means, the shelter and security of Lingmell Gill. Alternatively, follow the wall W until you find the large erratic boulder crowned by a ring of stones, where join the W ridge path.

Ridge Route to...

SCAFELL PIKE   DESCENT 280 ft   ASCENT 840 ft   1 mile

Descend SE to Lingmell Col, cross the broken wall, lead on through the irregular outcrops to link up with the Corridor Route (from the left) and then the path ascending from Hollow Stones (from the right). At a ledge slant half-right and then half-left, climbing with an excess of cairns the broad NW ridge (N of Pikes Crag) to a large cairn at the plateau edge. A stony but not too troublesome path leads to the summit, distinguished by an old trig pillar and crumbling walled tower.

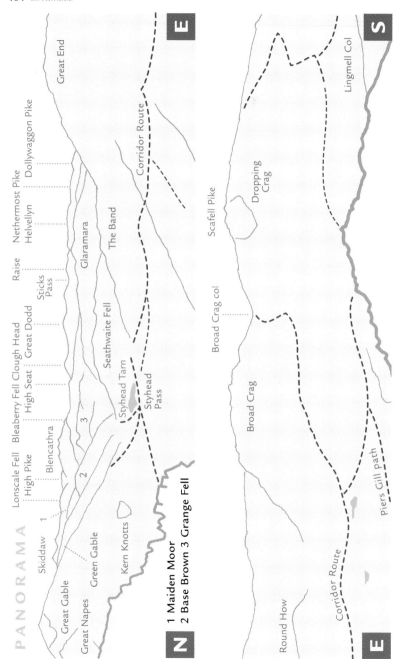

PANORAMA

N

Skiddaw · Great Gable · Great Napes · Green Gable · Kern Knotts
Lonscale Fell · Bleaberry Fell · High Pike · Blencathra
High Seat · Clough Head · Great Dodd · Sticks Pass · Raise
Nethermost Pike · Helvellyn · Dollywaggon Pike · Great End
Glaramara · The Band · Seathwaite Fell · Styhead Tarn · Styhead Pass
Corridor Route

1 Maiden Moor 2 Base Brown 3 Grange Fell

E

S

Scafell Pike · Dropping Crag · Broad Crag col · Broad Crag
Lingmell Col · Round How · Corridor Route · Piers Gill path

E

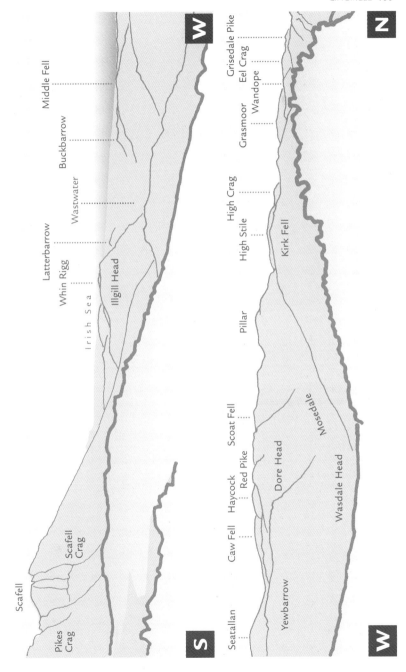

N

W

Middle Fell
Buckbarrow
Wastwater
Latterbarrow
Whin Rigg
Illgill Head
Irish Sea
Scafell
Scafell Crag
Pikes Crag

S

Grisedale Pike
Eel Crag
Wandope
Grasmoor
High Crag
High Stile
Kirk Fell
Pillar
Scoat Fell
Red Pike
Haycock
Caw Fell
Seatallan
Dore Head
Mosedale
Yewbarrow
Wasdale Head

W

LINGMOOR FELL

Sitting right in the middle of all the scenic action, with the valleys Great and Little Langdale to north and south, and three beautiful lakes nestling to east, west and south: Elterwater, Blea Tarn and Little Langdale Tarn. How could anyone not adore this lovely little fell? For good measure Lingmoor Fell cradles its own tiny sheet of water high amongst the rank heather that gave the fell its name. Wooded to the north and east, rugged to the south and west, the fell has much to merit a casual exploration, including slate workings old and new.

The east/west ridge does more than culminate upon the summit for in tapering to the west it throws up an eye-catching sturdy boss, Side Pike. A stout individualist, a fell in miniature, an excellent first-evening climb to start a fellwalking holiday based in the Langdales. Its east-facing crags effectively shut-off the ridge, forcing walkers onto a narrow ledge beneath the south-east face. The summit provides a peerless view of a famous valley-head: featuring the Langdale Pikes, Mickleden, Bowfell and the handsome heights about Oxendale, Crinkle Crags, Pike o'Blisco and Kettle Crag. The northern spur of the fell squeezes Great Langdale forcing it to contort. On the tip of this ridge is a blunt pinnacle, Oak How Needle.

There are seven lines of ascent around the compass detailed here, proving what a walker-friendly, approachable fell it is, enabling you to create your own peculiar circular walk from any given start-point.

470 metres   1,542 feet

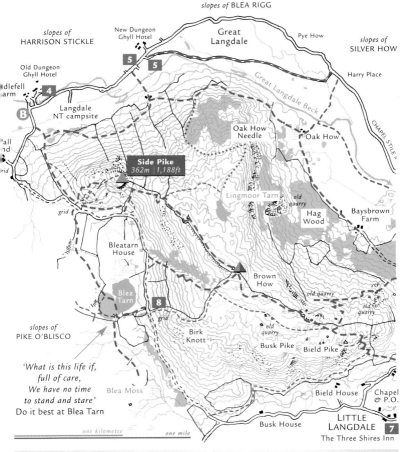

slopes of BLEA RIGG

slopes of
HARRISON STICKLE

New Dungeon
Ghyll Hotel

Great
Langdale

Pye How

slopes of
SILVER HOW

Old Dungeon
Ghyll Hotel

5

5

Harry Place

dlefell
arm

4

B

Langdale
NT campsite

Great Langdale Beck

CHAPEL STILE?

all
nd

Oak How
Needle

Oak How

rid

grid

Side Pike
362m | 1,188ft

Lingmoor Tarn

old
quarry

Hag
Wood

Baysbrown
Farm

Bleatarn
House

Brown
How

old quarry

old
quarry

Blea
Tarn

8

slopes of
PIKE O'BLISCO

grid

Birk
Knott

old
quarry

Busk Pike

Bield Pike

*'What is this life if,
full of care,
We have no time
to stand and stare'*
Do it best at Blea Tarn

Blea Moss

Bield House

Chapel
& P.O.

**LITTLE
LANGDALE**

7

Busk House

The Three Shires Inn

one kilometre

one mile

Lingmoor Fell from Little Langdale

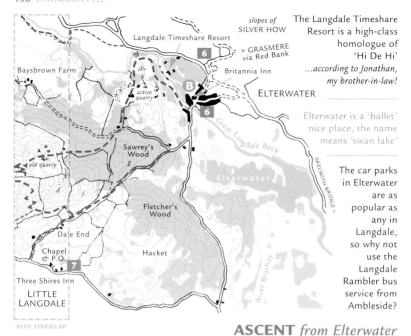

slopes of
SILVER HOW

Langdale Timeshare Resort

> GRASMERE
via Red Bank

Baysbrown Farm

active
quarry

Britannia Inn

ELTERWATER

Great Langdale Beck

SKELWITH BRIDGE >

old quarry

Sawrey's
Wood

Fletcher's
Wood

Dale End

Chapel
& P.O.

Hacket

Three Shires Inn

LITTLE
LANGDALE

River Brathay

MAP OVERLAP

The Langdale Timeshare
Resort is a high-class
homologue of
'Hi De Hi'
...*according to Jonathan,
my brother-in-law!*

Elterwater is a 'ballet'
nice place, the name
means 'swan lake'

The car parks
in Elterwater
are as
popular as
any in
Langdale,
so why not
use the
Langdale
Rambler bus
service from
Ambleside?

ASCENT *from Elterwater*

1 From the centre of the village, as much focused on the Britannia Inn as the river, cross the road bridge with a choice of two routes. Either bear right, branching right from the quarry access roadway, guided by signs, after taking a back view of the Langdale Timeshare Resort, partaking of a delightful wooded stroll near the River Brathay: note the waters backing up from a weir. Ignoring, if you can, the footbridge to Wainwrights Inn, continue upstream. The path is promptly drawn up a corridor path away from the river. Rising beneath slate tip, much of it naturalised by birch, continue to the busy entrance to Burlington's stone works (don your hard hat), a store and processing plant for decorative architectural slate. Pass a weighbridge and showroom, that might tempt you to inspect the stylish product: it is interesting to know the technique used to cut the stone is based on the principle of a cheese wire, hard cheese indeed!

   The path crosses into a quiet lane leading up to an open metalled road, still within the woods. This point can reached with equal facility by following the Colwith road from Bridge End, passing the Youth Hostel. Where the road forks, go right by Elterwater Hall; where this deteriorates into a track, keep to the metalled road which bears right by Ullet (owl) Nest Cottage. Join the route from Burlington's Quarry at the cottage, bear off the metalled road (bound for Baysbrown Farm). Follow the track half-left SW, rising further into Baysbrown Wood. This old track reaches a gate by the abandoned Bank

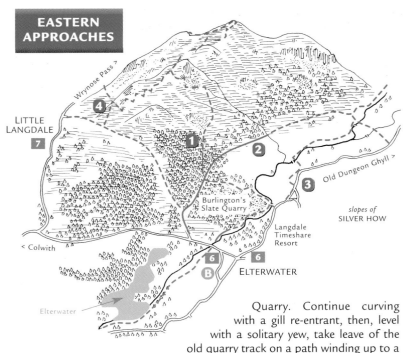

EASTERN
APPROACHES

Wrynose Pass >

LITTLE
LANGDALE
7

4

1

2

3

Old Dungeon Ghyll >

Burlington's
Slate Quarry

slopes of
SILVER HOW

Langdale
Timeshare
Resort

< Colwith

6

6

B

ELTERWATER

Elterwater

Quarry. Continue curving with a gill re-entrant, then, level with a solitary yew, take leave of the old quarry track on a path winding up to a ladder-stile in the ridge-top wall. Go up right, inspecting the ruin at the scarp edge above Lingmoor Quarry. Adhere to the ridge path running close to the wall. As Brown How swells ahead the wall is replaced by a fence and the path veers half-left before taking on the broken ground to reach the fence stile and the summit, immediately above the fence junction.

From Elterwater with the Langdale Pikes to the right

Great Langdale can be enjoyed as much from valley level as from on high. There are two principal foot-paths, each useful as means of avoiding traffic on the congested valley road, particularly useful when devising/constructing circular walks, incorporating with the ridge-top path. **2** The better of these hugs the northern base of the fell via Baysbrown Farm and is approached along the open road through Baysbrown Wood *(see right)* which becomes a walled lane to the farm. Pass on via a gate, where it branch-es off right, from the old Spoutcrag Quarry track; notice the odd road-sign directing to 'Great Langdale'! Approaching Oak How, fork left, via the old walled lane, leading via a gate beneath the steep northern

spur of Oakhow Crag. After a further hand-gate, descend a pasture to Side House. A permissive path has been created, via ladder-stiles, con-tinuing across the damp pasture slopes to slip through the Langdale campsite. **3** A pleasant alternative keeps closer to Great Langdale Beck, a route adopted in part by the Cumbria Way. In effect this begins from the Wainwrights Inn and follows a lane behind the school, then bears down to a track-bridge over the beck. The track continuing west either by Oak How, or a footbridge right onto the valley road. Going left a hundred metres, enter a bridle-lane which leads, rather neatly, direct to the NP Langdale/NT Stickle Ghyll car parks... and attendant hostelries.

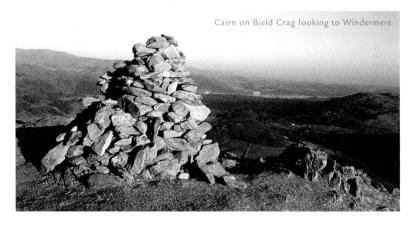

Cairn on Bield Crag looking to Windermere

ASCENT *from Little Langdale*

Be aware that casual car parking is strictly limited on this side of the fell; the village especially cannot cope. **4** From the vicinity of the Three Shires Inn follow the road up past the unusual first-floor church, leave the road right on the lane to Dale End Farm. Beyond the farm take a footpath signed left, leaving the lane, via a ladder-stile. Two further decrepit specimens are crossed before the path turns up a combe, zig-zagging in a measured progress: the ladder-stile in the wall up to the right only gives access to the ridge-end top. A prominent cairn on Bield Crag up to the left may be reached by a lateral path under the edge, beginning before the zig-zagging path reaches the easier gradient. The main path sweeps up the grassy ridge, meeting up with the path from Bank Quarry. Either opt to follow the ridge, or do a spot of detective walking, a path branches half-left, running through an area of small slate tips and ruined huts, the remnants of a cottage industry manufacturing roof slates: the slate is of excellent quality and possesses a lovely tone. The path levels and wanders along a lateral valley before meeting the path climbing from Bleatarn House at a stile in a marsh. Switch sharp right by the fence to the fragile stile at the fence junction and thus the summit cairn.

Looking north from below the summit, over Lingmoor Tarn

Oak How Needle
10
Great Langdale
Side Pike
Lingmoor Tarn
Little Langdale
Little Langdale Tarn
8
5
7
8
Blea Tarn
6
WRYNOSE PASS >
4
B
9
slopes of Pike o'Blisco
Wall End

WESTERN APPROACHES

ASCENT *from Blea Tarn*

Verge parking in this vicinity is unsightly, so resist such temptation. Use the Blea Tarn car park, a popular scenic spot; from here three routes naturally suggest themselves. **5** The most direct ascent embarks from the part-open road 400 metres north of the car park, and short of Bleatarn House, referred to as 'The Solitary' by Wordsworth. A clear grassy path climbs to a wall gap, then winds up the steep slope with larch engulfing a re-entrant close to the left. The path reaches a stile in a fence at the head of this gully; the wet ground is quickly left behind on the climb beside the fence to the summit.

6 The west ridge route: one may continue along the road from Bleatarn House, climbing the bank on a path that begins part-way round the left-hand curve in the road to reach the saddle east of Side Pike. However, the more pleasurable recourse is to follow the path via the hand-gate direct-

Looking along the west ridge to the Langdale Pikes

Side Pike from the path to Blea Tarn

ly opposite the car park entrance. The made-path saunters down to a kissing-gate and subsequent footbridge over the outflow of Blea Tarn. The luxuriant surroundings attract people and wildlife in almost equal measure. On a recent visit a peregrine falcon was audibly making its presence felt from the outcrop directly above the plantation. Rhododendrons love this place too, so are periodically hacked back. Across the lapping waters of the tarn one's attention is focused upon Side Pike and the backing Langdale Pikes: a composition to tempt the shiest camera from the pack. Keeping the lake in sight, head north to exit via a further hand-gate. The path traverses to a kissing-gate in a wall, reaching the road summit beside a cattle-grid. Climb the ladder-stile opposite and, passing the stone seat ascend, either rounding the slope to the right, scrambling up from the top of the wall ahead, or better still slant half-left to follow the regular path mounting more comfortably up to the ridge wall. The ridge path negotiates several small outcrops rising in harmony with the broken ridge wall to the summit cairn. A few paces further and the ground falls precipitously! There is absolutely no scope to continue directly up the ridge, unless you are equipped for, and practised at, abseiling!

Backtrack west, keeping a smart eye out for the narrow trod which sneaks left onto a shelf below the southern cliff. The shelf path ends at a firm flake *(see right)*, which will cause many walkers to question their chances of escape. Being less perfectly formed than I used to be, I resorted to poking my rucksack into the bottom of the crack before hoisting myself through the tight 'fat-man's agony': a sporting

Bleatarn House (The Solitary)
looking to a cloud-draped Bowfell

moment beneath the sheer rock wall which makes a conclusive defence of Side Pike. The subsequent path dips to a stile crossing a fence, here joining the path serving the less adventurous, rising direct from the road. The path proceeds with the undulating ridge wall climbing to cross a stile. A faint path bears left at this point; this is the natural means of reaching Lingmoor Tarn, a detour the solitary wanderer will savour. The vicinity of the tarn is pathless and damp; simply rejoin the ridge up the rough heather slopes. The ridge path scrambles up a rock step hugging the well-made wall, curving onto a prominent knoll, topped with a cairn; henceforward the wall is bettered by a straggled fence leading to the summit.

7 The most direct ascent from the Blea Tarn car park climbs straight up from the south side of the cattle-grid onto Birk Knott, following the skyline wall north. **8** A lovely path, which comes into its own when creating a circular outing with a southern bias, follows the intake wall off the open road, south of the car park. Find the barrier - slung across a green track on the left. Follow this track east, becoming a path in curving into a re-entrant. Ford the gill, keeping above the intake wall, climbing more steeply after High Bield; in so doing gain a superb view south across Little Langdale Tarn to Wetherlam, duly meeting up with the zig-zagging path beneath Bield Crag.

Oxendale and Mickleden from Side Pike

continuing ridge path
to unlock Side Pike

Side Pike *(above)* from the saddle at the foot of the west ridge and *(below)* from Blea Tarn

ASCENT *from Old Dungeon Ghyll*

9 Follow the valley road south from the bus stop. Join a footpath which leaves the road left, via the campsite wood, rise via kissing-gates onto the pasture, with a wall right. The path has two branches, the left option brings one up to the base of the Side Pike ridge, with a clear path climbing to the ridge wall and thus to the summit cairn on Side Pike (consult route **6** for the continuation up the west ridge). **10** Oak How Needle, a wanderer's route: follow the path leading east from Side House, rising to a hand-gate. Bear up right, keeping the wall close right. Don't be put off by the juniper, a way can be won through the dense foliage via an outcrop. Where the wall dips right, take the opportunity to climb straight on up the rigg. As the ground eases traverse left over a rough pathless fellside to locate the blunt Oak How Needle: there is little merit in getting too close, a rough scree gully inter-

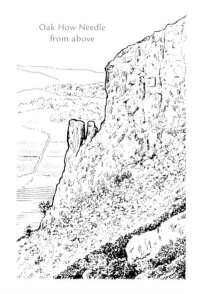

Oak How Needle
from above

The Langdale Pikes from the west ridge

venes. Climb back up the ridge to find the outflow of Lingmoor Tarn, where a path, largely holding a contouring line, wanders west to the ridge path by the wall at the stile below the inclined slab.

The Summit

The final rise above the fence junction is crowned with a modest cairn amongst ragged heather. The view is the thing, and a very fine thing it is too. One can see the Langdale Pikes in all their majesty, the prominent stack of Pike o'Stickle, Loft Crag surmounting Gimmer Crag, Harrison Stickle above the secretive ravine of Dungeon Ghyll, Stickle Beck falling in white fuming steps from the coy cragface of Pavey Ark. Elsewhere the bounty is no less exciting, westward Bowfell, Crinkle Crags and to the south the Coniston fells, all in startling contrast with the rolling, richly wooded country running east towards Windermere.

Safe Descents

The ridge wall-cum-fence offers all the security one needs in time of need. Westward to the saddle before Side Pike, keep left to reach the Bleatarn road for the ODG. Eastward descend steadily; for Elterwater find the ladder-stile after the quarry edge ruin; for Little Langdale follow the path which winds down the ensuing combe, cross three ladder-stiles to reach the lane above Dale End Farm. Go south for the quickest route to a road, follow the fence down to a stile in a wet hollow; the path bears half-left; avoiding the larch-filled gill, descend to the open road south of Bleatarn House *(contrast the images on pages 34 and 164).*

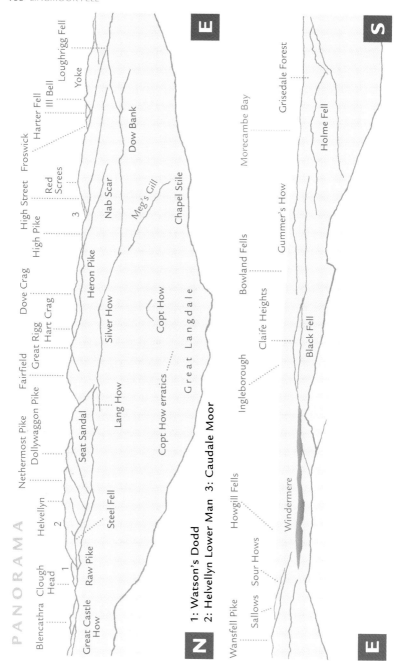

PANORAMA

N   **E**

Blencathra · Clough Head · Helvellyn · Nethermost Pike · Fairfield · Dove Crag · High Pike · High Street · Froswick · Harter Fell · Loughrigg Fell

Great Castle How · Raw Pike · Steel Fell · Dollywaggon Pike · Great Rigg · Hart Crag · Red Screes · Ill Bell · Yoke

Seat Sandal · Lang How · Heron Pike · Silver How · Nab Scar · Dow Bank

Copt How erratics · Copt How · Meg's Gill · Chapel Stile

Great Langdale

1: Watson's Dodd
2: Helvellyn Lower Man   3: Caudale Moor

E   **S**

Wansfell Pike · Howgill Fells · Ingleborough · Claife Heights · Bowland Fells · Morecambe Bay · Grisedale Forest

Sallows · Sour Hows · Gummer's How · Holme Fell

Windermere · Black Fell

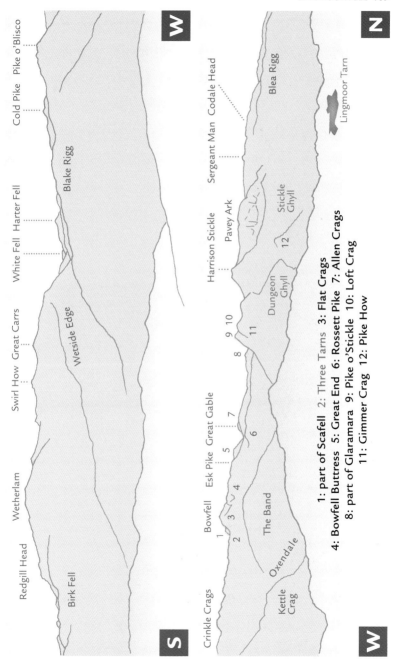

W

Pike o'Blisco Cold Pike

Harter Fell White Fell

Great Carrs Swirl How

Wetherlam

Redgill Head

Birk Fell

Blake Rigg

Wetside Edge

S

N

Sergeant Man Codale Head

Lingmoor Tarn

Blea Rigg

Harrison Stickle

Pavey Ark

Stickle Ghyll

Dungeon Ghyll

Bowfell Esk Pike Great Gable

Crinkle Crags

The Band

Oxendale

Kettle Crag

Pike How

W

1: part of Scafell 2: Three Tarns 3: Flat Crags
4: Bowfell Buttress 5: Great End 6: Rossett Pike 7: Allen Crags
8: part of Glaramara 9: Pike o'Stickle 10: Loft Crag
11: Gimmer Crag 12: Pike How

LITTLE STAND

By no stretch of the imagination can Little Stand be considered an intimate part of Crinkle Crags, though judgement has traditionally been deferred on whether it is a stand alone fell, or just a minor ridge adjunct of its more illustrious and elevated ridge partner. Not being in a mood to beat around the bush, this guide has no compunction in conferring separate fell status on what is clearly a prominent and distinct headland commanding the upper Duddon - a fell of standing.

There is a definite summit and much characterful plateau to explore before the northern run of the ridge leads to the impressive haystack upthrust of the fifth (southernmost) crinkle of Crinkle Crags. Travellers viewing the fell from Cockley Beck Bridge will see no comfortable ridge sweeping to the sky *(see above)*, though the direct rough ascent is fraught with little difficulty. Curiously, Ordnance Survey maps show bridle- and footpaths streaking up the fell from the dale bottom, but only the bridle-way, as far removed from a pony trail as can be conceived, has any credibility. Of greater antiquarian interest will be the course of the Roman Road between Hard Knott and Wrynose, picked out by the valley footpath over much damp ground. Immediately east of Gaitscale Gill, strictly on the slopes of Cold Pike, a definite causeway has survived. The adjacent Mosedale certainly lives up to the its name, keeping walkers firmly, more accurately softly, to the bridle-way.

739 metres   2,426 feet

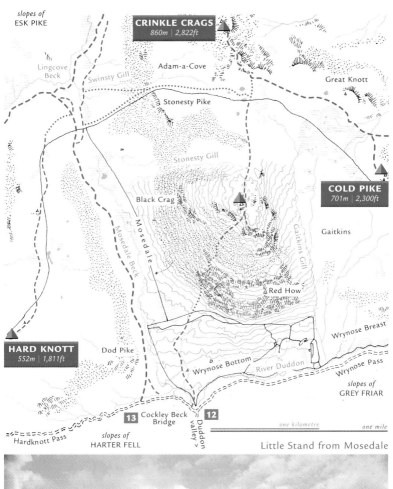

slopes of
ESK PIKE

CRINKLE CRAGS
860m | 2,822ft

Adam-a-Cove

Lingcove
Beck

Swinsty Gill

Great Knott

Stonesty Pike

Stonesty Gill

COLD PIKE
701m | 2,300ft

Black Crag

Gaitkins

Gaitkins Gill

Mosedale

Mosedale Beck

Red How

HARD KNOTT
552m | 1,811ft

Dod Pike

Wrynose Breast

Wrynose Bottom

River Duddon

Wrynose Pass

slopes of
GREY FRIAR

Hardknott Pass

13 Cockley Beck
Bridge

12

Duddon valley >

slopes of
HARTER FELL

one kilometre

one mile

Little Stand from Mosedale

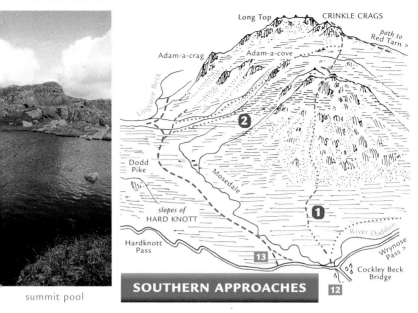

Long Top · CRINKLE CRAGS

path to Red Tarn >

Adam-a-crag

Adam-a-cove

Lingcove Beck

2

Dodd Pike

Mosedale

slopes of HARD KNOTT

1

River Duddon

Hardknott Pass

Wrynose Pass >

13

Cockley Beck Bridge

SOUTHERN APPROACHES

12

summit pool

ASCENT *from Cockley Beck Bridge and Mosedale*

1 Viewed from the walk's start the fell projects a quite rotten broken slope ameliorated by the inviting skyline which simply bristles with rock; given a swirling furtive cloud it is at times reminiscent of a remote Munro. Nonetheless, the direct approach, for the free-thinking independent fell-traveller, has a measure of pleasure. Ford the Mosedale Beck just west of Cockley Beck Bridge to a gate/stile (footpath sign); after fifty metres angle quarter-left across damp ground to find a track rising up the bracken bank with a gill right; this is all damp stuff, but it brings one to a wall gap and a little beyond a stile in the wire fence. Now set course up the rough slope, there is no obvious path up among the boulders, though as you emerge onto the upper pasture shelf as if by magic a path materialises, drawing one up to the apparent saddle between prominent skyline outcropping. Gaining the ridge path, an initial right turn enables one to enjoy the view from the ridge-end *(see right)*, while the summit cairn lies up to the left, off the more tangible path. **2** The Mosedale approach is labourious and might be thought more useful as a means of descent for a truncated circuit, which might nevertheless include the summit of Crinkle Crags, there and back to Swinsty Gill.

Long Top

Stonesty Pike

Crinkle Crags from Little Stand

The Mosedale bridle-path is signed off the open Hard Knott road. This leads purposefully and with some early pitching, keeping largely to the Hard Knott fell slope, reaching either the bridle-gate, or by a right turn some thirty yards earlier, the stile in the electric heaf fence. Go immediately right along the dale-head moraine ridge-top, accompanying the fence up the grass slope to Adam-a-Cove and the cluster of ridge-top tarns, which are skirted on the north side to reach the stile in the heaf fence from where the ridge path is joined leading south to Little Stand.

The Summit

The cairn rests upon outcropping just to the west of the ridge path. Beneath it to the west are lovely pools *(see top left),* while a large tarn sits in the hollow to the east cradled by a great slab. The view is fully worthy of the effort, though on balance it is better to venture to the southernmost limit of the ridge to appraise the Duddon valley.

Safe Descents

The fell-top is girdled with outcropping, making a comfortable descent extremely unlikely. Stonesty Gill leads to the worst of the Mosedale marsh, and be minded that bracken swathes lower Gaitkins Gill, making that equally unattractive in high summer. All the more reason to use the heaf fence north of Stonesty Pike (route **2**).

Ridge Route...

CRINKLE CRAGS   DESCENT 60 ft   ASCENT 450 ft   1.1 miles

In mist a compass is more than useful; in fact as the ridge path leads precisely due north, even the novice can find no problem in determining where the fifth Crinkle might be expected. Cross into the gap to tackle the bad step, or angle up left on a secure path to the saddle on the Long Top ridge west of the summit.

Wetherlam

Black Sails

Great Carrs ridge

Wetside Edge

PANORAMA

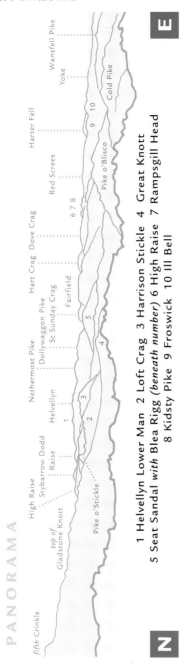

N

fifth Crinkle

High Raise
Stybarrow Dodd
Raise

Helvellyn

top of
Gladstone Knott

Pike o'Stickle

Nethermost Pike
Dollywaggon Pike
St Sunday Crag

Fairfield

1

2

3

4

5

Hart Crag Dove Crag

Red Screes

Pike o'Blisco

6 7 8

9

10

Cold Pike

E

Harter Fell

Yoke
Wansfell Pike

1 Helvellyn Lower Man 2 Loft Crag 3 Harrison Stickle 4 Great Knott
5 Seat Sandal *with* Blea Rigg *(beneath number)* 6 High Raise 7 Rampsgill Head
8 Kidsty Pike 9 Froswick 10 Ill Bell

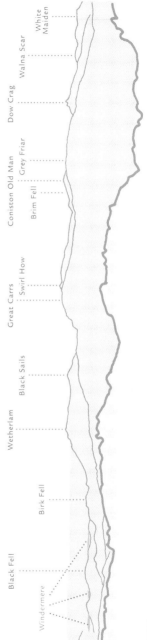

E

Black Fell

Windermere

Wetherlam

Birk Fell

Black Sails

Great Carrs

Swirl How

Coniston Old Man

Brim Fell

Grey Friar

Dow Crag

Walna Scar

White
Maiden

S

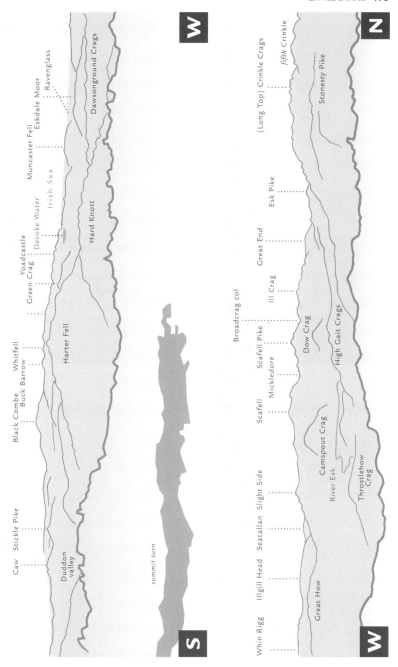

PIKE O'BLISCO

There is energy in the name, neatly matching the fell's sharply chiselled profile, particularly when viewed from Great Langdale *(see above)*: the sky-piercing summit cairn a clarion call to action, right from the moment one slips on one's boots. Alongside Blencathra, Glaramara and Helvellyn the name Pike o'Blisco spells romance. There is no surviving record of the fell-name before the 1865 Ordnance Survey map. Hence it remains an enigma befitting a noble and popular fell.

Pike o'Blisco is defined by Oxendale to the north, the deep trough of Blea Tarn beneath Blake Rigg to the east, while the Wrynose Pass road draws up its southern slopes, the top of the pass forming the natural bridge-head with the Coniston Fells. From this point the ground ascends north to the morainal hollow of Red Tarn which, with the Browney Gill ravine, makes the conclusive western limit of the fell.

Seen from Blea Tarn, Blake Rigg forms a formidable eastern façade; the better view of this aspect of the fell is from Side Pike, with Kettle Crag leading the eye up to the main summit mass. The rough southern slopes of the fell are known as Wrynose Fell, and for all that drivers' noses wryly twist with the hair-pin bends on the steep mountain road between Little Langdale and the Duddon, the name probably meant the

705 metres   2,313 feet

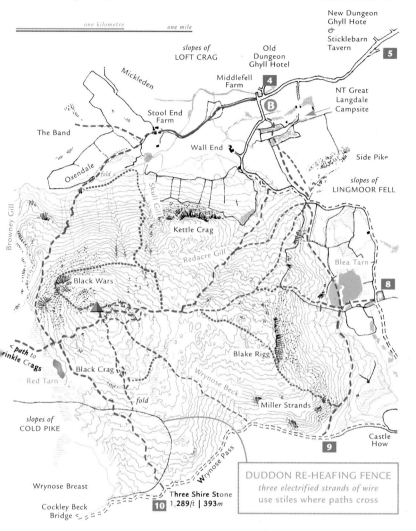

'stallion pass', the implication being extra horse-power was needed to negotiate the pass; the outcrops overlooking Wrynose Beck, Great and Little Horse Crags, adding to this equine connection.

Overlooking Oxendale are two bold crags. Kettle Crag – derived from 'the spring that issues like boiling water' – is infrequently climbed, being well-defended by bracken and has no clear-cut path. On the other hand Black Wars, situated below the summit, may have no recognised path, but is the more exciting quest. Strong walkers will see the fell as the first, or last, port of call on a grand circuit of the Great Langdale dale-head. A round that would feature Crinkle Crags, Bowfell, Rossett Pike, Martcrag Moor, Pike o'Stickle and Loft Crag: an excursion that could be termed the 'Great Langdale super-highway'... for it truly is superb!

There are six regular routes to the top with two bonus balls for the non-conformist fell explorer: clambering directly out of Oxendale, via Skull Gill and Black Wars, and from the common near Castle How, via the south-east ridge of Blake Rigg - they are both great fun.

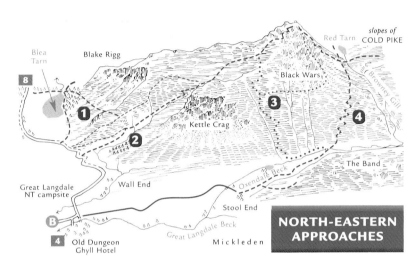

NORTH-EASTERN APPROACHES

ASCENT *from Old Dungeon Ghyll*

1 The conventional approach leads south from the ODG, follows the road beyond Wall End, squeezes by a roadside barn, crosses a cattle-grid, then winds up the hill. At the third bend a clear path leads off right; this is the main route up the Redacre Beck valley. As a variation one may follow the footpath leading up from the campsite to the ladder-stile onto the road pass. Go straight over the road, sweeping round the rigg ahead on a south-westerly course to join the Redacre path. **2** As the map shows, the Blea Tarn car park can play into the equation and, in many respects is the better start point. The path leading north from the Blea Tarn plantation arrives at a ladder-stile at the road pass. There are two options: either the contouring path to the Redacre path, or ascend the ridge, keeping a right-hand bias. This ridge can be

Blea Tarn

reached more energetically direct from the plantation, on a clear grass path climbing to cross a stile in the skyline fence. Traverse the slope on meeting the minor ridge path, angle up across a scarred bank to emerge on the edge, contour to join the Redacre path where it reaches the moor. Now in concert, the path ascends to the right of a large block slab. Weave up, via a tangle of routes through rock bands, to gain the summit.

3 Follow the farm-road leading to, and through, Stool End. Keep to the track into Oxendale leading, via a sheepfold gangway, to cross the footbridge. The popular path continues, via the stone-pitched staircase on a south-westerly line. Climb over a rigg, keeping above the Browney Gill ravine to reach the pass short of Red Tarn. Turn sharp left to complete the ascent. **4** There is an eminently practical middle way, seldom considered, leading up the rigg by Skull Gill to sate the alfresco spirit. From the footbridge bear left along the damp valley floor; as the delta debris of Skull Gill draws near, angle up right towards Kettle Crag. Reaching the ravine, bear right on a faint shepherds' trod; the zig-zags dissolve far too soon as the smooth rigg rears. At the top, either continue through the corrugated terrain to meet up with the main ridge path, or, keeping the 'at liberty' theme, drift right, holding to sheep trods drawing tightly under Black Wars. Slip under the tilted buttress, hugging the base of outcropping rising up a shelf. There are options to clamber onto the rocks, but the shelf serves well; either continue to link up with the path ascending from Red Tarn or angle left to climb the final arete direct to the summit.

The Langdale Pikes from the head of Skull Gill

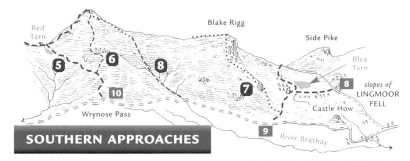

Blake Rigg

Side Pike

Red Tarn

Blea Tarn

slopes of LINGMOOR FELL

Castle How

Wrynose Pass

River Brathay

SOUTHERN APPROACHES

ASCENT *from Wrynose Pass*

5 With the ascent reduced to a tad over one thousand feet, many walkers buy into this approach. The popular path from the 'Lancashire' stone, currently encounters the heaf fence twice en route to Red Tarn. **6** The more attractive option veers right, on the early rise, to take the second fence crossing just below a fenced fold, attached to a large erratic boulder. The path winds up the bank to pass Black Crag, the cairn on the top worth visiting on a spur (of the moment). The cairn on the southern summit pike is easily gained through the final outcropping.

Black Crag, a popular climbers' playground

Three Shire Stone

Needle Rock

large slab

Pike o'Blisco in cloud-shadowed silhouette from Blake Rigg

ASCENT *from Castle How*

7 From Little Langdale the Wrynose road winds up by Fell Foot. Directly after Castle How the traveller's attention is struck by the beautiful view of the Langdale Pikes through the Blea Tarn gap. There is parking on the open ground at the wall corner where a footpath is signed right. Follow this path around the marsh/bracken fringe. Step off the path to climb the pathless, blunt ridge. A finger of bracken extends up this south-east

ridge of Blake Rigg, giving a clue to the key ramp higher up that gives easy access to the top of Miller Strands. The continuing ridge mounts onto Blake Rigg, giving scope to enjoy excellent views over Blea Tarn to Lingmoor Fell. A prominent cairn marks the top. There is no path across the marshy outcrop-interrupted ridge to meet up with the path from Redacre Gill. **8** Walk up the Wrynose Pass road to cross Wrynose Bridge, bear off right on an evident path which accompanies Wrynose Beck to its marshy source and beyond mounts the craggy final feet to the fell summit.

Blake Rigg from the head of Wrynose Beck

Coniston Old Man   Great Carrs
Black Sails   Swirl How   Grey Friar
Hell Gill Pike

The Coniston Fells from a pool near Blake Rigg

The Summit

The ultimate ground is reminicient of a battleship with cannon station cairns at the north prow and southern aft, set on an irregular bare rock deck. The northern cairn, the summit, has had a hard life, and deserves to be reconstructed with durable intent. One is reminded of Andy Goldworthy's stone sheepfolds sprinkled around the county, resonating of the heritage of fell country. It is time this talent was turned to the edifices that mark the popular focus of fellwalking endeavour, reflecting a contemporary heritage 'outdoor Cumbria'. That the summit is a land-mark can be further judged by the alignment of the old Cumberland county boundary which made a darting visit to the southern cairn, taking a 35 degree slice out of Westmorland before falling back over

The summit cairn looking to the south top, backed by Wetherlam

Black Crag to Wrynose Pass, where the two counties came face to face with the Lancashire: from 1974 the line on the map fell back to nothing more than a parliamentary constituency division. Visitors to the summit perch on many a ledge to witness a particularly fine view, Crinkle Crags receiving most admiration.

Crinkle Crags and Bowfell from near the top of the Black Wars ascent

Safe Descents

The easiest escape is SW. A popular path descends to the depression N of Red Tarn; either follow the path N, by rough steps initially beside the headstream of Browney Gill, then over a rigg shoulder onto a pitched staircase leading down to the footbridge in Oxendale, bound for Stool End. Alternatively, go S, passing Red Tarn, crossing the heaf fence twice to reach the road at the top of Wrynose Pass. E from the summit, a tortuous mangle of paths seek various lines of weakness via a series of rock bands, none of which are too terrible. They all coalesce on the regular path to Redacre Gill; descend easily until the steep gill is entered, fortunately now well furnished with stone stair pitching.

Ridge Route to...

COLD PIKE   DESCENT 660 ft   ASCENT 650 ft   1.25 miles

Follow the popular path SW down to the depression. Ford the gill, continuing W on an easy gradient, crossing a small exposure of red soil. As the path shapes to ford a gill issuing from the moor, bear off left, ascending directly to the summit - a matching twin with Pike o'Blisco.

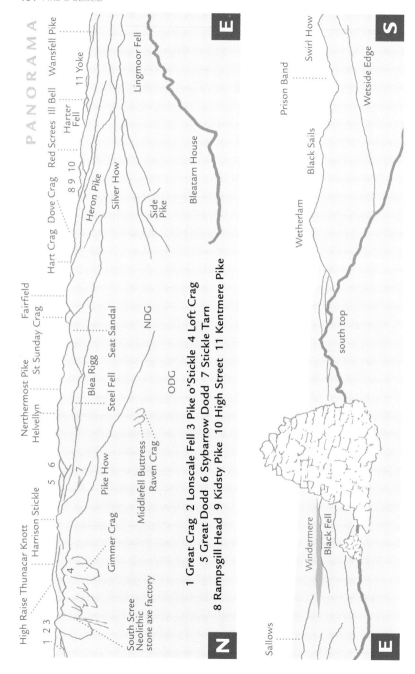

PANORAMA

E

High Raise Thunacar Knott
Harrison Stickle
Nethermost Pike   Fairfield
St Sunday Crag
Helvellyn

Red Screens Ill Bell
Hart Crag Dove Crag
Harter Fell
11 Yoke   Wansfell Pike

8 9 10

Heron Pike

Gimmer Crag
Pike How
Steel Fell
Blea Rigg
Seat Sandal

Silver How

Middlefell Buttress
Raven Crag

5 6
7

Side Pike

Lingmoor Fell

ODG

NDG

Bleatarn House

South Scree
Neolithic
stone axe factory

1 2 3
4

N

1 Great Crag 2 Lonsdale Fell 3 Pike o'Stickle 4 Loft Crag
5 Great Dodd 6 Stybarrow Dodd 7 Stickle Tarn
8 Rampsgill Head 9 Kidsty Pike 10 High Street 11 Kentmere Pike

S

Prison Band
Swirl How

Wetherlam
Black Sails
Wetside Edge

south top

Sallows

Windermere
Black Fell

E

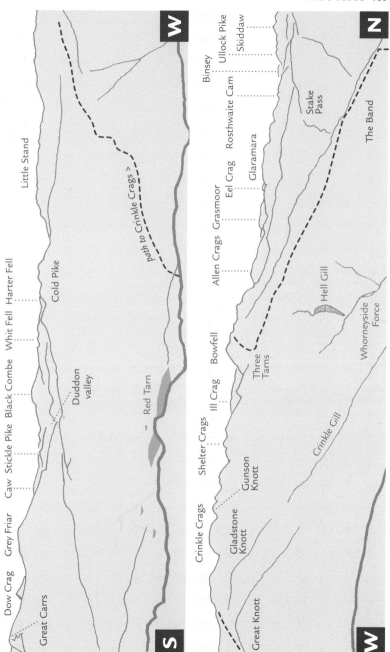

W

Little Stand

Harter Fell

Whit Fell

Black Combe

Stickle Pike

Caw

Grey Friar

Dow Crag

Great Carrs

Cold Pike

Duddon valley

Red Tarn

path to Crinkle Crags >

S

N

Binsey

Ullock Pike

Skiddaw

Rosthwaite Cam

Eel Crag

Glaramara

Grasmoor

Allen Crags

Stake Pass

The Band

Hell Gill

Whorneyside Force

Three Tarns

Bowfell

Ill Crag

Shelter Crags

Crinkle Crags

Gunson Knott

Gladstone Knott

Great Knott

Crinkle Gill

W

ROSSETT PIKE

With two age-old pony routes switching out of Mickleden at both ends of this dale-head ridge there can be little surprise that the fell-name has an equine connotation, 'peak of the horse shieling'. It would seem logical that the implied stable bothy would have stood at the head of Mickleden: the situation, comparatively remote from habitation, would have been vital for man and beast during any journey overtaken by darkness or bad weather. The two paths, recent recipients of restorative pitching, are quite different in character. The Rossett Gill route, a popular access to the Scafells, takes an extravagant double zig-zag, while the Stake Pass route, the saddle connection with the Central Fells, has an unusual intensity of hair-pins on both sides of the ridge *(see opposite descending by Stake Gill, while page 207 shows the Stake Beck side of the pass)*.

In the company of so magnificent an array of peaks, Rossett Pike may be thought a minor party; for all the labour in ascent and conservative attributes, it nonetheless is liberally green in its scenic outlook, notably to the east down Mickleden. Rossett Pike forms a conclusive headwall to the classic 'U'-shaped glacial valley of Mickleden, 'the big narrow valley'. The moraine directly beneath is characteristic of this origin, as too the amazing collection of pillow moraine in the hanging valley of Langdale Combe.

651 metres   **2,136** feet

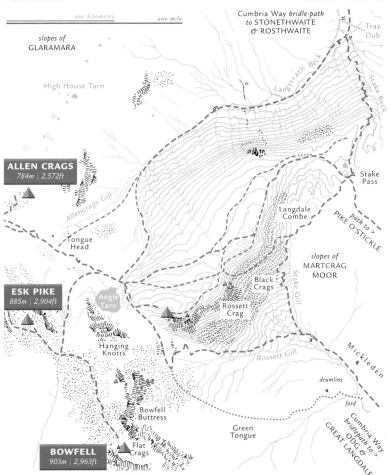

one kilometre   one mile

Cumbria Way *bridle-path*
to STONETHWAITE
& ROSTHWAITE

Tray Dub

slopes of
GLARAMARA

High House Tarn

Langstrath Beck

Stake Beck

ALLEN CRAGS
784m | 2,572ft

Stake Pass

Langdale Combe

path to >
PIKE O'STICKLE

Allencrags Gill

Tongue Head

slopes of
MARTCRAG MOOR

ESK PIKE
885m | 2,904ft

Angle Tarn

Black Crags

Rossett Crag

Stake Gill

Hanging Knotts

Rossett Gill

Mickleden

drumlins

ford

Bowfell Buttress

Green Tongue

Cumbria Way
bridlepath to >
ODG *&*
GREAT LANGDALE

BOWFELL
903m | 2,963ft

Flat Crags

The easily gained summit can give a truncated day some sense of achievement when higher brethren are wreathed in mist and worse.

The fell can figure in walks from both Great Langdale and Langstrath, this latter as a modest digression from the Cumbria Way.

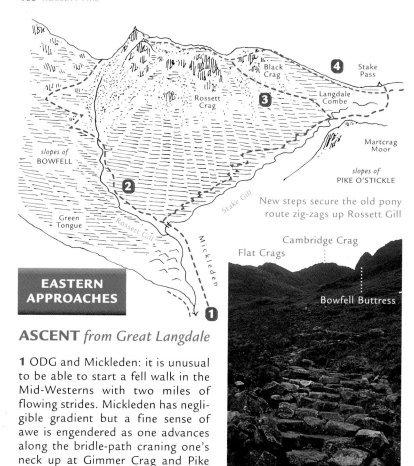

Black Crag

4 Stake Pass

Langdale Combe

3

Rossett Crag

Martcrag Moor

slopes of PIKE O'STICKLE

slopes of BOWFELL

2

Green Tongue

Rossett Gill

Stake Gill

Mickleden

New steps secure the old pony route zig-zags up Rossett Gill

Cambridge Crag

Flat Crags

Bowfell Buttress

EASTERN APPROACHES

1

ASCENT *from Great Langdale*

1 ODG and Mickleden: it is unusual to be able to start a fell walk in the Mid-Westerns with two miles of flowing strides. Mickleden has negligible gradient but a fine sense of awe is engendered as one advances along the bridle-path craning one's neck up at Gimmer Crag and Pike o'Stickle. Bowfell grudgingly reveals its prized craggy possessions, high to one's left, Bowfell Buttress a distant object of admiration. Rossett Pike, on the other hand, contrives to dominate the dale-head itself, a simple focus of attention. If the cloud is sufficiently low to obscure the crags of Bowfell, then Rossett Pike will seem alone, now all the more likely a fellwalk scalp. Crossing the footbridge at the bottom of Stake Gill a slate sign marks the fork in the bridle-path.

2 A left turn traverses up to a fording point in Rossett Gill from where a smart new pitched path levitates us (how we wish!) up a double zig-zag to the head of Rossett Gill. Forget all thoughts of ascending the gill itself, many's the walker who, in the past, has scrabbled up leaving a sad, ugly,

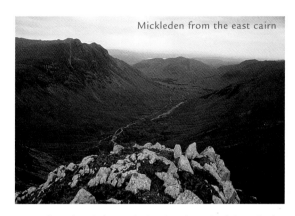

Mickleden from the east cairn

unstable mess... *a jumble of letters in fact!* Advance to the level ground of the saddle and bear up right onto the easy ridge – couldn't be sweeter!

3 A right turn signed 'Stake Pass' and the turning starts in earnest. The path, engineered in the tightest hair-pins imaginable, winds up under Black Crag. As the path shapes to ford the beck, on entry to the hanging valley of Langdale Combe, branch immediately left. Take the path climbing directly up the grassy slope. This mounts onto a grassy shelf and, with the encouragement of small cairns, traverses above Black Crag to Littlegill Head. A path climbs from this saddle keeping to the ridge-top which is comfortably rough.

4 Continue with the old bridle-path as it curves round the wide hollow of Langdale Combe, littered with an amazing collection of drumlins (glacial moraine). A cairn marks the top of Stake Pass. Turn left (west), skirting a large peaty pool, which is only redeemed when sunlight, sky and cloud are reflected in its otherwise unscenic waters. There is a strong path curving round the head of the combe; however you may notice a 'retired path' forking right to contour the upper slope, thus ignoring the Rossett Pike ridge altogether. By 'retired', I mean that during the autumn of 2001, once public access had been resumed after the Foot & Mouth outbreak, this path was not re-adopted by fellwalkers. My plea - don't use it, it was something of a scar anyway, slicing through peat and bare ground. Let it heal, the ridge path to the top is far more scenic anyway.

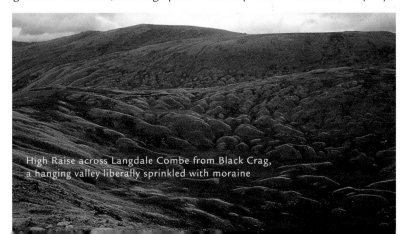

High Raise across Langdale Combe from Black Crag, a hanging valley liberally sprinkled with moraine

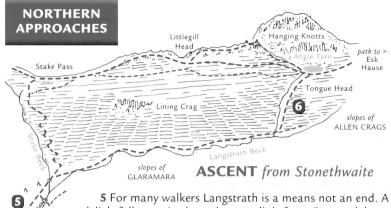

NORTHERN APPROACHES

Littlegill Head

Hanging Knotts

path to > Esk Hause

Angle Tarn

Stake Pass

Tongue Head

Lining Crag

6

slopes of ALLEN CRAGS

Stake Beck

Langstrath Beck

slopes of GLARAMARA

ASCENT *from Stonethwaite*

5

bridle-path from Stonethwaite

5 For many walkers Langstrath is a means not an end. A delightfully scenic through-route link from Borrowdale to Great Langdale. Frequently they are congenially engaged on the Cumbria Way, or less specifically making the adept round-trip connection using local buses. The Langdale and Borrowdale Rambler services combined with the 555 Keswick to Ambleside service, make the perfect car-free day out, witnessing at close quarters the heart of the district. The key objective, Stake Pass (1575ft/480m), is also the best route to Rossett Pike. The Cumbria Way chooses the bridle-path on the east side of the valley, the better path is the footpath on the west side which crosses Tray Dub and Stake Beck footbridges. The ascent is entertained hugely by the vibrant cascades of Stake Beck, then becomes engrossed in the technical twists of the upper section of the path. You don't have to wait for the pass-top cairn to branch onto the ridge, though for a consistent path it is best. The natural ridge path, mounting onto the crest above Black Crag, dips into Littlegill Head and then becomes rougher on Buck Pike above Rossett Crag leading to the east cairn. **6** Crossing

Bubbles boil beneath Stake Beck footbridge

Stake Beck footbridge one may keep in the valley tracking up the narrowing dale with at least one fine waterfall in view below. At the confluence with Angletarn Gill, find a convenient ford. My last visit coincided with a July deluge and I simply couldn't get across, proving that this can happen at any season. The south bank had to suffice! The popular path ascends to the outflow of Angle Tarn, turns left on the regular path to the saddle, then veers half-left onto the summit.

The Summit

A rocky east/west crest the perfect place to survey the cliffs of Bowfell, with the great slab of Flat Crags prominent. The east cairn an airy place to comprehend the relationship of the Langdale Pikes with Mickleden.

Safe Descents

Backtrack west to the saddle and follow the Rossett Gill bridle-path left.

Ridge Route to...

PIKE O'STICKLE   DESCENT 590 ft   ASCENT 780 ft   2.7 miles

Wedded to the Mid-Western group, yet for most walkers intrinsic to the Great Langdale circuit, hence this is the natural and popular ridge connection. Follow the ridge north-eastwards to Stake Pass. A clear path continues from the cairn on a southerly line over the marshy Martcrag Moor. From the head of Troughton Beck a cairned path has recently been consolidated to the northern base of the famous Pike. The summit is gained only by hands-on scrambling.

Refreshment over, time to leave the summit and head to the east cairn viewpoint

PANORAMA

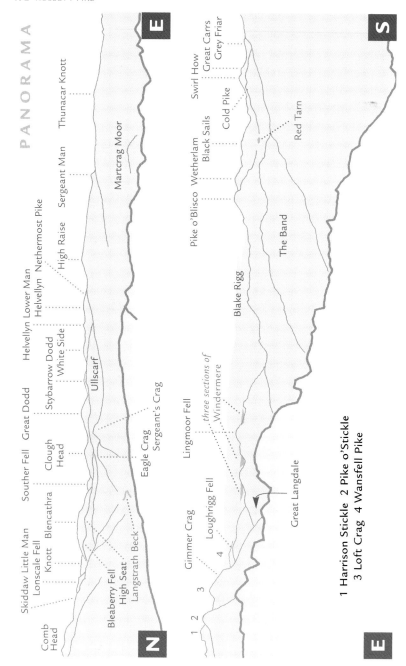

N

Comb Head
Skiddaw Little Man
Lonscale Fell
Knott Blencathra
Souther Fell
Great Dodd
Clough Head
Stybarrow Dodd
White Side
Helvellyn Lower Man
Helvellyn Nethermost Pike
High Raise
Sergeant Man
Thunacar Knott

Martcrag Moor

Bleaberry Fell
High Seat
Langstrath Beck
Ullscarf
Eagle Crag
Sergeant's Crag

E

S

Pike o'Blisco Wetherlam
Black Sails
Swirl How
Great Carrs
Grey Friar
Cold Pike

Lingmoor Fell
three sections of
Windermere

Gimmer Crag
Loughrigg Fell

Blake Rigg

The Band

Red Tarn

Great Langdale

E

1 Harrison Stickle 2 Pike o'Stickle
3 Loft Crag 4 Wansfell Pike

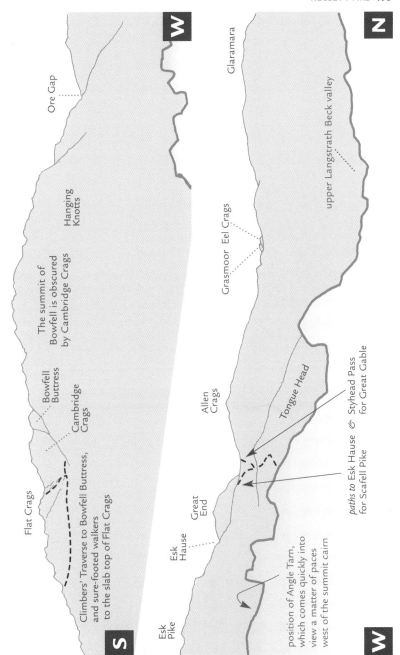

W

Ore Gap

Hanging
Knotts

The summit of
Bowfell is obscured
by Cambridge Crags

Bowfell
Buttress

Cambridge
Crags

Flat Crags

Climbers' Traverse to Bowfell Buttress,
and sure-footed walkers
to the slab top of Flat Crags

S

N

Glaramara

upper Langstrath Beck valley

Grasmoor Eel Crags

Allen
Crags

Tongue Head

Esk
Pike

Great
End

Esk
Hause

paths to Esk Hause & Styhead Pass
for Scafell Pike   for Great Gable

position of Angle Tarn,
which comes quickly into
view a matter of paces
west of the summit cairn

W

ROSTHWAITE FELL

The fell rather undeservedly receives scant attention from walkers. There are no popular paths on this intricate tangle of rough fell and only a sketchy ridge path giving a clue to the passage of the occasional intrepid soul. The plaintive call of peregrine frequently pierces the air about its craggy tree-shaded northern slopes, forming the beautiful backdrop to the attractive hamlet of Stonethwaite. This fellside convincingly hides the one prime staircase to the top by Stanger Gill, beginning from the entrance to the National Trust's Stonethwaite campsite.

Elsewhere scramblers may revel in the airy arete of Cam Crag and the sun-warmed curiosity of Dovesnest Crag. Fellwalkers may also find interest in Dovesnest, and two other side slope approaches, via Dry Gill out of Comb Gill, and from Blackmoss Pot in Langstrath. The obvious re-entrant of Woof Gill proves even less appealing on close acquaintance than that surmised from the valley view, being defended by bracken on approach and remorsely steep at its headwall. I actually descended from the Great Hollow beside Woof Gill and regretted my inquisitiveness: I was very grateful for my son's walking poles!

As the ridge rises in steps it is no wonder that there are several piked tops, Bessyboot, the traditional summit, is but the second of four.

551 metres   1,808 feet

Seatoller has a
National Park
Information Centre
and a pub/tearoom;
Stonethwaite lacks
only the former.

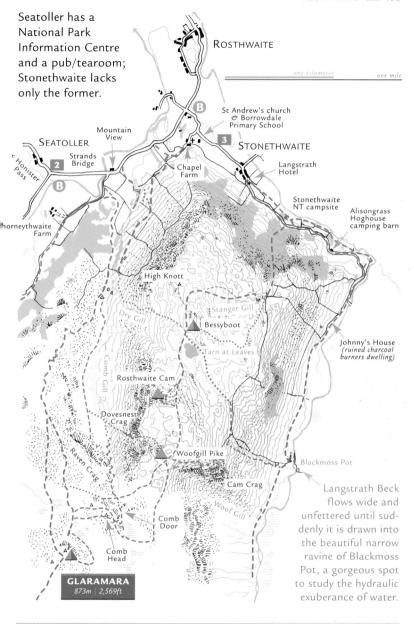

ROSTHWAITE

one kilometre

one mile

St Andrew's church
& Borrowdale
Primary School

Mountain
View

SEATOLLER

STONETHWAITE

Strands
Bridge

Chapel
Farm

Langstrath
Hotel

Honister Pass

Stonethwaite
NT campsite

Alisongrass
Hoghouse
camping barn

horneythwaite
Farm

High Knott

Stanger Gill

Dry Gill

Bessyboot

Tarn at Leaves

Johnny's House
*(ruined charcoal
burners dwelling)*

Rosthwaite Cam

Comb Gill

Dovesnest
Crag

Woofgill Pike

Raven Crag

Cam Crag

Woof Gill

Blackmoss Pot

Comb
Door

Langstrath Beck
flows wide and
unfettered until sud-
denly it is drawn into
the beautiful narrow
ravine of Blackmoss
Pot, a gorgeous spot
to study the hydraulic
exuberance of water.

Comb
Head

GLARAMARA
873m | 2,569ft

The fell, liberally dispersed with attractive pools, has one main shining
level, Tarn at Leaves... which sounds like an early attempt at a website!

Tarn at Leaves and Rosthwaite Cam from Bessyboot

High Knott forms the northern crest, quickly followed by Bessyboot, then beyond the hollow of Tarn @ Leaves *(sic)*, the slope mounts to a distinctive undulating east/west crest *(see above)*, with Rosthwaite Cam the eye-catching western top some 70 metres higher than the acknowledged summit. A further depression is crossed before the fell yet again reaches for the sky upon a mighty mass of craggy ground. This top, some six metres higher still. Therefore I have ventured to lend it the dignity it deserves by ascribing it Woofgill Pike, both because it is the true top of the fell and an exceptional fine viewpoint, quite distinct from Bessyboot. From here the Great Hollow separates Rosthwaite Fell from Comb Head, the northern stand of Glaramara. Rosthwaite Fell is sheer delight is clear weather... something of a nightmare in swirling hill fog!

Lane running through Stonethwaite

Stanger Gill

Eagle Crag

Stonethwaite and Borrowdale
from the Stanger Gill path
looking across Hanging Haystack

Catbells

King's How

Rosthwaite

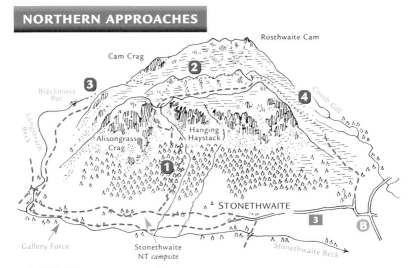

NORTHERN APPROACHES

Rosthwaite Cam

Cam Crag

Blackmoss Pot

Langstrath Beck

Comb Gill

Alisongrass Crag

Hanging Haystack

STONETHWAITE

Galleny Force

Stonethwaite NT *campsite*

Stonethwaite Beck

ASCENT *from Stonethwaite*

Car parking in the hamlet is limited, best to use the lay-by in the approach lane after Borrowdale primary school **1** This, the principal ascent, begins at a green gate opposite the entrance to the National Trust campsite, situated a quarter of a mile east of Langstrath Hotel along the rough tracked lane. Climbing into light woodland, the partially-pitched path rises close to Stanger Gill, slippery tree roots demanding caution when wet. Mount via a wall stile, as the path hugs Bull Crag by a minor arete-top col; the view back over the Stonethwaite vale *(see pages 6 & 197)* providing all the excuse one needs for frequent pauses to catch the breath - exacted by the height of the stone steps! A final zig-zag brings the walker into a small amphitheatre. Keep right via a wall-end, pass on to ford the gill before a fall. Switch right and quick-ly left to ascend the damp slope, with the rock ribs of Racomb Bands up to the left. The path swings left at peat groughs skirting boggy ground. One may either visit the cairned top of High Crag just to the west, keep south on the shelf below Bessyboot, or even scramble straight onto the rigg direct to the summit. **2** From the wall-end bear up left squeezing through the tight step gap between the wall and outcrop, climb onto the pathless ridge - the route is not an exact science! The eastern top of Racomb Bands has a beautiful pool and a lovely view to Eagle and Sergeant's Crags. The ridge west undulates pleasantly to culminate on Bessyboot. **3** For an unusual 'catch-it-unawares' route via Blackmoss Pot *(see facing page)*; follow the footpath that continues from the campsite approach lane. Entering Langstrath, keep with the west side track to the gate/ladder-stile at Blackmoss Pot. Beyond bear immediately right,

The eastern slopes from Blackmoss Pot in Langstrath Beck

Turquoise waters of Stonethwaite Beck at Galleny Force

climbing by the fence fold. Ascend the gill, with a wall right; after this tackles a rock slab, find evidence of a path contouring right in harmony with the top of the wall to go through a gate in the fence. Keep beside the wall to the next gill, follow this, Tansey Gill, into the hollow wherein lies the enigmatically named Tarn at Leaves. Bessyboot, climbed from the ridge path, is encountered at the western end of the tarn.

4 Follow the cul-de-sac by St Andrew's Church, pass through Chapel Farm via gates. Bear off the track left to the gate in the left-hand field corner, entering the fringe of a shelter belt of larch. Turn promptly left via the kissing-gate. The concessionary path goes right passing through a gateway, washed by a gill. The path angles up half-left with waymark posts, it contours as a green track above Comb Gill, via old wall gaps to a gate by a partial fold. The path disappears, but no matter, angle up half-left to accompany the first watercourse, Dry Gill (seems a misnomer!). A path materialises during the ascent, emerging into a nick in the ridge below a knoll surmounted by an erratic: the conical peak of Bessyboot rises immediately left. **5** Via Dovesnest Crag - *for the route to the sheepfold at the very head of Comb Gill see GLARAMARA route* **2** *on page 93*: from the sheepfold a steep slope presages the approach to the foot of Dovesnest Crag. A path materialises as height is gained, slanting to the right of the cliff. Walkers might make a cursory visit, clambering onto the

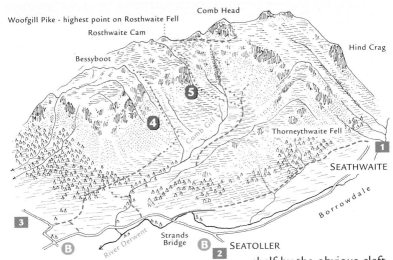

Woofgill Pike - highest point on Rosthwaite Fell

Comb Head

Rosthwaite Cam

Hind Crag

Bessyboot

5

4

Comb Gill

Thorneythwaite Fell

1

SEATHWAITE

Borrowdale

3

B

River Derwent

Strands Bridge

B

2

SEATOLLER

NORTH-WESTERN APPROACHES

shelf by the obvious cleft, but go no further. The cliff has been a popular rendezvous for climbers and competent scramblers for as long as recreational climbing has been abroad. The chimneys and cave-like lateral rifts are a fascinating maze caused by a rock shudder possibly several thousand years ago that settled on a firm base, unlike all other such cliff-quakes. Ascend the steep ground beside the outcropping, don't get caught in the short but wet gully; keep right. Above, as the cliff eases, clamber left to complete the ascent via the final brow outcropping. The marshy shelf at the top offers the option of visiting the two hen-comb crests of either Rosthwaite Cam left or Woofgill Pike right. Rosthwaite Cam is a real characterful chunky square boss of rock. The name derived from its likeness to the stones used to cap local walls, known as cams. Access only from the west side.

Dovesnest Crag

The Summit

With a name as endearing as Bessyboot who would deny this as a delightful spot. Yet the name is heaped with vitriol, for the summit knob was likened to Queen Elizabeth's taxes on local miners - her highness Bessy's booty. A cairn set on a small outcrop registers this as a place to rest and count the loot of a fine view. One can forgive Rosthwaite Cam, and the backing Comb Head, for imposing a sense of inferiority on this knott. The avid fellwanderer will cast off such notions as they peruse the wonderful view. Pike o'Stickle will intrigue eastward but it is the scene to the west that will hold the greatest admiration: Honister Crag backed by High Stile with Dale Head and the North-Western Fells all held dramatically in a tight camera shot.

Safe Descents

In deteriorating conditions the best way off is via Dry Gill (reversing route **4**). Descend south from the summit to the initial nick, before the erratic-topped knoll. Descend due W, there is some rough ground but progress is uncomplicated. Short of Comb Gill bear right to the gate in a down wall (and partial sheepfold); joining a green track, contour N, en route to the valley pastures at Chapel Farm and St Andrew's Church.

Bessyboot

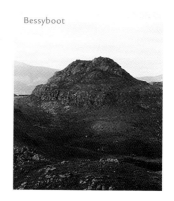

Bessyboot   Tarn at Leaves

Rosthwaite Cam

Ridge Route to...

GLARAMARA   DESCENT 280 ft   ASCENT 200 ft   1.9 miles

A less than orthodox ridge turns navigation into a challenge in misty conditions. Mountain Leadership certificate holders and entry-level Mensa candidates will enjoy the deviousness of what passes as a ridge path. Others, me included, have to concentrate, even on sunny days. There are paths, but they are never strong enough to give confidence that it is *the* ridge path. Descend S, skirting the knoll W of Tarn at Leaves. Slant half-left up the ensuing slope to cross the E shoulder of the Rosthwaite Cam ridge. There is a path that aims half-right towards a notch in the ridge close to the Cam, if you wish to pay a visit this eye-catching high point and I think you should! The main path weaves on, rounding the bank beneath Woofgill Pike; you'll know you've passed it as the path slips over a short length of broken wall immediately after. Now either cross Great Hollow diagonally half-right, mounting the ensuing bank. Contour along the shelf beneath Comb Door and directly above the top of the Comb Gill ravine to join the path climbing Thorneythwaite Fell, angling left to the summit bastion. Alternatively: from the broken wall, keep left, skirting the marshy ground to avoid the apparently impenetrable ridge-top outcropping, proceed up a ramp onto Comb Head from the E.

Upper falls of Stanger Gill

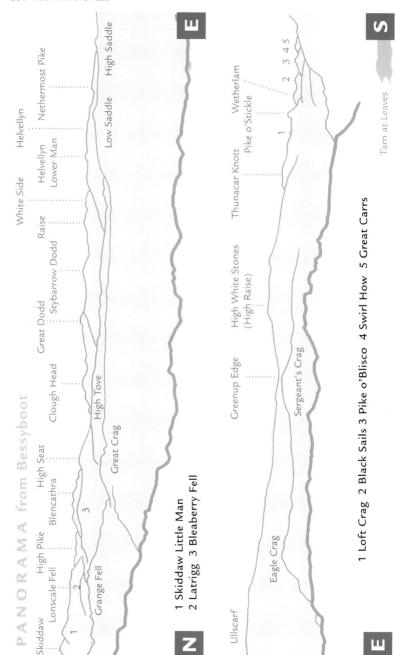

PANORAMA from Bessyboot

Skiddaw   High Pike   High Seat   Clough Head   Great Dodd   Raise   White Side   Helvellyn   Nethermost Pike
Lonscale Fell   Blencathra   Stybarrow Dodd   Helvellyn   Lower Man
Grange Fell   Great Crag   High Tove

1 Skiddaw Little Man
2 Latrigg 3 Bleaberry Fell

High Saddle   Low Saddle

N   **E**

Ullscarf   Greenup Edge   High White Stones   Thunacar Knott   Wetherlam
(High Raise)   Pike o'Stickle
Eagle Crag   Sergeant's Crag   Tarn at Leaves

1 Loft Crag 2 Black Sails 3 Pike o'Blisco 4 Swirl How 5 Great Carrs

E   **S**

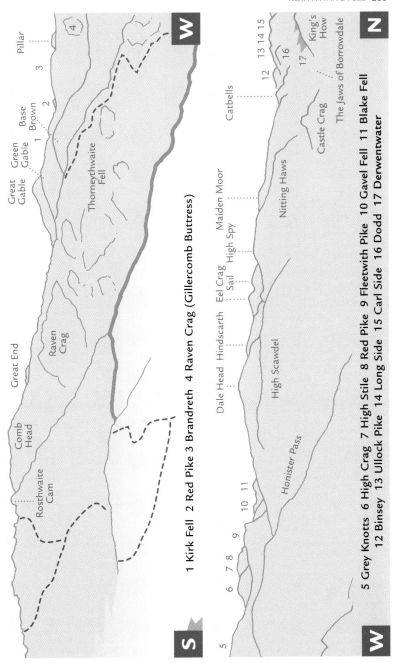

1 Kirk Fell 2 Red Pike 3 Brandreth 4 Raven Crag (Gillercomb Buttress)

5 Grey Knotts 6 High Crag 7 High Stile 8 Red Pike 9 Fleetwith Pike 10 Gavel Fell 11 Blake Fell 12 Binsey 13 Ullock Pike 14 Long Side 15 Carl Side 16 Dodd 17 Derwentwater

WOOFGILL PIKE

626m   2,052ft

Walkers embroiled in the Cumbria Way heading north over the Stake Pass and winding down the zig-zags *(see facing page)*, looking down the Langstrath Beck valley will admire, above all, the crag and ravine on the far side of the dale, culminating upon a jagged peak. It seems strange that this, the highest point on that portion of fell pasture, long known as Rosthwaite Fell, has not been credited with a name. The bare rock ridge is known as Cam Crag, a popular expedition for accomplished scramblers, the ravine is Woof Gill, 'the ravine of the wolf'. *(The scene above is a reverse view – and right – the top from above Dovesnest Crag)*

The author pleads guilty to inventing the name for what is, without question, one of the best viewpoints on Rosthwaite Fell.

Rosthwaite Cam
from Woofgill Pike

Woofgill Pike

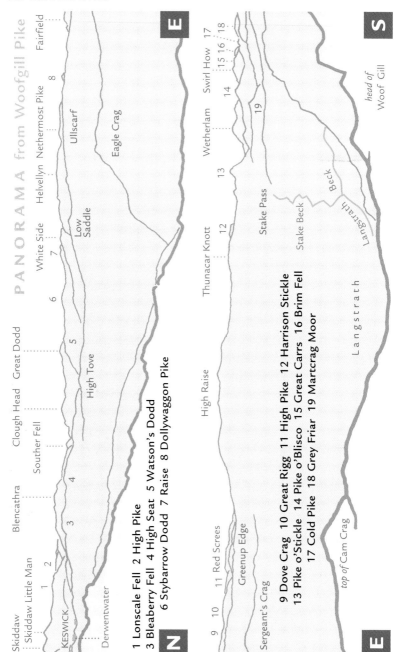

PANORAMA from Woofgill Pike

N / E

Skiddaw · Skiddaw Little Man · Blencathra · Souther Fell · Clough Head · Great Dodd · White Side · Helvellyn · Nethermost Pike · Fairfield

KESWICK

Derwentwater · High Tove · Low Saddle · Ullscarf · Eagle Crag

1 Lonscale Fell 2 High Pike
3 Bleaberry Fell 4 High Seat 5 Watson's Dodd
6 Stybarrow Dodd 7 Raise 8 Dollywaggon Pike

E / S

High Raise · Thunacar Knott · Wetherlam · Swirl How

Red Screes · Greenup Edge · Sergeant's Crag · Stake Pass · Stake Beck · Beck · Langstrath · head of Woof Gill

top of Cam Crag · Langstrath

9 Dove Crag 10 Great Rigg 11 High Pike 12 Harrison Stickle
13 Pike o'Stickle 14 Pike o'Blisco 15 Great Carrs 16 Brim Fell
17 Cold Pike 18 Grey Friar 19 Martcrag Moor

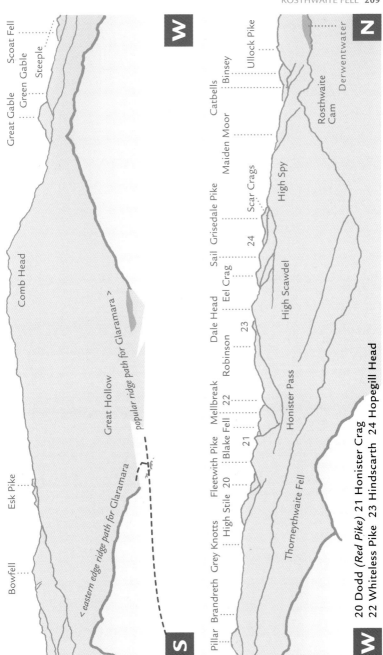

W

Pillar Brandreth Grey Knotts Fleetwith Pike 20 Mellbreak 22 Dale Head Sail Grisedale Pike Maiden Moor Catbells Binsey Ullock Pike

High Stile Blake Fell Robinson Eel Crag Scar Crags

21

23 24

W 20 Dodd (*Red Pike*) 21 Honister Crag
22 Whiteless Pike 23 Hindscarth 24 Hopegill Head

Bowfell Esk Pike Comb Head Great Gable Green Gable Scoat Fell
Steeple

Great Hollow

popular ridge path for Glaramara >

< eastern edge ridge path for Glaramara

W

S

N

High Spy High Scawdel Honister Pass Thorneythwaite Fell Rosthwaite Cam Derwentwater

SCAFELL

Scafell was historically thought to have had height advantage over Scafell Pike, hence the latter has the adjunctive name. Whether from Crinkle Crags or Wastwater the summit contrives to look more elevated that the Pike; however, triangulation proved the eye wrong. Of the two mountains it is the one with the most peak-like quality, its convex slopes, craggy to the east and north, plain to the west, enable the summit to be constantly in view. Prospects from the summit are not hindered by foreground. All and sundry home-in on Scafell Pike, only the determined mountain lover includes both tops in any one day's walk. The mere mention of Scafell brings forth thoughts of mighty crags; the view from Hard Knott across lonely upper Eskdale *(see above)* holds the promise of likely rewards for the adventurous fellwalker of this the wildest aspect of the second highest mountain in England.

The north-facing Scafell Crag, plummeting from Symond's Knott, was until recently the focus of the bolder fellwalker's attention, with Lord's Rake and West Wall Traverse accessing Deep Gill, thrilling hands-on sporting routes. Special mention of Lord's Rake is necessary because alongside Jack's Rake it is *(was)* a remarkable route, a fellwalking experience to place upon one's mental mantel-piece. Regrettably it could not be included in the research for this guide for a rock-fall in 2002 rendered it far too dangerous for everyone, competent climber

964 metres   **3,163** feet

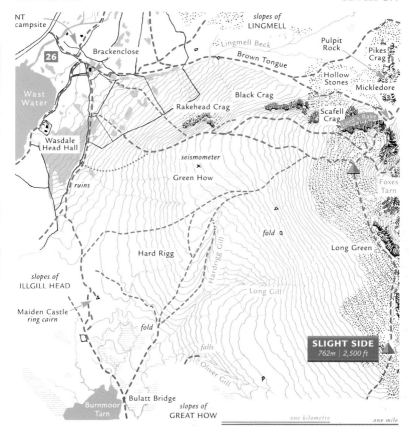

NT campsite

Brackenclose

26

Wast Water

Wasdale Head Hall

ruins

slopes of LINGMELL

Lingmell Beck

Brown Tongue

Pulpit Rock

Pikes Crag

Hollow Stones

Mickledore

Black Crag

Rakehead Crag

Scafell Crag

seismometer
×
Green How

fold

Foxes Tarn

Long Green

Hard Rigg

Hard Rigg Gill

Long Gill

slopes of ILLGILL HEAD

Maiden Castle
ring cairn

fold

falls

Oliver Gill

SLIGHT SIDE
762m | 2,500 ft

Bulatt Bridge

Burnmoor Tarn

slopes of GREAT HOW

one kilometre   one mile

and adventurous rambler alike. The present delicate situation will eventually resolve itself, the gravity that pulled the rocks down will continue to take its toll, progressively the place will become relatively secure. But I hasten to add that it could be a number of years before the rake is rendered safe, mindful that the word 'safe', in this context, will remain of dubious relativity! The rake is a striking feature, well seen during the latter stages of the ascent to Mickledore from Hollow Stones. The main gully rearing from the foot of Scafell Crag, always notoriously full of loose rock, is now dire, so access to the West Wall Traverse has been compromised too. The apparent top and bad step are followed by a dip and another col at the head of Tower Buttress before a final dip leads to deliverance (see right).

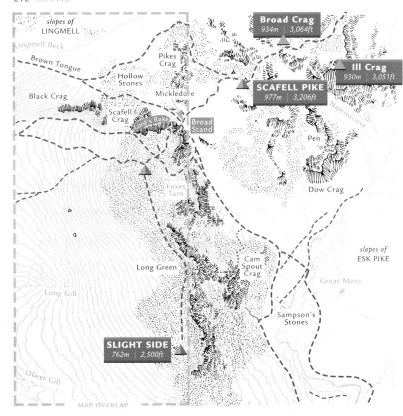

slopes of
LINGMELL

Lingmell Beck

Brown Tongue

Broad Crag
934m | 3,064ft

Pikes
Crag

Hollow
Stones

Mickledore

Ill Crag
930m | 3,051ft

SCAFELL PIKE
977m | 3,206ft

Black Crag

Scafell
Crag

Lord's Rake

Broad
Stand

Narrowcove

Pen

Foxes
Tarn

Dow Crag

slopes of
ESK PIKE

Long Green

Cam
Spout
Crag

Great Moss

Long Gill

Sampson's
Stones

SLIGHT SIDE
762m | 2,500ft

Oliver Gill

MAP OVERLAP

For map continuation south see SLIGHT SIDE page 249

South-western aspect from Bulatt Bridge at the outflow Burnmoor Tarn

The Scafells from Long Top, from which point Scafell looks the senior partner

ASCENT *from Brotherilkeld & Wha House*

The journey into upper Eskdale from the road-end, effectively the foot of the Hardknott Pass, is one of Lakeland's dale-approach treats. In terms of reaching Scafell the key point is Cam Spout; three paths draw in to this point. Two accompany the Esk on either bank, while a third makes for the moorland intent on getting to the massif with minimum of distraction, difficult in these surrounds! The scenery both within and without the dale is pure fell delight.

1 The speediest route is via the Cowcove zig-zags. Embark either along the farm track direct to Taw House (GR 202 009), or the corresponding farm-track to Brotherilkeld from the red telephone kiosk (GR 212012), guided left of Brotherilkeld farmyard to a hand-gate, and a matter of a few metres on, go left, crossing the wooden footbridge spanning the wonderfully tree-shaded Esk. Traverse the pasture, with a wall right, to a ladder-stile entering the farmyard at Taw House. The farm-track approach to this farm has a permissive path option signed left, via a gate (avoiding the farmyard) this leads by a wall on a rough track, wet at the start, to a ladder-stile. Though to be frank this vicinity is better reached through the farmyard. So, as with the path from the footbridge, leave the Taw House farmyard by the gate at its northern end and follow the lane to a gate, thereafter upon an open track, via two gateways, to a gate/ladder-stile below the aforementioned ladder-stile at a sheepfold. A clear track continues to Scale Bridge, crossing the embowered cascades of Scale Gill. The footpath is signed further along the track, though an intermediary path takes a cavalier direct diagonal line up to the zig-zags from the bridge. **2** The footpath track becomes the lesser used west side valley route, rougher than its parallel path to Lingcove Bridge, particularly above Esk Falls, but nonetheless fascinating to tramp.

If keeping to the strict line of the Cowcove zig-zag footpath, watch for

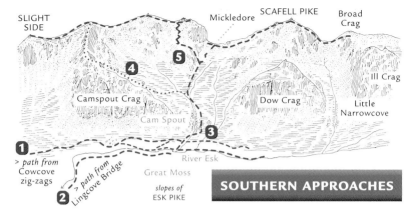

SLIGHT SIDE · Mickledore · SCAFELL PIKE · Broad Crag · Ill Crag · Camspout Crag · Dow Crag · Little Narrowcove · Cam Spout · River Esk · > path from Cowcove zig-zags · path from Lingcove Bridge · Great Moss · slopes of ESK PIKE

SOUTHERN APPROACHES

the acute turn left up through the bracken, the path is clear enough. Higher, the zig-zags afford a view into the Cowcove Beck ravine laced with birch and rowan, before entering the first of two marshy hollows. Keep to the dry western edge, crossing a plank over Damas Dubs, the natural drainage for the two, apparently separate, hollows. The path, well-evidenced underfoot, leads into the Esk catchment and meets up indistinctly with the west side valley path. The combined path leads through what could be mistaken for a remote deserted farmstead, but in reality is a multi-penned sheepfold, curving round a low spur, littered with huge erratics, known as Sampson's Stones, set beneath the massive cliff of Camspout Crag. Keeping to the fringe of Great Moss marsh, the path now bears up half-left to reach the foot of Cam Spout *(see below)*, the most handsome of pencil thin waterfalls.

2 The main valley approach, this is held tight to the Esk by a fence; notice the curious erosion that has left an oak tree's roots bare some 20 metres short of the hand-gate releasing the path into the pastures. A clear path leads, via a gate in a wall, continuing to a ladder-stile beside a gate and small fold, where a path, that began above the cattle-grid at the foot of Hardknott road converges. The valley soon constricts with three great cliffs catching the eye, Yew Crag up to the right on Hard Knott, and Brock (badger) Crag and Heron (sea eagle eyrie) Crag to the left; the latter has a large free face that must have attracted climbers' attention. Quickly The Steeple is visible up to the right. The undulating path varies from rough to smooth in approaching the sheep-wash fold at the elegant single-span Lingcove Bridge. From here The Steeple takes on the appearance of a Roman 'thumb's up'. Close to the bridge is quite the most excited passage in the Esk's beautiful career. Deep pools and falls abound, and in high summer it is the happy scene of swimmers and dippers in the crystal cool waters.

Cross the bridge and follow the path up Throstle Garth, passing too high to catch a glimpse of Esk Falls; these are known only to the infrequently followed and infinitely rougher west side path. As the mass of Throstlehow Crag is left behind we see the river taking wide meandering sweeps through a landscape reminiscent of a remote Highland glen, the path keeping close company under Scar Lathing. As the vast amphitheatre surrounding Great Moss takes centre-stage, see a turf-topped

Scafell Pike from the summit ridge above Foxes Tarn

wall close right; this is the remnants of a medieval deer compound built by the monks of Furness Abbey. Wet marsh is unavoidable, but once the Esk shallows are forded the sponge is less of a problem trending north-west to the foot of Cam Spout, where the real rigours begin!

3 The path climbs steeply upon naked rock close to the falls - two thin tails of water spilling down the gully, intermingled with a few smaller spills. **4** As the slope eases the first of three routes appear, though one may continue to the first path ford of How Beck. The objective: the little visited delights of the Camspout Crag ridge. Angle across the grassy slope avoiding a band of rock to the right. Work up through the skyline outcropping, no trace of a path until at last the ridge is joined. This is a stunning, safe, grassy arete leading handsomely to the cairned ridge-top of Long Green; take in the fine views across Green Cove to Scafell's East Buttress and south to the craggy eastern declivity of Slight Side. An easily found stony trail leads north to the summit.

Scafell from Long Green

5 The normal recourse is to follow the path up the combe beneath Mickledore, branching into a gully below East Buttress. Steep, stony but not rotten, this clambering stair leads to Foxes Tarn; a small dam ensures a constant horse-shoe of water surrounds the large boulder. A pitched path, more pitching is needed, zig-zags up the loose fellside south of East Buttress reaching the skyline at a cairn. The summit is located left upon a final rough stony rise. First-time visitors should know that while the summit is the firm objective, they should not miss the head of Scafell Crag located right from this saddle. The prominent headland of Symond's Knott should be climbed to tentatively gaze over the brink into the abyss of this famous climbing arena. Passing on by the head of Deep Gully *(see above),* one can now be petrified or impressed by the temerity of your recent actions! Stride cautiously a little further, gaze over the Broad Stand brink to Scafell Pike and down upon Pikes Crag towards Lingmell and Great Gable, a supremely beautiful prospect.

The combe path climbs, normally close under East Buttress, to Mickledore (the big gap), the narrow saddle connection linking the two Scafells. At the time of writing, Lord's Rake, and by implication its associated West Wall Traverse, are ruled out-of-bounds. A rock-fall near the top of the Rake threats even greater catastrophe and walkers are strongly advised to keep clear. This is a great shame; for generations it has been the one really stunning route to the top, sharing with rock climbers the thrill of a crag environment, which is matchless in Lakeland.

Broad Stand may seem a modest step from the saddle. I remember climbing this route during my formative years as a hillwalker... with a tight top rope! There are several exposed moves involved, so for heaven's sake, don't try your luck!

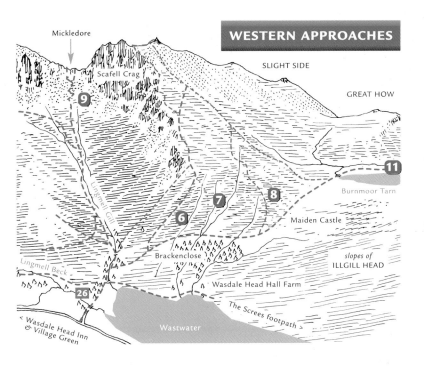

ASCENT *from Wasdale Head*

There are two main lines of ascent, either via Green How or the much more exciting route up Lingmell Gill. The latter is made the more taxing because it is necessary to cross over Mickledore, descending some ninety metres to climb a gully on the east side of the mountain. One may begin from the Village Green car park, following the footpath through to the National Trust campsite. This can be difficult when Lingmell Beck is flowing strongly; then it is necessary to follow the road, or the path by the footbridge traversing the lower slopes of Lingmell into the Lingmell Gill valley. The National Trust car park, accessed off the farm-track to Wasdale Head Hall, gives the more direct start for either ascent.

6 Green How: from the car park go left crossing the broad bridge, leave the farm-track following the gorse-lined path beside Lingmell Gill. Enter the Brackenclose enclosure with a Fell and Rock Club Hut in its midst.

A left turn leads up to a footbridge, from where a very poor path embarks, climbing the steep pasture via stiles to tackle the excessively steep scarp slope on the west side of Rakehead Crag: the path is horrid in ascent and wretched beyond words in descent, so be kind to the fell and leave it alone. Better bear right with the Eskdale bridle-way via a gate onto a green track into a field. Approaching the next gate, bear up the shallow hollow-way to a gate in the fence. Slant half-left up the pasture interspersed with thorn scrub to a stile in the intake wall/fence. A steep grassy trod leads directly up the scarp; at the brow keep along the edge above Rakehead Crag. **7** But the kindest option, for fell and feet, is to continue up the track to where it crosses Hollow Gill by a twin-arched stone bridge. Climb left, initially beside the gill, slanting pathless across to the left to join the scarp edge path. **8** One might even continue higher up the bridle-way and branch onto the broad open ridge climbing to join the Hard Rigg path, though it is tediously easy walking. The best views inevitably exist from the northern edge above Rakehead Crag leading up to the top of Lord's Rake: where the views are absolutely stunning.

9 The popularity of the Lingmell Gill path has necessitated considerable pitching works. Keep to the right-hand fork on Brown Tongue leading up to Hollow Stones, a real stony hollow beneath the huge shadowed north-facing Scafell Crag. A loose gravel gully leads up to the Mickledore saddle. Broad Stand should not be considered unless you have a high level of climbing competence. A torrid ninety metre descent, beneath the East Buttress, leads to an obvious gully on the right-hand side (see route **5** for the remainder of this ascent).

ASCENT *from Boot*

There are two routes. In combination they make the perfect circular.

10 Via Eel Tarn consult SLIGHT SIDE route **1** on page 250.

11 Via Burnmoor Tarn - and the preferable return leg to any round walk: cross the stone bridge passing Eskdale Mill to a gate; the succeeding path zig-zags, go through the gate on the right beneath a pine tree. A gated path leads through the enclosures onto the open moor. Keep to the principal path, crossing Ramshaw Beck hold to the right fork, leave the hardcore path leading to the Eller How barn. The green way reaches Bulatt Bridge, a humble sleeper bridge spanning the outflow of Burnmoor Tarn. Take the path forking half-right NNE across the low ground to reach a sheepfold. The path forks, take the ascending left-hand path out of the bracken onto the grass prairie of Hard Rigg; the right-hand path leads up Hardrigg Gill; any shelter this more minor route provides is lost when the two paths combine at its head. A further variant **9** uses a thin path mounting Hard Rigg from the marsh north of Maiden Castle - an intriguing circular cairn of unknown origin. The paths meet up, climbing in straightforward fashion onto the stony western slope, aiming to the high saddle some forty metres north of the summit.

Walkers with a wanderlust may find the solar-powered seismometer on Green How; nothing earth moving about that... or is there?

bridle-path to Wasdale Head

Green How

SLIGHT SIDE

Burnmoor Tarn

GREAT HOW

11

Lambford Bridge

ESKDALE MOOR

bridle-path to Brat's Moss Bronze Age stone circles

Whillan Beck

10

Eel Tarn

Great Barrow

Eskdale Mill

BOOT

La'al Ratty

SOUTHERN APPROACHES

For the diagram of the approaches from Wha House *(The Terrace Route),* Taw House and Brotherilkeld consult SLIGHT SIDE *page 251*

At the time of going to press C18th Eskdale Mill's future hangs in the balance, much as the new shaft being worked on by David King *(on the left)* in this scene of August 2003.

The Summit

Marked by a modest cairn on a tilted pedestal, close by a low circular wind-shelter all set up upon a rough rocky crest. On the north side  two short walls serve as shelters from contradictory winds. The view matches up to expectations. Anyone who makes the serious effort to combine the two Scafells in one expedition, and it is no light undertaking, will recognise this as a distinctly different point of view. More than just different, it might be thought the pick of the two, being the point of culmination on a narrow ridge, and sufficiently set apart to give perspective on Scafell Pike and upper Eskdale. The Western Fells about Wastwater and Mosedale are well displayed, as too Burnmoor Tarn and Miterdale, with the Isle of Man, as if afloat in the Irish Sea, beyond.

View down the Long Green ridge to Slight Side

Safe Descents

There are two simple ways off. The easiest of all heads for Wasdale Head (2 miles) and leaves the summit immediately N of the summit outcrop. A cairned path takes to the stony fellside heading due W, the loose trail easing as grass takes over on the route down Green How; ankles are less stressed by linking to the Burnmoor bridle-path at the foot of Hollow Gill, rather than by being drawn off the scarp beyond Rakehead Crag. For Eskdale (4.5 miles) follow the stepped ridge SSE, then due S to Slight Side, a well-marked path leading off that top into Cow Cove following the Terrace Route bound for the Whahouse car park.

Camspout Crag and the Esk
an ideal wild country camp

Ridge Routes to...

SCAFELL PIKE　　DESCENT 900 ft　ASCENT 945 ft　　　　1.25 miles

Ignore old guides and maps, there is only one way to Mickledore. The mouth-watering delights of Lord's Rake and the real rock route of Broad Stand are rendered out-of-bounds. From the shallow saddle 60 metres north of the summit, turn abruptly SE (right) by the cairn descending the zig-zags to Foxes Tarn. Follow the tarn outflow down the bouldery gully; at its foot, bear up left, clambering the gravelly slope below East Buttress to reach Mickledore. Go right passing the Mountain Rescue stretcher box, the stony ground seldom relenting, though the slope eases heading NE to the summit, identified by an old Ordnance Survey column and a crumbling, low walled tower – the whole process will take at least one hour and considerably more if you are tired!

SLIGHT SIDE　　DESCENT 680 ft　ASCENT 90 ft　　　　1.2 miles

The ridge falls in easy stages with some rough bouldery ground, but nothing to trouble an accustomed fell-foot. Should you be tempted to curve with the initial ridge to take advantage of the splendid view from the ridge-end above Green Cove, viewing Foxes Tarn and Scafell Pike beyond, you may notice evidence of old aeroplane wreckage on the scree. Mid-point on the ridge is the shapely summit of Long Green (marking the top of the Camspout Crag ridge, and a novel route down into Eskdale). A simple, if occasionally loose path, leads on S. The ground levels before the final easy scramble on this perfect termination of the massif.

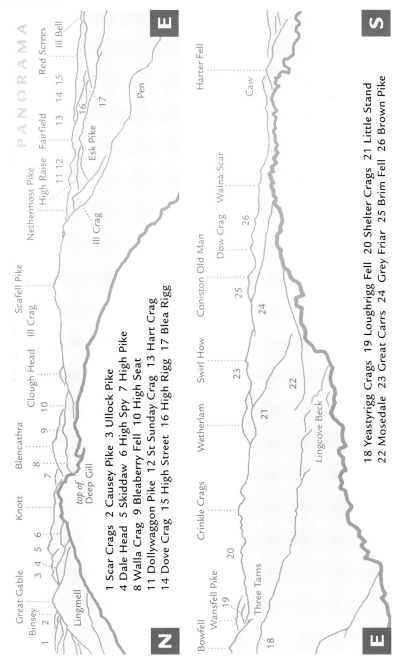

PANORAMA

E

N

Great Gable

Binsey

Knott

Blencathra

Clough Head

Scafell Pike

Ill Crag

Nethermost Pike

High Raise

Fairfield

Red Screees

Ill Bell

Lingmell

top of Deep Gill

Ill Crag

Esk Pike

Pen

1 Scar Crags 2 Causey Pike 3 Ullock Pike
4 Dale Head 5 Skiddaw 6 High Spy 7 High Pike
8 Walla Crag 9 Bleaberry Fell 10 High Seat
11 Dollywaggon Pike 12 St Sunday Crag 13 Hart Crag
14 Dove Crag 15 High Street 16 High Rigg 17 Blea Rigg

S

Harter Fell

Caw

E

Bowfell

Wansfell Pike

Crinkle Crags

Three Tarns

Swirl How

Wetherlam

Coniston Old Man

Dow Crag

Walna Scar

Lingcove Beck

18 Yeastyrigg Crags 19 Loughrigg Fell 20 Shelter Crags 21 Little Stand
22 Mosedale 23 Great Carrs 24 Grey Friar 25 Brim Fell 26 Brown Pike

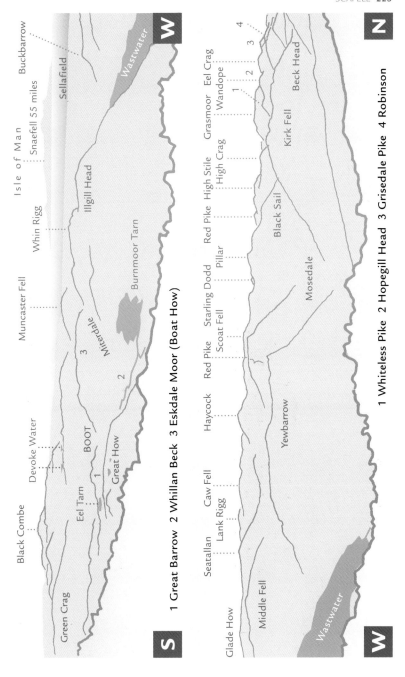

Black Combe · Muncaster Fell · Whin Rigg · Isle of Man · Snaefell 55 miles · Sellafield · Buckbarrow

Green Crag · Devoke Water · Eel Tarn · BOOT · Illgill Head · Wastwater

Great How · Miterdale · Burnmoor Tarn

W **S** 1 Great Barrow 2 Whillan Beck 3 Eskdale Moor (Boat How)

Glade How · Middle Fell · Seatallan · Lank Rigg · Caw Fell · Haycock · Red Pike · Scoat Fell · Starling Dodd · Pillar · Red Pike · High Crag · High Stile · Grasmoor · Eel Crag · Wandope

Yewbarrow · Mosedale · Black Sail · Kirk Fell · Beck Head

Wastwater

W **N** 1 Whiteless Pike 2 Hopegill Head 3 Grisedale Pike 4 Robinson

SCAFELL PIKE

The monarch of all Lakeland mountains. Following hard on the heels of Helvellyn as the most popular climb of the major fells. Not the most beautiful, not the very best ascent, not the finest panorama, not the most challenging crags, but the highest, roughest, toughest and assuredly the most revered ground. In a district simply bristling with shapely peaks there is inevitably a strong impulse to stand atop the highest of the lot. Scafell Pike is in every dimension a real mountain, no mock facades here, crag and scree abound on all fronts. Caution is therefore demanded both in ascent and descent. The summit contrives to keep itself remote from the gaze of valley observers; hence historically Scafell was thought to be the superior peak. From the closest spot it comes to a motorable road, at the head of Wastwater, all one can see is Pikes Crag which completely shields the fell-top. In fact from this vantage point Pikes Crag actually looks subservient to Scafell Crag.

One's judgement on when to go, and by which route, needs to be tempered with much forethought. The fell can be climbed from four directions, Wasdale Head, Seathwaite in Borrowdale, Great Langdale via Esk Hause and lonely Eskdale. There are two hot favourite ascents, two paths come together in the vicinity of Lingmell Col, from Lingmell Gill

977 metres   3,206 feet

Scafell Pike from the Esk Gorge

and the Corridor Route; both may start from Wasdale Head, though most walkers set sail from Seathwaite. The second approach is from Great Langdale via Rossett Gill and Esk Hause. With the M6 motorway as the principal feeder into the National Park inevitably this route is exposed to disproportionate pressure, but is nonetheless a grand route.

Broad Crag from Lingmell Col

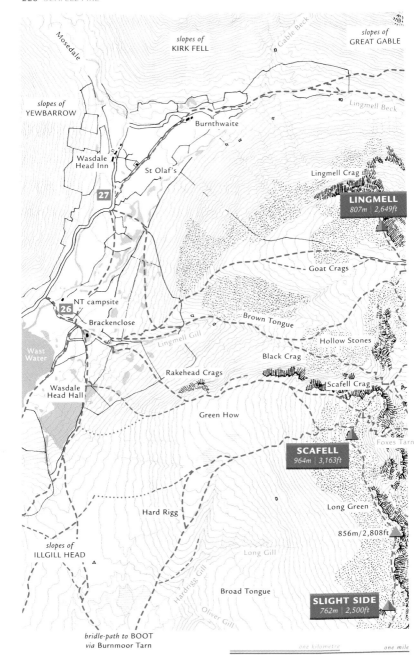

slopes of MOSEDALE

slopes of KIRK FELL

slopes of GREAT GABLE

Gable Beck

Lingmell Beck

slopes of YEWBARROW

Burnthwaite

Wasdale Head Inn

St Olaf's

Lingmell Crag

LINGMELL
807m | 2,649ft

27

Goat Crags

NT campsite

26

Brackenclose

Brown Tongue

Hollow Stones

Lingmell Gill

Wast Water

Black Crag

Rakehead Crags

Scafell Crag

Wasdale Head Hall

Green How

Foxes Tarn

SCAFELL
964m | 3,163ft

Hard Rigg

Long Green

856m/2,808ft

slopes of ILLGILL HEAD

Long Gill

SLIGHT SIDE
762m | 2,500ft

Hardrigg Gill

Broad Tongue

Oliver Gill

bridle-path to BOOT
via Burnmoor Tarn

one kilometre

one mile

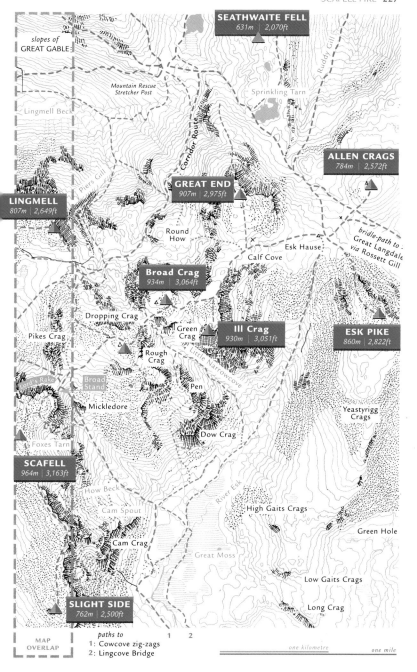

slopes of
GREAT GABLE

SEATHWAITE FELL
631m | 2,070ft

Ruddy Gill

Mountain Rescue
Stretcher Post

Sprinkling Tarn

Lingmell Beck

Piers Gill

Corridor Route

ALLEN CRAGS
784m | 2,572ft

GREAT END
907m | 2,975ft

LINGMELL
807m | 2,649ft

Round
How

Esk Hause

Calf Cove

bridle-path to
Great Langdale
via Rossett Gill

Broad Crag
934m | 3,064ft

Dropping Crag

Green
Crag

Ill Crag
930m | 3,051ft

ESK PIKE
860m | 2,822ft

Pikes Crag

Rough
Crag

Little Narrowcove

Broad
Stand

Pen

Mickledore

Yeastyrigg
Crags

Lord's Rake

Foxes Tarn

Dow Crag

SCAFELL
964m | 3,163ft

How Beck

River Esk

High Gaits Crags

Green Hole

Cam Spout

Cam Crag

Great Moss

Low Gaits Crags

Long Crag

SLIGHT SIDE
762m | 2,500ft

MAP
OVERLAP

paths to
1: Cowcove zig-zags
2: Lingcove Bridge

1   2

one kilometre

one mile

ASCENT *from Great Langdale*

Scafell Pike is a distant, almost surreal, notion from the ODG, with the added fear that it is a lost kingdom in the clouds! The adage 'it is better to travel hopefully' applies, as too 'retreat is the better part of valour', an option if, having reached Esk Hause, it looks a lost 'befogged' cause.

1 In positive vein, pick up your stride in Mickleden, don't overdo it, energy levels will be tested today. Crossing the footbridge at the foot of Stake Gill, engage on the newly restored pony path which fords Rossett Gill, then via an exaggerated double zig-zag steps ascend to the saddle at the head of the gill. The path declines to the outflow of Angle Tarn, a moment to pause and study the the reflections of Hanging Knotts in the hanging waters. The continuing path rises westward up Tongue Head.

Closing in on the saddle; drift half-left to the cross-wall shelter. This is an important landmark, its existence is no co-incidence; the terrain has a nasty habit of confusing even confident ramblers and is a meeting of the winds too! Be aware there are two saddles, the east/west link to Sprinkling Tarn and Styhead *and* the higher col of Esk Hause, situated 250 metres to the south-west of the wind-shelter. Esk Hause, the broad depression between Esk Pike and Great End is littered with cairns; most are superfluous, their only message that 'many people come this way' bound for Calf Cove, they direct there with undeniable precision! Go west on the all too palpable trail - shades of the American Wild West. Thoughts turning to youthful television addiction to watching the wildly romanticised tales of *Wagon Train*, *Laramie*, *Boots and Saddles*, *Rawhide*, *Gunslinger*, *Bronco*, *Maverick*, and so on. They were fantasies but this path is not, it winds up the damp hollow wherein lies a small bield shelter and the last running water for 'High Noon' thirsts.

Climbing onto the plateau saddle, so far so good, as far as underfoot conditions go, matters are about to take a turn for the worse. The ridge draws up south-westward to an innominate rocky crest; weave through the boulders, the path inevitably becomes vague, though there is no inherent problem. The boulders relent as the summit of Scafell Pike comes tantalisingly into eye shot - more distant that hoped in many hearts! The path sweeps majestically over the gravelly shoulder of the Ill Crag plateau, dipping into Illcrag Col, before yet more boulders on the traverse of the east shoulder of Broad Crag into Broadcrag Col. Views from the col, left down Little Narrowcove to the Pen and right to Lingmell, are quite stirring. Wearying legs need to make one final effort on the sorely-eroded scramble up the narrow arete leading to the summit boulder-field. The recent memory of the route from Esk Hause will cause most walkers to dally long on the summit, perhaps wandering to the various plateau brinks for differing perspectives, knowing it all has to be repeated. Though I have met walkers, with energy reserves to match a gazelle, who blithely wander down to Cam Spout and across Great Moss, destination Three Tarns, thinking nothing of such a line on the map!

BROAD CRAG

Weather-bleached, bright lichened
rocks adorn the fortress summit

This is an opportune moment to make a sales pitch for Ill Crag and Broad Crag, both considered part and parcel of the Scafell Pike ensemble. The tiresome trek across the plateau causes the majority of walkers to ignore their very existence, but as summits to visit they fully deserve the attention of well-informed fellwanderers and the high country connoisseur. Broad Crag is a serious adjunct, serious in the sense of its utter rockiness *(judge its qualities from the image on page 225)*. One may count the grass by the blade! The cairnless top lies only a matter of yards to the west of the ridge path, easiest access from the north. Ill Crag is different. In fact but for its relationship with Broad Crag and their traditional harmony with Scafell Pike the case for separate entity is very strong. Witness Ill Crag from Pen across Little Narrowcove and the sensation is magnified tenfold. Of the four dependent summits associated with Scafell Pike, Pen and Ill Crag rate as personal favourites, being removed situations, yet at one with the mountainous setting.

ILL CRAG

The eye-catching summit tor

ASCENT *from Seathwaite*

For all its tantalising distance from the target summit a circular expedition can easily be created courtesy of forking paths at Stockley Bridge. The valley to the left leads to Esk Hause, while that to the right makes unerringly for Styhead Pass and the Corridor Route.

2 For the approach to Styhead Pass consult GREAT END page 104 and SEATHWAITE FELL page 242. For the Corridor Route see route **4**.

3 The Esk Hause route follows the left-hand path up Grains Gill, becoming Ruddy Gill after a footbridge. New pitching is evident right up to the point where the upper ravine is forded; link to the path rising from Sprinkling Tarn and Styhead. Take the first branch path right, leading up to Esk Hause. Hereon consult route **1** on page 228.

ASCENT *from Wasdale Head*

4 Consult GREAT END route **7** on page 110 for the route to Styhead Pass. There is nothing hemmed-in or passage-like about the Corridor Route, it is a deceptively long and quite tough traverse, frequently congested with human traffic. On-going pitching works on the steep open sections have brought it nearer the comfort zone. One may start directly from the Styhead stretcher box, angling half-left, short-cutting across the

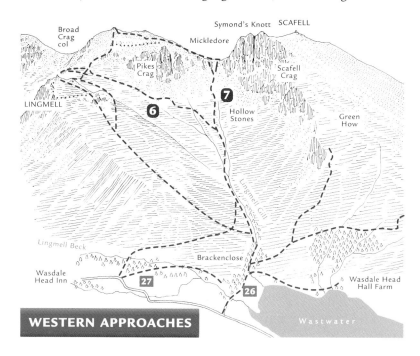

WESTERN APPROACHES

headstream of Spouthead Gill, though it is better to take the original route which branches right after the initial rise on the eastbound path, as to Sprinkling Tarn. Cross the vestige of a short wall, dipping and contouring to the mouth of the Skew Gill ravine. Climb the facing slope, pass through a short cutting on a hard staircase rising to a ridge crossing. Watch the far side step down is awkward. The path weaves on by two headstream fords of Greta Gill before a parting in the way.

5 A clear set of steps marks the start of a less than savoury direct route to Broadcrag Col. The latter stages of the climb up the wild combe to the narrow, rough saddle, test the tempo and temper. The summit lies up the eroded arete to the right.

The Corridor Route continues, fording the Piers Gill ravine just where it spills almost innocently into its notoriously deep and treacherous ravine. Eschew the dubious trace of a path that branches up the rough northern slopes west of Dropping Crag. Having been tempted to follow a clear path coming off the summit above Dropping Crag, I know only too well the pitfalls of the descent, and by implication ascent, on this area of the fell – give it a wide berth. The main path avoids the Lingmell Col; work up among the outcropping to link with the path from Hollow Stones on the broad, stony, but otherwise unthreatening, north-west ridge.

Scafell Pike from the upper section of Piers Gill

6 The shortest and most trouble-free ascent follows Lingmell Gill up into Hollow Stones, the most dramatic arena beneath the impressive face of Scafell Crag and Pulpit Rock. The left fork on the Brown Tongue ridge is imperative to locate; this leads the well-worn trail below Pikes Crags, onto the north-west ridge, winding up to a large cairn on the lip of the summit plateau. **7** The right branch on the Brown Tongue rigg leads up to quite a breathtaking intimacy with Scafell Crag. The path to Mickledore is not exactly a joyous amble, and may never have been all that sweet, but certainly the day after day scouring of fell boots has taken its toll: repair of this section is unlikely to be all that effective, even if attempted; expect some discomfort and know it is not actually difficult to achieve. Once on the narrow neck of ridge connecting the two great Scafells, turn left, passing the Mountain Rescue stretcher box; the path

Ill Crag from Pen

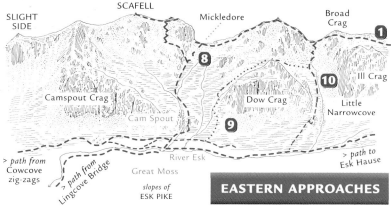

SLIGHT SIDE

SCAFELL

Mickledore

Broad Crag

1

8

Ill Crag

10

Camspout Crag

Dow Crag

Little Narrowcove

Cam Spout

9

> path from Cowcove zig-zags

> path from Lingcove Bridge

River Esk

Great Moss

> path to Esk Hause

slopes of ESK PIKE

EASTERN APPROACHES

Lingmell and Great Gable from the top of Dropping Crag

to the summit remains clear. As a worthwhile variation, once onto the plateau, bear half-left and with modest effort and a handful of bravery, clamber onto the top of Pulpit Rock. A cairn marks the spot, and enjoy a jealously guarded and airy new angle on Scafell Crag.

ASCENT *from Brotherilkeld*

For the approaches to Cam Spout consult SCAFELL pages 213-217.

8 There are three lines to consider from Cam Spout. The normal practice is to clamber up the bare rocks to the right of Cam Spout, ascending the increasingly rough combe above beneath Scafell's East Buttress. There is a path all the way, though it is inevitably loose nearing the saddle. **9** While some intrepid fellfolk may contemplate tackling the Pike via the craggy south-east ridge above Pen, more rewarding options are to be found in reaching Broadcrag Col via the shy wild hollow of Little Narrowcove. One must presume that the comb above Cam Spout is an unrecorded, or at least, unspoken Great Narrowcove! Arguably the most impressive of Scafell Pike's chest of crags is Esk Buttress (Dow Crag), the Central Pillar face commanding upper Eskdale *(see title view on page 224)*. It is quirkily surmounted by a pimple of banded rock bearing a distinctly Celtic name, Pen. The route to this fabulous little top is arduous and largely pathless, but well rewards the effort. A path contours along the edge of Great Moss, fording How Beck and, after the second subsequent gill, it is time to bend to the ascent. The rigg tapers to a gill to the left of

Little Narrowcove

Dow Crag, a worn path materialises, this being none other than the climbers' descent route off the back of the crag. Don't be drawn into the gully, keep on the steep rigg. As the slope gradually eases drift right to scramble to the top of Pen. There is a cairn and cause for much inner revelry at reaching this less than orthodox viewpoint. Ill Crag's stunning southern buttress simply steeples even from this elevated spot. Briefly follow the spine of the ridge, then work round to the left to find the breach in the ridge; a sheep path leads easily through into Little Narrowcove. **10** The direct route into Little Narrowcove does not hug the outflowing beck. To find the point of entry continue beside the infant Esk; after a large cairn, angle up the rigg left. A path emerges on approaching a gully. Clamber up, exiting right then left on a path drawing up in harmony with Little Narrowcove Beck. The rarely seen beauties of this secret corrie deserve to be savoured. The final stages of the ascent zig-zag up the scree at the head to reach Broadcrag Col. It's a feather in your cap to have made this point, by this means. Walkers coalesce here from Esk Hause and up the combe from the Corridor Route, but precious few indeed, from Little Narrowcove!

Looking down Little Narrowcove to Pen from Broadcrag Col

Pulpit Rock from Scafell

The Summit

A domed plateau proliferating with boulders and a few precious grassy patches culminates on a blunt circular drystone-walled tower. A few paces to the west an old Ordnance Survey column looks eminently dignified beside the sad crumbling memorial. As I have mentioned elsewhere, there are a few fell high points around the district that deserve to be tidied up; they merit a fresh start. I would like to see carefully selected summits identified for such special treatment, their summit cairns recreated with existing stones, respecting the honourable tradition of the cairn-builders' craft. All summits with loose rock seem to attract windbreak-makers, Scafell Pike is no exception. There are several of the normal, tumbledown type and one, situated towards the eastern brink, which lacks only a roof. I recommend visitors to make the effort to wander around the plateau edge and enjoy some stunning new perspectives, the pick of the bunch that from above Dropping Crag *(see page 233)*.

View north over Broad Crag to Great End

Safe Descents

For all its many year-round visitors, in nasty weather, there can be no lonelier place than the summit of Scafell Pike. And while it is true you have got here, getting back can be an altogether different proposition. Psychologically, the energy that drove you ever upward disappears in the instant you turn back, you may be tired and objectives are down beat. Great Langdale, for instance, lies to the east, smack into the teeth of winter winds. Wasdale Head, by contrast, catches the prevailing ocean-borne breeze, by definition warmer, if potentially no less fierce.

The securest lines are for WASDALE HEAD 2.75 miles: start from the extra large cairn on the plateau edge 250 metres W of the summit. Descend the cairned path down the NW ridge. Short of Lingmell Col the path veers left down into Hollow Stones, drawn naturally onto Brown Tongue and then into close company with Lingmell Gill. For SEATHWAITE 4.25 miles: instead of veering left, go right, off the NW ridge, following the Corridor Route NE to Styhead Pass. From the stretcher box the old bridle-path leads unerringly down to Stockley Bridge. For GREAT LANGDALE 5.4 miles: the tiresome bouldery ridge N dips by two small staccato saddles of Broadcrag and Illcrag Cols before leaving the high plateau, via Calf Cove E down to Esk Hause. Aim NE to the cross-wall wind-shelter, now E to merge with the bridle-path to the outflow of Angle Tarn and ever onward to descend the Rossett Gill zig-zags into Mickleden. For ESKDALE 4.75 miles: go SE to Mickledore, descend the combe SE, the awkard slabs beside Cam Spout requiring some care at the foot. One may either bear right, onto the path leading to Cowcove zig-zags, or ford and follow the Esk through its gorge to Lingcove Bridge and Brotherilkeld.

Ridge Routes to...

GREAT END   DESCENT 600 ft   ASCENT 330 ft   1.4 miles

Descend N via the narrow sorely eroded arete into the tight neck of Broadcrag Col. Traverse the ensuing bouldery shoulder into Illcrag Col, sweep up the gravelly slope to a short boulder section over a crest and then down onto the broad saddle. Divert half-left, off the popular path to Esk Hause which leads down Calf Cove, keep on the easy ground on the ridge heading N to a choice of two summit cairns.

SCAFELL   DESCENT 945 ft   ASCENT 900 ft   1.25 miles

Aim SE, a cairned path leads to the narrow connecting ridge of Mickledore, passing the stretcher box. The drama of Scafell wonderfully apparent; Broad Stand blocks off the ridge-end to walkers. Descend left into the combe beneath Scafell's East Buttress. Find an easy gully to the right, there is but one, climb this to Foxes Tarn, then tackle the partially restored zig-zag path climbing up onto the saddle, go left to the summit.

PANORAMA

Binsey · Dale Head · Ullock Pike · Longside Edge · Carl Side · Skiddaw · Skiddaw Little Man · Knott · Lonscale Fell · High Pike · High Spy · Derwentwater

Base Brown

Gillercomb Buttress

Sty Head

Styhead Tarn

Blencathra · Clough Head · Great Dodd · Raise · Helvellyn · Nethermost Pike · Dollywaggon Pike · High Street · Red Screes

Great End

Broad Crag

Ill Crag

Esk Pike

Little Narrowcove

path from Esk Hause

E

N

1 Binsey 2 Dale Head 3 Ullock Pike 4 Longside Edge 5 Carl Side 6 Skiddaw
7 Skiddaw Little Man 8 Knott 9 Lonscale Fell 10 High Pike 11 High Spy 12 Derwentwater
13 Seathwaite Fell 14 Grange Fell 15 Bleaberry Fell 16 Souther Fell 17 Stybarrow Dodd 18 Sergeant's Crag
19 Ullscarf 20 High Raise 21 St Sunday Crag 22 Fairfield 23 Ill Bell 24 Harrison Stickle (*The Langdale Pikes*)

S

Loughrigg Fell

Bowfell

Pike de Bield

upper Eskdale

Three Tarns

Crinkle Crags

Wetherlam

Adam-a-Crag

Little Stand

Swirl How

Grey Friar

Mosedale

Duddon Valley

Dow Crag

Walna Scar

Caw

Walney Island

Harter Fell

25 Shelter Crags 26 Black Sails 27 Brim Fell 28 Coniston Old Man 29 Hard Knott

E

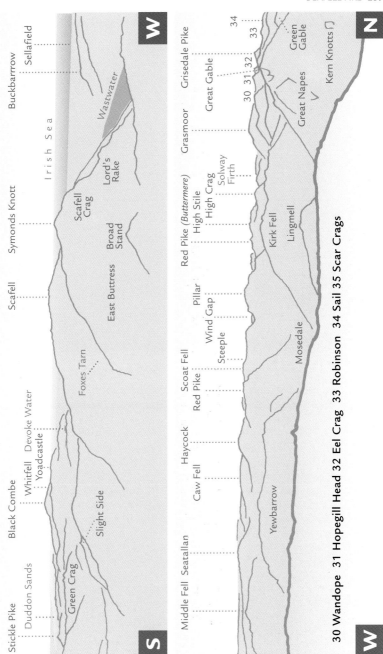

W

Sellafield
Buckbarrow

Irish Sea

Wastwater

Lord's Rake

Scafell Crag

Broad Stand

Symonds Knott

Scafell

East Buttress

Foxes Tarn

Black Combe
Whitfell Devoke Water
Yoadcastle

Slight Side

Stickle Pike

Duddon Sands

Green Crag

S

N

Grisedale Pike

34
33

Green Gable

30 31 32

Great Gable

Great Napes

Kern Knotts

Grasmoor

Red Pike (Buttermere)
High Stile
High Crag
Solway Firth

Kirk Fell
Lingmell

Scoat Fell
Red Pike

Pillar
Wind Gap
Steeple

Mosedale

Haycock
Caw Fell

Middle Fell Seatallan

Yewbarrow

W

30 Wandope 31 Hopegill Head 32 Eel Crag 33 Robinson 34 Sail 35 Scar Crags

SEATHWAITE FELL

So long the butt of jibes about Lakeland's inclement weather, for years a rain gauge situated near Sprinkling Tarn affirmed this as the wettest sector of Lakeland: 120 inches compared to 50 inches in Keswick. One might consider 'sea' thwaite to be well named. Yet, without the wetness we wouldn't have the beautiful lakes, so we have much to thank Seathwaite Fell and its neighbouring heights for.

Resolutely defended east and west by crags and rough slopes, there is little encouragement for a walker to divert from either of the two popular paths that track up the flanking valleys of Styhead Gill and Grains with Ruddy Gills. Where the fell merges with Great End the going becomes more lenient. At Sprinkling Tarn, which lies beside the Sty Head to Esk Hause trail, a path weaves onto the undulating plateau. The ridge-top is quite irregular, pleasantly so if your visit coincides with fair weather, the pools and knobbly tops making this a joyous quest. The highest point is situated due north of the Sprinkling Tarn, a smaller unnamed pool and rocky ground passed en-route. However, the traditional summit, suggested as such when viewed from Seathwaite Bridge, lies further north and is some thirty metres lower, an abrupt little pike crowning the slope above Aaron Crags, and a peerless viewpoint for upper Borrowdale.

631 metres   2,070 feet

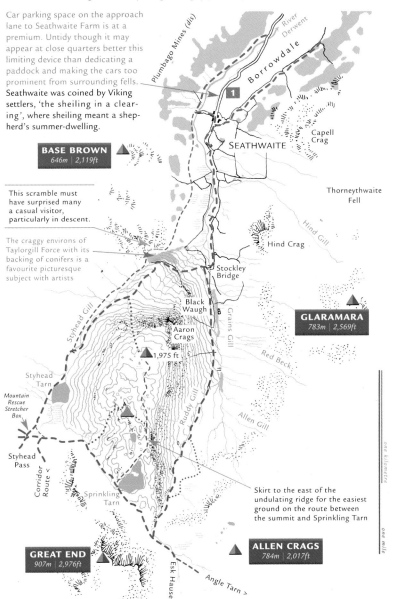

Car parking space on the approach lane to Seathwaite Farm is at a premium. Untidy though it may appear at close quarters better this limiting device than dedicating a paddock and making the cars too prominent from surrounding fells. Seathwaite was coined by Viking settlers, 'the sheiling in a clearing', where sheiling meant a shepherd's summer-dwelling.

Plumbago Mines (dis)

River Derwent

B o r r o w d a l e

1

Capell Crag

SEATHWAITE

BASE BROWN
646m | 2,119ft

Thorneythwaite Fell

This scramble must have surprised many a casual visitor, particularly in descent.

Hind Gill

The craggy environs of Taylorgill Force with its backing of conifers is a favourite picturesque subject with artists

Hind Crag

Stockley Bridge

Styhead Gill

Black Waugh   B

Grains Gill

GLARAMARA
783m | 2,569ft

Aaron Crags

1,975 ft

Red Beck

Styhead Tarn

Ruddy Gill

Mountain Rescue Stretcher Box

Allen Gill

Styhead Pass

Corridor Route <

Sprinkling Tarn

Skirt to the east of the undulating ridge for the easiest ground on the route between the summit and Sprinkling Tarn

GREAT END
907m | 2,976ft

ALLEN CRAGS
784m | 2,017ft

Esk Hause v

Angle Tarn >

one kilometre

one mile

From Sprinkling Tarn issues the River Derwent. Was ever a river born with more aplomb? The tarn sprinkles a moment's serenity and calm on fellwalkers bent to the sweaty task of climbing Scafell Pike, or traversing from Langdale to Wasdale or Borrowdale. Wander along the northern shore to the peninsula and admire the cliffs of Great End across the choppy waters.

Seathwaite Farm and Fell

ASCENT *from Seathwaite*

Road signs to Seathwaite from Seatoller imply a dale-head village, but in reality it is nothing more than a farm. A busy farm for all that, where cattle and sheep vie with B&B guests and an army of walkers and climbers traipsing through the farmyard to the craggy roof of Cumbria. **1** The primary valley route leads through the farmyard, via gates, heading for Stockley Bridge, a typical packhorse bridge (*see* GREAT END page 113), well-maintained and focal to two popular routes; the bridge is probably named after the builder of the first elegant stone structure. Pass through the succeeding hand-gate and consider your options, either left via Grains and Ruddy Gills towards Esk Hause, or right via the ancient pony route towards Styhead Pass and Wasdale.

   2 The direct ascent of the fell takes the right-hand path. After the next hand-gate you will see Aaron Crags. Go right with the main winding trail above Taylorgill Force (unseen from this angle). A minor ford gives the clue to the direct route to the traditional summit. There is no path on the ground, the gill dwindling as a weakness in the skyline gives cause for confidence that easy ground is at hand. The summit knoll lies directly ahead, defended by modest outcropping.

3 A walled lane leads right from the midst of the buildings (under the roof canopy) at Seathwaite Farm. Crossing the Derwent footbridge turn left via the hand-gate; the path traverses under trees and above marshy rough terrain to a ladder-stile crossing a wall at the top of a small plantation. Slant across the fellside to climb more steeply to a hand-gate as the gorge constricts facing the Taylorgill Force amphitheatre. A short scramble ensues, awkward in descent. The path continues on the true left-bank until, at a footbridge, the pony route from Stockley Bridge joins. Keeping to the west bank pass above Styhead Tarn to reach the stretcher box at Sty Head, the pass-name referred to the 'top of the steep path from Wasdale'. There was a time when road engineers eyed this pass as a likely through route, mercifully wise counsel prevailed and the sanctuary remained sacrosanct.

Scramble on the path opposite Taylorgill Force

Sty Head Pass is a point of elation and decision, a high saddle subjugated by the immensity of Great Gable and the massive bastion of The Band leading up onto the Scafells. **4** Turn east mounting a bank and as a ravine comes close to the left slip across and slant up the pathless grass slope, passing under outcropping, rounding to reach the summit from the north. **5** Alternatively, for an even easier life, keep to the main path to ford the outflow of Sprinkling Tarn, the first issue of the River Derwent. Follow the northern shore path venturing onto the ridge, the path diminishes, keep right of the nameless tarn to avoid outcropping, skirting round to approach the summit from the east.

6 A left turn at the hand-gate beyond Stockley Bridge leads onto the path up Grains Gill. This leads via a hand-gate, and subsequently a footbridge, up the east bank of Ruddy Gill to meet the path from Sty Head to Esk Hause. Fording the gill, as it bends south-east, follow this path right to reach the outflow of Sprinkling Tarn and accompany route **5** to the summit (see white dashes below).

Approach to the south top from Sprinkling Tarn

South top cairn

The Summit

Now let's clear things up: can a fell have more than one summit? The firm rule that a summit is the highest point falters where there are rising ridges of the character of Rosthwaite and Seathwaite Fells. It is hard to justify one high spot above another. There are perceptual as well as strict structural considerations at play. When viewed from Seathwaite Bridge the fell culminates assuredly at the northern pike above Aaron Crags. Stand upon that pike and you know precisely why tradition has ordained this to be the summit. The view down Borrowdale is peerless. A new generation of fellwalkers may arrive seeking to overthrow the traditional per-

North top cairn - the commonly accepted summit

ception and feeling no compunction at adopting the highest ground as a summit. The south top may be a brilliant viewpoint, but it lacks that intimate visual relationship with upper Borrowdale. You will note that the ridge path from the north top to Sprinkling Tarn has no truck with the ridge proper, nor the south top, preferring to wend near the eastern edge: a lovely link to higher things.

Safe Descents

Steep rough ground runs away from the summit, most notably to the north and east. In favourable conditions one may descend pathless route **1**, west from the summit, then from the scarp edge north by the emerging gill. The better choice is to follow the ridge south linking up with the Esk Hause/Styhead path at the outflow of Sprinkling Tarn. This also gives options for your valley return, dependant on prevailing winds, a stiff westerly encouraging one to track down the sheltered Ruddy and Grains Gill path, in preference to the more popular and more exposed Styhead Pass trail bound for Stockley Bridge and Seathwaite.

Ruddy Gill's crashing conversion to Grains Gill

PANORAMA

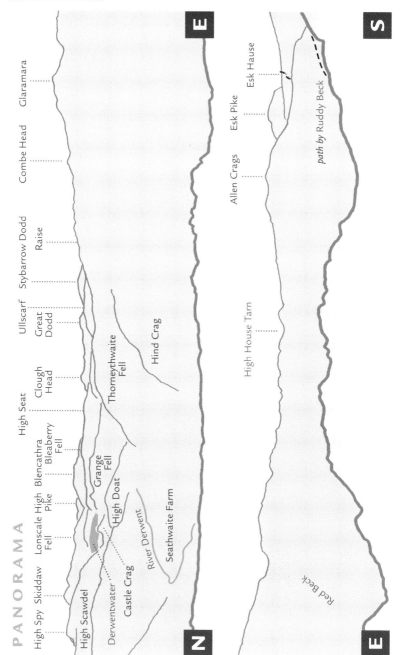

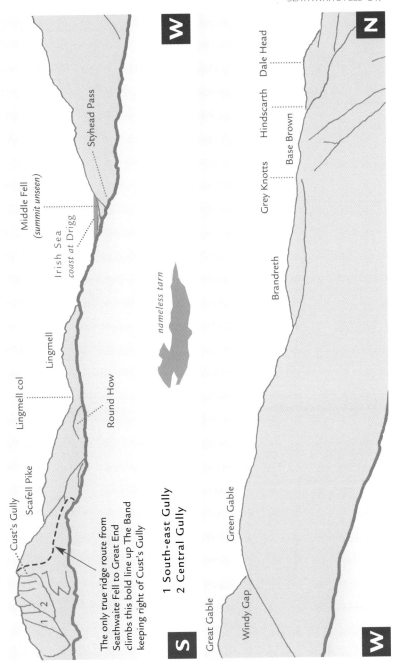

W

N

Styhead Pass

Middle Fell
(summit unseen)

Irish Sea
coast at Drigg

Lingmell col

Lingmell

Round How

Cust's Gully

Scafell Pike

nameless tarn

The only true ridge route from
Seathwaite Fell to Great End
climbs this bold line up The Band
keeping right of Cust's Gully

1 South-east Gully
2 Central Gully

S

Great Gable

Green Gable

Windy Gap

Dale Head

Hindscarth

Grey Knotts

Base Brown

Brandreth

W

SLIGHT SIDE

Of the several less than courteous expressions of slight, 'a broad expanse of flat ground' does not leap to the front of the mind. The name means the 'long slope' from such an area; in all probability a reference to Cow Cove 'the summer grazing of suckler cattle'.

The summit effectively terminates the main Scafell massif. It is a remarkable viewpoint, reached by sleight of foot. A real peak, albeit a shoulder of Scafell. Unlike most fells, it has but one natural ascent line, with a two-pronged approach, from Boot and Wha House. The latter, the Terrace Route, is a gem, a comparatively easy going fell trail, until the abrupt final slopes most inviting, dare one say, a joy - anyone for Pimm's on the Terrace? The long lead in by either route gives the walker time to adjust to the beautifully wild setting and the pull to the top, largely on grass, is achieved in remarkably quick time. As an exit gate from perilous weather on Scafell it serves the walker well. The eastern slopes are consistently cragbound, be ye so warned!

762 metres   2,500 feet

SCAFELL
964m | 3,163ft

Cam Spout

River Esk

Cam Crag

Long Green

Great Moss

Long Gill

Sampson's Stones

fold

Broad Tongue

Scar Lathing

Horn Crag

Quagrigg Moss

High Scarth Crag

GREAT HOW
523m | 1,716ft

Es
Fal

Lingcove Bridge

Damas Dubs

Brockshaw Beck

Heron Crag

Catcove Beck

Cowcove Beck

Brock Crag

Dawsonground Crags

slopes of
HARD KNOTT

Stony Tarn

Peelplace
Noddle

Yew Crags

Terrace Route

Taw House

Hardknott
Roman Fort

Brotherilkeld

HARDKNOTT & >
WRYNOSE PASSES

15

Eskdale
Youth Hostel

River Esk

Two good agricultural names derived
from the Norse are: Taw = 'manured land'
Wha = 'cattle enclosures'

Wha House

18 **17**

16

Slight Side from Cow Cove

ASCENT *from Boot*

Anyone contemplating climbing Slight Side from Boot, will actually have Scafell in their sights. Kicking off from this base a natural circuit is conjured by returning off the higher summit, via Hard Rigg. The out-walk, via Eel Tarn and the curiously name Peelplace Noddle, has much the same feel as the approach to a remote Munro so it will ring a happy chord with hillwalkers forth of Scotland.

1 From the short village street, passing the Burnmoor Inn, bear right, signed 'Eel Tarn'. A roadway winds up behind the tree-shaded mill, the thunderous thrashings of Whillan Beck making an early impression. As the tarmac ends leave the farm-track - leading to Gill Bank, with its two specimen monkey puzzle trees. Take the gate right, go left at the three-way footpath sign, again directing to 'Eel Tarn'. The green track threads through a walled passage *(see opposite)*, the immediate surroundings reminiscent of Yorkshire limestone country, minus the limestone of course! The path curves right up, do not be lured left onto the path to Lambford

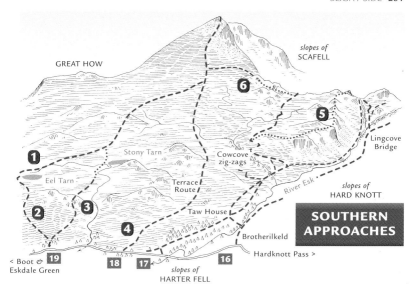

Bridge, but keep right to reach Eel Tarn. The boggy ground on this northern side has to be traversed before skirting to the east of the tarn, from where a path weaves on up through a confusing terrain leading by Peelplace Noddle. In mist you certainly do have to use your noddle, a compass would not come amiss. The path mounts onto a more definite ridge above Stony Tarn, and generally contours across marshy ground due north-east, fording several minor gills, latterly a grasssy trod that meets up with the Terrace Route, as the slope steepens... now gird your loins for a final push for the top.

Lane on the approach to Eel Tarn from Boot

Horn Crag from high on the Camspout Crag ridge

The south-western approach can also begin from the Woolpack Inn via either **2** Eel Tarn or **3** Stony Tarn - consult GREAT HOW on page 118.

ASCENT *from Wha House*

4 The Terrace Route: a small car park (GR201009) has been made specifically for walkers embarking on this popular route to Scafell and, by implication, Slight Side. Cross the fence stile and mount the slope diagonally right to go through a cluster of stone sheepfolds via four hand-gates. The path continues, initially with the intake wall close right, then gradually rises above it and beneath the rough slopes of the Goat Crag ridge. A succession of rock steps are taken in the stride, with every good reason to pause from time to time to admire this truly handsome aspect of the heather-clad Harter Fell and Hard Knott with its Roman Fort and craggy front to south and east. Fording a gill the path moves through irregular terrain in a natural manner, the sense of a terrace-cum-corridor evident to the point where the path comes above the Catcove Gill gorge and Slight Side comes strikingly into view *(see above right)*. The path steps over a shallow stony ford, continuing north in lower Cat Cove – 'the wild cat lair' – and fords the beck, now no more than a minor gill. It works steadily across the slope with the great bowl of Cow Cove to the right, meeting up with the path from Boot at a small cairn above a large erratic. The climb has the occasional gravelly passage, but nothing of note; the summit can be reached either from a breach up to the left or by skirting round to climb from the north. The key word is climb, as the summit is naked rock, though there is nothing perilous.

5 Cowcove zig-zags and **6** the Round Scar ridge:

A matter of 150 metres further east along the valley road a farm-track leads off; there are two recess car parking spots just a few yards beyond (with a signposted track linking up). This, the access to Taw House, suggests two intriguing variant routes exploring Slight Sides's craggy sub-scarp ridges west of the Esk Gorge. Either follow the permissive path signed left just prior to the farmyard, or go through the farmyard and along the gated lane. Follow an open track up pasture, via gates, to a fold where the two routes come together; proceed to Scale Bridge to admire the sheltered falls upstream. Keep faith with the proper green path which leads on at a fork, curving up left through the bracken. There are some pitched sections on this, the Cowcove zig-zags. One may either

Taw House, backed by Hard Knott

The ridge leading up over Long Green to the summit of Scafell

keep with the regular path, ultimate destination the upper Esk and Cam Spout beneath the mighty Scafells. Or, **6** take the fellwanderers line by stepping off the regular path just where it draws up onto the moor. Venture to follow the scarp edge right above Brock Crag, the name evidently associated with an ancient badger sett, as brock is a Celtic term - as in Brocolitia Roman Fort on Hadrian's Wall. There is no hint of a path, other than that created by cloven feet. Work your own instinctive way either over the highest ground, or do like me, and find the top of Heron Crag, the more airy eyrie. Angle west, skirting a tarn, to join the undulating ridge leading north via Round Scar, a classic remnant volcano plug; there are numerous similar plugs forming outcrop blocks, the greatest being Silverbield Crag. **5** The direct path is joined beyond the buttress of Silverbield Crag at the threshold to the great amphitheatre of the upper Esk. The Cowcove path, having skirted the marshy hollow of Damas Dubs, crosses a plank bridge at the outflow in the combe's midst. Follow the main path, as into the upper Esk, though, as the rough slope up to the left eases, branch off on a whim to climb the pathless grass fellside, with Slight Side's craggy upper face, Horn Crag, glowering from on high. Wander up to a notch, created by a large slab, to find a path in all probability established as much by contouring sheep as off-beat walkers. This path works across the rough slope on a south-easterly line, alternating between clear and vague until the ascending Terrace Route path is encountered on the steepening slope above the junction with the Boot path. Yes, I know, I know, all the paths are boot paths. Not so! The majority of walks I have done this summer, whilst covering the entire Mid-Western Fells, have been undertaken in strong trainers, supported by walking poles, it's been that dry!

The Summit

The summit cairn rests on top of a natural fortress *(see below)*, exhibiting the same white-flecked surface as occurs on Esk Pike. The rocky spine an appropriate final flourish ensures the Scafell massif ends impressively. The view is special, from Bowfell to the Coniston Fells and down to Black Combe - to a large extent the Southern Fells, my next area of quest. It is a wide prospect that includes a long horizon of the Irish Sea, typically gorgeous when evening sun lights up the ocean with golden hues.

Safe Descents

The E declivity is precipitous. Keep it simple; unsurprisingly the one way up, becomes the one way down. Leave the summit, rounding the eastern end of the main outcrop, taking an initial SW line, the path is clear. The scree soon relents and the path descends uneventfully. A small cairn marks the point where the Boot path veers half-right, traversing on a consistent SW line to Eel Tarn. The main path runs S down the W side of Cow Cove to briefly accompany Catcove Beck, thereafter keeping to the natural terrace of the Terrace Route to reach the Wha House car park.

Ridge Routes to...

SCAFELL   DESCENT 90 ft   ASCENT 680 ft   1.2 miles

The ridge just could not be more simple. There is nothing but the occasional gravelly patch to the top of the Long Green ridge, an intermediate high point which should definitely be savoured with the same relish one treats a separate fell. The ridge dips then climbs again, with moderate toil, to the skyward crest of Scafell - now you're talking!

PANORAMA

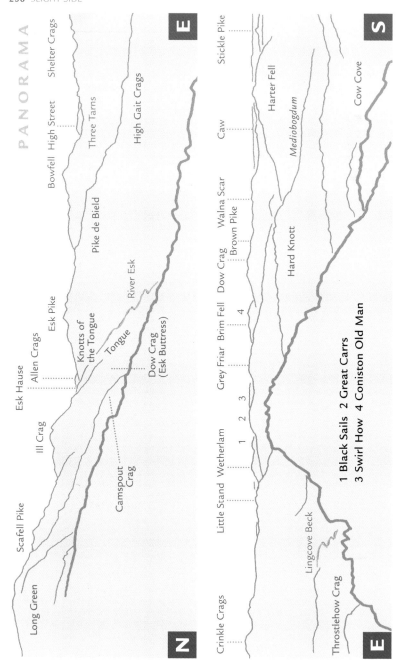

E

Shelter Crags
Bowfell   High Street
Three Tarns
Pike de Bield
High Gait Crags
Esk Pike
Knots of
the Tongue
River Esk
Tongue
Allen Crags
Esk Hause
Dow Crag
(Esk Buttress)
Ill Crag
Camspout
Crag
Scafell Pike
Long Green
Crinkle Crags

N

S

Stickle Pike
Harter Fell
Caw
Mediobogdum
Cow Cove
Walna Scar
Dow Crag   Brown Pike
Grey Friar   Brim Fell
Hard Knott
4
Little Stand   Wetherlam
3
2
1
Lingcove Beck
Throstlehow Crag

E

1 Black Sails 2 Great Carrs
3 Swirl How 4 Coniston Old Man

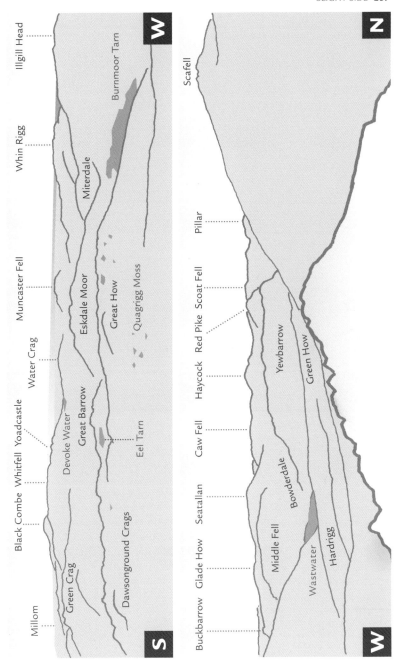

W

Illgill Head · · · · · · ·
Whin Rigg · · · · · · ·
Muncaster Fell · · · · · · ·
Water Crag · · · · · · ·
Yoadcastle · · · · · · ·
Whitfell · · · · · · ·
Black Combe · · · · · · ·
Millom · · · · · · ·

Burnmoor Tarn
Miterdale
Eskdale Moor
Great How
Quagrigg Moss
Devoke Water
Great Barrow
Eel Tarn
Green Crag
Dawsonground Crags

S

N

Scafell
Pillar · · · · · · ·
Scoat Fell · · · · · · ·
Red Pike
Haycock · · · · · · ·
Caw Fell · · · · · · ·
Seatallan · · · · · · ·
Glade How · · · · · · ·
Buckbarrow · · · · · · ·

Yewbarrow
Green How
Middle Fell
Bowderdale
Wastwater
Hardrigg

W

WHIN RIGG

The most ferocious sequence of crags and gullies dominates the lower reaches of Wastwater forming a majestic northern frontage to an otherwise lacklustre ridge. Illgill Head may be the highest point but Whin Rigg is certainly the most hairy-chested of the twin fell brotherhood forming the Wastwater Screes massif. The summit marks the western termination of this famous mountain facade. The massive fans of scree hold Wasdale-bound travellers' spell-bound attention, courting colourful light and shadow effects above the dark waters of this the deepest lake in the National Park.

In a sense Whin Rigg is an odd name for the fell, as it would seem a far-fetched idea that gorse, 'whin', can ever have grown anywhere near the summit. When viewed from the roadside near Wasdale Hall *(see above)* the imposing buttresses seem to insist they call the tune. The westernmost portion of the cliff is called Pens End, strongly suggesting the Celtic name for the main mass was in fact Pen; my grand-mother's maiden-name Penna, a Cornish variant of this word, meant 'bold brow'

536 metres   1,759 feet

as indeed this summit most certainly is. Born from the sylvan woods and meadows of the lower Irt, growing from Irton Pike, gaining confidence and stature it casts off the conifers to reach this proud moment.

Easthwaite Farm

Routes to the top are defined and confined by crags, scree, enclosure, forestry and boring bracken to access points along the spine ridge running up from the west. The principal ascent climbs Greathall Gill, with the bridle-path linking Eskdale Green with Nether Wasdale a solid alternative approach with the full ridge, off the Santon Bridge road beneath Irton Pike, a further natural choice.

But, without question, the first thought on fellwalkers' minds will be to combine the Screes Footpath with a high-level traverse of the two fell tops from Nether Wasdale. When the weather is iffy and cloud shrouds the tops one may enjoy the eight-mile circuit of the lake, as I did in a torrential storm in August! I met a guy, on another occasion, on Illgill Head who said he had walked the Scree Footpath with crampons in snow and ice. Now that's a concept I find quite mind-boggling!

Wastwater from Greathall Gill

Miterdale is a mightier dale than may be suspected; from Eskdale Green it forms the portals to an unusual view to Scafell, the afforested slopes lending a touch of alpine drama. Miterdale Forest is undergoing change, as the Forestry Commission bring their woodlands into closer harmony with both the environment and the lives of people. Presently Cumbria has an important stake in the Commission, with its current chairman, Lord Clark, also a director of Carlisle United Football Club - a man of the people indeed!

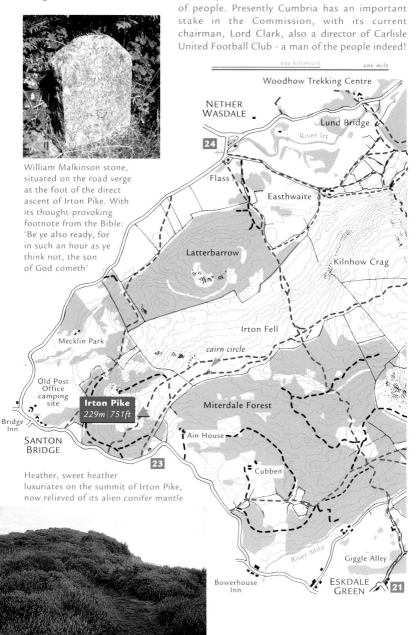

William Malkinson stone, situated on the road verge at the foot of the direct ascent of Irton Pike. With its thought-provoking footnote from the Bible: 'Be ye also ready, for in such an hour as ye think not, the son of God cometh'

Heather, sweet heather luxuriates on the summit of Irton Pike, now relieved of its alien conifer mantle

one kilometre   *one mile*

Woodhow Trekking Centre

NETHER WASDALE

Lund Bridge

River Irt

24

Flass

Easthwaite

Latterbarrow

Kilnhow Crag

Irton Fell

cairn circle

Mecklin Park

Old Post Office camping site

Irton Pike 229m | 751ft

Miterdale Forest

Bridge Inn

SANTON BRIDGE

23

Ain House

Cubben

River Mite

Giggle Alley

Bowerhouse Inn

ESKDALE GREEN

21

There is no formal parking anywhere between Santon Bridge and the head of Wastwater, though there is scope for some casual parking on the verges at Nether Wasdale and, through almost daily custom, along the open road running beside Wastwater.

ILLGILL HEAD
609m | 1,998ft

WASDALE HEAD

25

Wastwater

Wasdale Hall
Youth Hostel

Lund Bridge

Greathall Gill

Tongue
Moor

In descent watch you
don't find yourself
lured off the ridge
proper by this wall
(as the author did!)

Great Bank

Low Place

Miterdale

22

Low Holme

Giggle Alley

Outward Bound School

21 ESKDALE GREEN

MAP OVERLAP

Scarp edge tear
slump, presaging
another future major
collapse of the Wastwater
Screes: timescale?
*no one alive today
will witness it!*

bridle path to
Miterdale *&*
> Eskdale Green

Wastwater

7 The Screes

1

6 Wasdale
Hall YH

< WASDALE HEAD

Greathall Gill

> ridge path
to Irton Pike

Lund
Bridge

River Irt

Easthwaite

2

Latterbarrow

24

NETHER
WASDALE

GOSFORTH >

Flass

SANTON BRIDGE >

**WESTERN
APPROACHES**

ASCENT *from Nether Wasdale*

1 Park on the verge near Forest Bridge. From the signpost 'Wastwater' stride out along the lane leading to Easthwaite Farm with Whin Rigg firmly in view. Pass on by the barns and farmhouse, via a gate on the continuing track. As the track bears left through a gateway go straight on via stile/gate, entering a narrow walled path. At the end 'no path' on gatepost means you must turn up right, keeping the wall to the left to reach a kissing-gate. Go right to a stile, ford the gill to embark on a firm path mounting the really steep rigg on the east side of the deepening Greathall Gill ravine. Zig-zag up on a path sufficiently well used to beat back the bracken. The bracken relents, though it is some time before the grass slope follows suit! A large cairn heralds the junction with the ridge path. Go left, north-east on a steady plod to the summit.

  2 To the right of the Easthwaite lane-end stands a white house called 'Flass'; right of this is a bridle-path signed 'Eskdale' at the hand-gate. Head straight ahead, traversing a parkland liberally landscaped with Scots pine. Pass the occasional Flass Tarn, a tautological name, to a stile in the corner entering woodland at the north-eastern tip of Latterbarrow. Latterbarrow meant 'craggy lair'... and the setting may still harbour its fair share of wild creatures, with pole cat and peregrine falcon high on the list! Keep the wall left, on an oft muddy track, leading through via a footbridge and on to a railed path to exit the afforested enclosure at a hand-gate. The path negotiates marshy ground before heading up the steep fellside, bracken and a stony roughness putting a brake on progress. At the brow a path short-cuts half-left off the formal bridle-path, leading, via a hand-gate, into a plantation of Miterdale Forest,

Buckbarrow   Seatallan   Haycock   Scoat Fell

Middle Fell

Wasdale Hall Youth Hostel from the first gully east of the summit

the planation currently reaching maturity. The ridge path winds steadily up following the wall; at a ladder-stile crossing a lateral ridge-wall, continue up the damp moorland, slip over a broken wall onto the final open mass of fell to the summit.

ASCENT *from Santon Bridge*

The Irton Fell ridge leads up from above the former deer enclosure of afforested Mecklin and Irton Parks. Start from the large parking area at (GR122013) on the Santon Bridge to Eskdale Green road. There is a choice right at the outset. **3** Follow the easily graded track from the gate by the road, signposted 'Wasdale Head'. This reaches a fork in the track; either go left to the ridge-top or right, closer to the forestry wall, to a gate in the fence. The two paths remain separate for quite some distance, re-uniting at a damp patch close to the wall, short of the final rise to meet the cross-ridge bridle-path. **4** Alternatively, and this is recommended, climb Irton Pike. Walk along the road some 220 metres to an opening into the woodland, four short paces after the roadside Malkinson memorial stone. With minimal subtly this path makes a steep assault on the hill, crossing a

Frozen tarn east of the summit

Illgill Head and Whin Rigg from the Santon Bridge road

forest track, it runs up a slope, curves right, then climbs out of the trees onto the heather-capped hilltop. In late summer when the ling is doing its thing *(see below)* this is a delightful place to rest and soak up a wonderful view *(see PANORAMA on page 269)*. Thankfully, Irton Pike's ridge-top conifers have recently been felled - though the stumps need sprucing up! The ridge path declines, meets the forestry track and advances to step over a cross-ridge fence at a stile. Notice the fine view of Latterbarrow down to the left, then shortly the pile of stones over to the right which are the remnants of a Bronze Age burial mound. The path next crosses a rake dyke, former mining excavation, before rising to join the ridge wall and meet up with the bridle-path as it enters the forestry at the ridge wall. Join the course of route **2** and continue along the ridge.

Looking down Greathall Gill from the ridge path

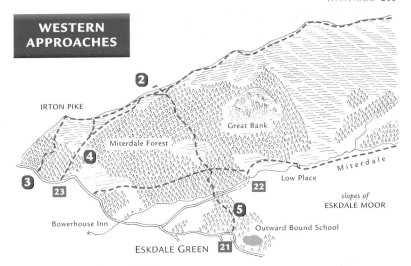

WESTERN APPROACHES

IRTON PIKE

Great Bank

Miterdale Forest

Miterdale

Low Place

slopes of
ESKDALE MOOR

Bowerhouse Inn

Outward Bound School

ESKDALE GREEN

ASCENT *from Eskdale Green*

5 From the village car park turn up the Giggle Alley lane, passing Low Holme via a gate; descend to cross the by-road into Miterdale. Enter Miterdale Forest, crossing the stone bridge over the River Mite. A clearly marked path winds up, initially among deciduous woodland, then crossing various tracks and newly opened (felled) areas before being consumed in the higher, mature plantation to reach the hand-gate and the open ridge. Go right, following route **2.**

Whin Rigg from Irton Pike

The Illgill Head west top cairn lies just back from the edge at this point

The infamous section of The Screes Footpath negotiates this massive fan of boulders

And now for something a little different... The Screes Footpath

By and large a walk around a Cumbrian lake is a gentle alternative to climbing a fell, a lazy Lakeland day. The Screes Footpath, as part of a full seven-mile circuit of Wastwater is no doddle! The western approach leads in either by Easthwaite Farm from Nether Wasdale, giving a lovely view of Whin Rigg itself, or Woodhow (no parking in the vicinity of the

trekking centre, please note) where the mighty wall of crags and screes are softened by an under-mantel of trees.

6 The most attractive start utilises the shoreline path from the ladder-stile off the open road north of Wasdale Hall youth hostel (GR 148048). Akin to the sugar on a pill, this delightful woodland passage is in stark contrast to the rigours of the screes path itself. From in front of the handsome youth hostel the serried ranks of crags, gullies and near vertical screes can be studied with some perspective - and the whole notion of following the screes path considered... or re-considered!
7 Uniting with the Woodhow path at the Lund Bridge, the path runs along the tree-shaded banks of the River Irt, via gates and along a track as the lake emerges from the river. On reaching the pumping house, emitting a steady hum, it is time to focus on the path.

The path dwindles to a narrow trod, weaves through an area of light tree growth to face *(see grim image on facing page)*, as face you must, the most awful tilt of boulders nature bequeathed a Lakeland path. Not even Broad Crag, on a bad hair day, can match the sheer mind-boggling maze of boulder problems. There is no visible path, in fact one might have thought a recent massive rock-fall had consumed it. Not a bit of it. The peril might always be there but the path never was! The natural tendency is to gradually climb, though this only exacerbates your hassle as you will have to work your way back down at some point and this is harder than angling up. When the stones are wet they are slick and the whole process becomes painfully slow; each step is taken with little certainty of a firm footing. If a common line can be explained, then it keeps between the central twin masses of large boulders. The time taken over this first scree fan can vary from twenty to forty minutes. They say time flies when you are engrossed! What follows this torment, while intermittently troublesome, is never again quite as consistently bad, which is solace of sorts. Wastwater was never more imminent nor ominous. The dark waters lapping at your feet run down consistent with the acute angle of the screes, reaching some eighteen metres below sea-level - a fjord indeed. No need to invent a Nessie, the landscape itself is on a monster scale. As the scree recedes and bracken takes over (recent herbicide spraying on either side of the dale challenging its dominance) the beauties of Wasdale Head fill the senses with anticipation of greater things to come. A field-gate heralds the advent of in-by pasture passing Wasdale Head Hall farm. Cross a stile, join the access lane leading to the valley road beyond the tree-screened National Trust car park and camping ground below Brackenclose.

Middle Fell from the scarp edge above Broken Rib

The Summit

A small shelter cairn sits on top of the knoll a few paces north of the ridge path. A second cairn rests on the south top, looking towards Eskdale. The main top is a wonderful spot, and if you know the situation from viewing it from the shores of Wastwater below, then you will know you are on a significant summit, culminating a mighty craggy fortress. Gingerly visit the top of Great Gully, a matter of a few paces north.

Safe Descents

Clearly there is no way N and extensive bracken and forestry blanket the S slopes into Miterdale. Therefore, you are bound to follow the ridge W to Greathall Gill, a steep grassy path. As an alternative, continue to the cross-ridge bridle-path linking Eskdale Green S, through the forestry, destination a footbridge over the River Mite, or N down the scarp, passing through the plantation fringe of Latterbarrow for Nether Wasdale.

Ridge Route to...

ILLGILL HEAD   DESCENT 240 ft   ASCENT 440 ft   1.4 miles

How you undertake this walk probably depends as much on whether you are alone or have conversational company. If the latter you'll stride E with the well defined ridge path, or should that be paths, it being braided as it passes the brace of attractive tarns in the broad saddle. If, like me, you find the escarpment compelling, then whether you have distractive friends or not, you'll be irresistably drawn to follow the ragged, jagged edge. There are places where one can teeter out on aretes. This can be great fun – in calm conditions. The W top cairn of Illgill Head stands only thirty metres in from the N awesome edge. The E top wind-shelter cairn is better placed for one to relax and consider the impressive circle of fells about Wasdale Head. One of the natural homes of British mountaineering and an iconic landscape for fellwalkers.

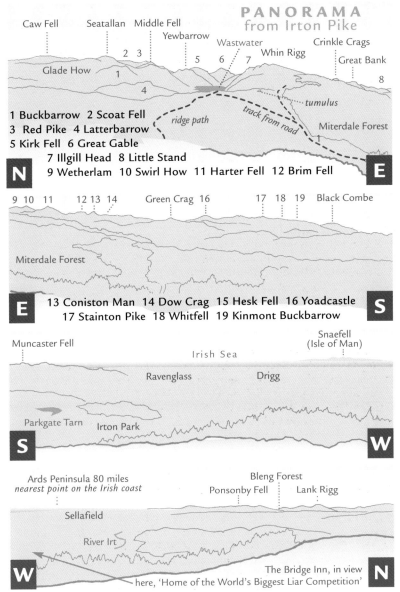

PANORAMA
from Irton Pike

Caw Fell Seatallan Middle Fell
Yewbarrow Wastwater
2 3 Whin Rigg Crinkle Crags
Great Bank
Glade How 1 5 6 7
4 8
··· tumulus

1 **Buckbarrow** 2 **Scoat Fell**
3 **Red Pike** 4 **Latterbarrow** *ridge path* *track from road*
5 **Kirk Fell** 6 **Great Gable** Miterdale Forest
7 **Illgill Head** 8 **Little Stand**
9 **Wetherlam** 10 **Swirl How** 11 **Harter Fell** 12 **Brim Fell**

N **E**

9 10 11 12 13 14 Green Crag 16 17 18 19 Black Combe

Miterdale Forest

E 13 **Coniston Man** 14 **Dow Crag** 15 **Hesk Fell** 16 **Yoadcastle** **S**
17 **Stainton Pike** 18 **Whitfell** 19 **Kinmont Buckbarrow**

Muncaster Fell Snaefell
(Isle of Man)
Irish Sea
Ravenglass Drigg

Parkgate Tarn Irton Park

S **W**

Ards Peninsula 80 miles Bleng Forest
nearest point on the Irish coast Ponsonby Fell Lank Rigg

Sellafield

River Irt

W The Bridge Inn, in view **N**
here, 'Home of the World's Biggest Liar Competition'

It is a little known fact that the Ards Peninsula in Northern Ireland can become a magical addition to the view on evenings of superlative visibility. Confirmation of this fact may be judged from the plaque set to the right of the front door of the Bridge Inn at Santon Bridge *(see note above)*.

PANORAMA

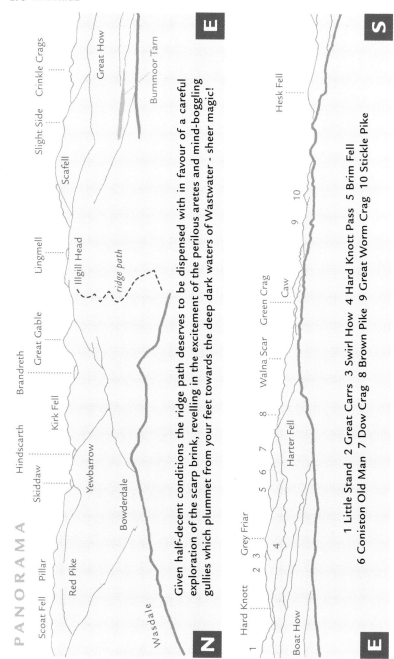

N

Scoat Fell Pillar Red Pike Bowderdale Skiddaw Hindscarth Yewbarrow Kirk Fell Brandreth Great Gable Lingmell Illgill Head *ridge path* Slight Side Scafell Crinkle Crags Great How Burnmoor Tarn Wasdale

E

Given half-decent conditions the ridge path deserves to be dispensed with in favour of a careful exploration of the scarp brink, revelling in the excitement of the perilous aretes and mind-boggling gullies which plummet from your feet towards the deep dark waters of Wastwater - sheer magic!

E

Hard Knott Grey Friar Boat How Harter Fell Walna Scar Green Crag Caw Hesk Fell

1 Little Stand 2 Great Carrs 3 Swirl How 4 Hard Knott Pass 5 Brim Fell
6 Coniston Old Man 7 Dow Crag 8 Brown Pike 9 Great Worm Crag 10 Stickle Pike

S

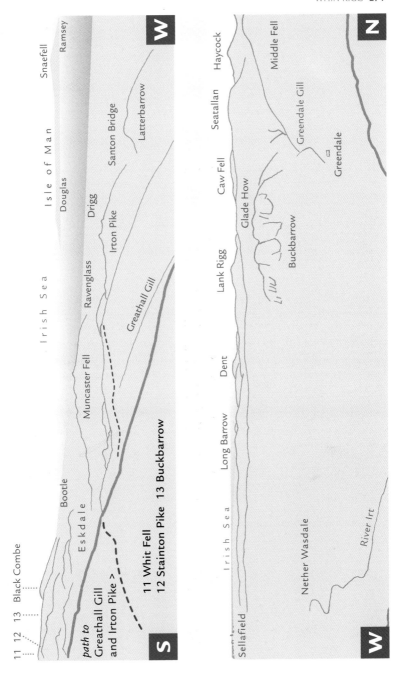

W

Snaefell
Ramsey
Douglas
Isle of Man
Irish Sea
Black Combe

11 12 13 Black Combe

Bootle
Eskdale
Muncaster Fell
Ravenglass
Drigg
Santon Bridge
Latterbarrow
Irton Pike
Greathall Gill

path to
Greathall Gill
and Irton Pike >

11 Whit Fell
12 Stainton Pike 13 Buckbarrow

S

N

Haycock
Middle Fell
Seatallan
Greendale Gill
Caw Fell
Greendale
Glade How
Lank Rigg
Buckbarrow
Dent
Long Barrow
Irish Sea
Nether Wasdale
River Irt
Sellafield

W

A Precious Place

The long practised freedom to roam over our beloved fells has exacted its toll with worn paths. We may turn a blind eye but when descending some familiar fell-top the scored surface gives pain to our ankles and knees. At such times we re-focus our attention on the issue of path erosion. The metalling of roads we take for granted; traditionally pack-horse trails were given a similar treatment, but in stone pitching. This work has thankfully been re-invented and the activity given new impetus in Lakeland following the traumas of the 2001 foot and mouth outbreak, when Heritage Lottery Funding gave a partnership of the National Park, the National Trust and English Nature sufficient cash for a five-year programme of works. There is much to do: at present the Upland Path Landscape Project is in full swing. Large white bags full of boulders can be spotted at many locations around the district, waiting for helicopter relay to target paths. Pitching is sometimes criticised for its slickness when wet or hardness when dry, but the truth is on steep ground this is the one sustainable means to ensure the fells are both accessible and well kept. To find out more visit: www.lake-district.gov.uk

For casual visitors and fellwalking enthusiast alike, perhaps no other organisation more surely represents their values and interests than the Friends of the Lake District, for 70 years the ever-vigilant guardians of the whole Cumbrian landscape. My suggestion, affirm your affinity. Join and lend them your much valued support: www.fld.org.uk

For the Lakeland Fellranger series to serve its readership better, it needs to be dynamic and alert to changes. Although I only have one pair of legs and eyes, the users of the series represent a massive resource of such limbs and lenses to witness errors, omissions and serious changes that affect the course of walking routes on our fells. You are invited to email your observations to me at authors@harpercollins.co.uk – please ensure you write 'Mark Richards' in the subject line.

Haytime at Brotherilkeld, a working farm in upper Eskdale